The BEST

of Team Ruptured Buzzard Rally Raids (so far...)

A compendium of mayhem and folly through motorcycle ride reports and other shenanigans

By David J. Jankowsky

(aka Stovebolt)

First published in 2012 by David J. Jankowsky, P.O. Box 656, Victor, Idaho 83455 USA

Copyright 2012 David J. Jankowsky
ISBN-13: 978-0615697550
ISBN-10: 0615697550

The information in this book, although it is fact-based, represents the opinions of the author. The navigation information contained herein, in generalized representation, graphical depictions and technical data, is shared with the reader for entertainment purposes only and does not represent necessarily sound guidelines for the planning of any travel by anyone. The route information represented, described throughout the reports and the graphical depictions, in no way constitutes travel advice or implies legal access and/or egress anywhere. Following any route information contained in this book should be considered proscribed rather than vetted. It is up to the reader to research all travel routes and GPS tracks thoroughly, and carefully adhere to all laws respective of land use with all government land stewards and private property owners. Failure to properly plan for and navigate through public lands as well as private property can lead to serious injury, trespass, and incarceration in the case of violating federal statutes covering secured ground by our nation's military. One may also be subject to being killed to death on the spot by legal use of deadly physical force. Know where you are, and where you are going. Many times, others know more about that than you do. Plan accordingly!

Adventure riding and participation in dual-sport motorcycling is dangerous. Readers join all others in assuming personal responsibility for their actions while riding and navigating, and do so at their own peril. Discomfort, injury and death can and do occur while adventure riding.

Do not assume that possession and use of a personal tracking and emergency locator beacon device will keep you safe or save your life in the event of mishap. Signals for cell phones are also unreliable in many remote regions at the time of publication, and should not be relied upon as the sole means for assistance or rescue.

Some words, manufacturer names, descriptions and designations mentioned herein are the property of the trademark holders and reference to them is for identification purposes only. This is not an official publication endorsed by any manufacturer of any product. Use and mention of any products in this book constitutes no advertising or contractual relationship between product manufacturers and the author or publisher.

I gratefully acknowledge the use of maps in the public domain obtained from the National Atlas (Nationalatlas.gov) and of public domain satellite images from NASA (commons.wikipedia.org).
I am grateful for and respectful of the words of fighter pilot John Gillespie Magee Jr. (1922-1941); for his poem *High Flight*, a work of art also currently in the public domain.

Editor and designer: Dorothy Jankowsky • Vetted and petted by "Captain Fur-illo"
On the front cover: Photo by Marshal Bird; Back cover: Photo by Keith Briggs

Contents

RAIDS:

~

For Dorothy

~

Stovey exits the Arroyo Grande in Baja California Norte. *(Joe Watsabaugh photo)*

Preface

Why anybody would deliberately expose themselves to harsh elements within the hostile landscapes of our world — with wind, weather, dehydration, hunger, filth, disorientation and potential for bodily injury — is a worthy topic. But it is not the subject of this book. I am sure a topic such as that is well covered in mental health literature and has been beaten to death by all kinds of worm-heads all over the globe. And it's likely been studied and had the studies' expenses landed on the backs of taxpayers for many decades. I would also hazard a guess that the beak-nosed lab-coats who beat their skinny little chests over their results and theories are pretty proud of themselves for having "bettered mankind" for their efforts — their tireless, sacrificial, altruistic enthusiasms. Their "understanding" of the human psyche so well perfected that we all live better, richer lives because we have their knuckleheaded psycho-logical "science" to fall back on should we ever need it to treat ourselves for some kind of "mental illness."

And I'd bet Aunt Betty's last bottle of gin that they've all got it completely wrong. But that's just me. I am an adventure rider, and they call me "Stovebolt." For the duration of these humble passages, I will remain, at your service.

These are some of my best ride reports so far, and some have already been published on the Internet on various forums. The reason I am publishing them here in a hard copy format is because there are friends and family who are interested in reading some of them, but who may not have the interest or savvy to wander around on the Internet trying to chase them down. Some folks would also rather have a hard copy of anything, regardless of its availability online, and so there was the impetus to just compile some of these little vignettes and hash them down onto a piece of paper, and call it good.

Meanwhile, the ride reports are really small escapist vignettes that allow a reader to drift down the trail with me for awhile anyways, whether they have ridden a dual-sport motorcycle before or not. The reports aren't in and of themselves any kind of a "Shakespeare" in terms of literature, but I don't claim that status. I leave that kind of braggadocio to the worm-headed psychologists who think all the nuances of the human condition have been explained. A spirit of adventure needs no analysis or explanation – rather it is its own cause for celebration, and worthy of an honest pursuit. Having what I've been able to share through these stories about dirt-biking adventures being vetted by some of my peers has given me great satisfaction. And it is my hope that through taking these journeys with me in prose, it may cause a spark and ignite the desire in some folks to follow through on a hidden compulsion to explore on their own, and go out and just "do it." After all, living ain't living, unless you are making a commitment to yourself to do just that.

For me, riding a motorcycle across vast tracts of untamed rural America where no established routing already exists is a passion that I share with many, many other adventure riders. My experiences are only as unique as I've made them – they are not unique to the human condition. But most cube farmers don't even know about "adventure riding," let alone understand it or do it themselves. Surely, there is something to think about other than data entry and the most up-to-date sales correspondences "needing to be done" via Facebook and Twitter. To those who live that kind of "quiet life of desperation" day in and day out, I appeal to you to set the earbud down, and step away from the keyboard. The internet router can wait… entertain yourself for a few moments, and consider what life might be like on a trail you have yet to ride down, on a summit you have yet to achieve. Think about the possibility of trying something as a one-time thing, or even as a pastime – that something is out there you can do that will fill your soul, and defy words to describe. Something that will embrace you and never let you go, as you take a chance on yourself, to rally on.

A few words about some of the Internet forums might be in order, by way of information and insight. Online forums are cyber-meeting grounds to share, gather and trade all kinds of information, and in the case of dual-sport and motorcycle-adventure riding, there are quite a few URLs dealing with the subject. There are "boards" ("bulletin boards" from the early days' nomenclature) that specify loads of different subjects in a variety of categories – all with varying degrees of interest to any given reader. But, a guy can trawl around on Adventure Rider or Ride Dual Sport and learn all about how to replace the water pump seal on a KTM 640A in fine detail, with pictures, as well as download GPS tracks to a route you might be interested in taking in Mexico. Ride reports are a big draw for many readers of the forums, and following along vicariously with some of the most intrepid adventurers on the planet as they wail their ways across the back and beyond of Siberia or Indonesia, or jumping the Darien Gap from Central to South America, is a hoot! My favorites are Adventure Rider, Ride Dual Sport, My2Wheels and Horizons Unlimited. But there are literally hundreds of related Internet websites devoted to all aspects of motorcycle travel and in particular, off-road and adventure riding.

Anyway, as I gathered steam on this project, it became clearer and clearer to me that if nothing else, putting together a few of my riding experiences might at least serve to "explain" why *I* do it, and allow a little insight as to what kind of things motivate me. Then I can share it with my in-laws – give them a map so to speak – so they can finally figure me out after all these years.

So, if a bit of what I've shared here resonates with some of my peers, people who actually ride dual-sport motorcycles, or do adventure riding casually, or have even made solo trips around the world… then maybe some of this shared passion will reflect a little bit of that experience, and they might take their copy of this book along with them on the weekend getaway with their girlfriend, and say "hey, sweetheart… you were asking me about this trip I wanted to take, and this book has some of what I feel like when I ride written in it, and I'd like you to read it. Maybe it will say it better than I tried to. . . . Now pass me that 'joy lotion' and I'll give you that special back rub you've been waiting for. . ." Or maybe some other wives, sisters, brothers, fathers and mothers will be able to glean a little insight into the workings of that 'rider relative' of theirs, for whatever that might be worth. I dunno.

For some, it's about the bikes, the machines — the performance. Hearing that engine roar. For others it's all about miles, and making lots of them; sometimes fast and sometimes slow. For many it can be about the solitude — the getting away from it all. For still others it's about the many colorful characters we meet and can ride with, the sharing of a journey — traveling with friends, or just your riding buddy. There are as many reasons why we all do it as there are riders who do. It's not for everybody, and sometimes even relating what we do is next to impossible to achieve on any really meaningful level. Perhaps by being enriched from our rides we can in some way convey our sparks to our non-riding companions. These shared experiences resonate amongst the adventure riding community, and I hope to push that great stentorian BOOM on down the line, and share some moments from the journeys with non-riders as well. Good luck with that, dear readers. . .

"Team Ruptured Buzzard" — the beginning. . . My cousin Jim is the inspiration behind the name, having come up with it decades ago during a comedy session we were having at our grandparents' home in Manlius, New York. His sense of humor is unstoppable, unless of course, you stop it.

How "Stovebolt" got his name, from the "Bustedcompass.com" website:

"Stovebolt"

"I am 'Stovey' but you can call me whatever you want. I go by Dave, "Janks" and "Janko," too, and of course I didn't pick any of these names — they have been bestowed upon me. When I was a young motorcycle enthusiast, I lacked proper funds to support the motocross-racing habit I desperately wanted to form. My weekly pre-race rituals included repairs with whatever nuts, bolts, tape and wire I could find lying around, and many an empty hole where a part had fallen off my Suzuki was stuffed with either carriage or stove bolts. Mystery gone there on that. I won't let any of the other guys write my bio, it's not happening here.... Some of them know way too much for my own good. Suffice it to say, I am a grand fellow, a supreme adventure companion and the humblest one of the group. I am also married to the only female buzzard so far, (only "female" so far, not "married" so far) — Dorothy. She says I am handsome, but that's only because I am. I have this website. I love my dogs."

Good luck and good hunting in your adventure travels, and I hope to meet you out on the trail, on a ride somewhere, someday. And I will listen to your report around the campfire, and have something in my soul ignite as I hear YOUR tale of adventure.

All the best to you, my friend.

Dave Jankowsky
"Stovey"

Foreword

Growing up in the Pacific Northwest teaches a person how to endure the elements in order to enjoy one's outdoor endeavors. For me that endeavor was motorcycling and I did it for 30 years mostly in the rain, fog and snow. Why did I keep riding despite ice-cold water seeping into my pants and down my neck with my boots skimming the snow-covered road like outriggers? I ride to live, to escape, to wander, to find myself, and to find our Country.

These days, the internet does a lot of the finding for me, and life is every bit as rich and colorful as it was pre-internet. The RideDualSport motorcycle forum is laced with Stovey's adventures. Even in the age of the internet, I believe that printed books remain one of life's true comforts. Books engage us, soothe us and calm us in this age of mass-media saturation.

Reading Stovey's adventures will entertain you, give you an escape, take you to distant places, and most importantly, tell you what kind of man he is. Stovey is man who does not give up, a man who transcends beyond where two wheels can take him. He is a man who revels in each grain of sand as it slips between the future and the past. His adventures capture the now, those infinite microseconds of pure being.

You can grab it too.

Motorcycling brings us closer to the things that matter most in life, one of which is good friends in adventurous places. Motorcycling is really about the people you meet and the experiences you share. Stovey's book will get you away from the computer, and into the now of life.

Patrice Ninaud, KosmicKLR on RideDualSport.com

My riding buddy, "Stovebolt," aka "Janks," "Mike," "Mikey," "Michael J. Witowski," "Malcolm J. Witowski"....
Most famous quote: "Here I sit and started thinking, suddenly shit and started stinking."
Professional Experience: None.

Well, actually, he has worn many hats; rock climber, cop, park ranger, range master, master baiter, landscaper, cable locator, sprayer of the paint, security system installer (voyeur), tree doper, bike mechanic, welder, machinist, and others.... But most currently he's a fabricator of the most excellent motorcycle safe sex accessories made.

"Malcolm" has two loves: Dorothy and their dogs, period. Nothing else, period. Except bikes, biking, working on bikes, looking at bikes, writing about bikes, sometimes bikes writing back and, in what some would say is not 100 percent abnormal: lubricating, greasing, massaging a bike. Sometimes when he's all alone save the presence of maybe a fresh fart, he could be found mounting something on his, or maybe one of your bikes. That is a frightening thought, isn't it?

"Mikey" can tell a tale no doubt, but given the bullshit I personally have waded through while listening to him occasionally, any stories, logs, blogs, tracks, cookies, bread crumbs, quotes, verses, songs, sonnets, scriptures, hymnals, audio or visual recordings of Mikey's past transgressions, unless verified by a court-appointed officer, is and always will be considered bullshit. Basically, anything Mikey says that I did not personally witness with my own two fooking eyes and ears that can't be proven in a court of law is most likely to be TOTAL BULLSHIT. Given that, one time at band camp....(oooops)

Mikey is pretty fun to ride with. He is a little stinky, hauls way too much shit on his bike, paints himself up with red, white and blue zinc oxide resembling the American flag (no shit, a real patriot) and he requires stilts to mount and dismount any fooking motorcycle chosen for the ride. That makes riding with him not only a pleasure, but also a comedic foray all day long. He has been known to roll on the throttle a little heavy at times. I personally have been passed like I was going fooking backwards, once... but enough of that. I can honestly say that no motherhumper enjoys bikes more than I do, period... of course except for Mikey, or I mean, "Malcolm."

His latest testament to a man's time and money used poorly (like most bike nuts or the rest of us) is a 2010 KTM 450 Six Days. This motorcycle is so thoroughly equipped it makes me laugh and cry. I am so jealous and envious, I want one, too. One or two things might be missing on my bike that exist on his, but mine would still haul ass. Unfortunately, mostly when someone else is riding mine....

I have done quite a bit of riding with the fooker, so I say that someday he will likely be referred to as the "Whiskey-Throttled Ballchinian Dickhead from Arffgone." He smokes too much, drinks too much and burns through fooking fuel near as bad as Jay, but that is another story. (A couple of Whiskey Throttled fookers like you have never seen...) I will conserve fuel like a priest all day long, then have to fuel their bikes, only to guarantee I run out next; starting to get the picture? Mike is about as fooked up as everyone else in our riding group. Most of us are over-the-hill no-shows to begin with. There might be one or two decent riders, but as a rule, even the younger guys whiskey throttle off cliffs at times, making me smile. I once watched Malcolm, (yes — he and others once passed me in Red Wash, once) going so fooking fast it wasn't funny. Until he decided to bulldog his KTM 300 EXC, then it was funny. The fooker took the bars straight in the chest in a low-side; it looked like he was trying to complete the first sideways carb fook on a virgin KTM... he and his bike skipping down Red Wash looked like a stone thrown across a calm pond. It was fooking fuuuunnnnnyyyyyy. Then, he could not breathe nor get up, so like any concerned riding buddy I graciously offered him a precordial kick to the ribs, but he passed on that. That crash cost him a year, mostly. I have reenacted that crash myself once or twice, it sucks. So as he/we age, the rides become more important. We just returned from a three-day Moab trip; typical Utah red rock country, fooking incredible. (Oh, I almost forgot, the asshole along with bbriggs held me down and poured beer down my throat, good times....) We are currently in conference about a Spring Red Desert mud massage and more. I hope we get 'em all. Here's to you, you fooking fook.

Joe Watsabaugh, Jackson, Wyoming

Route of Baja Raid

NASA satellite image of Baja in the public domain obtained from Wikipedia Commons.

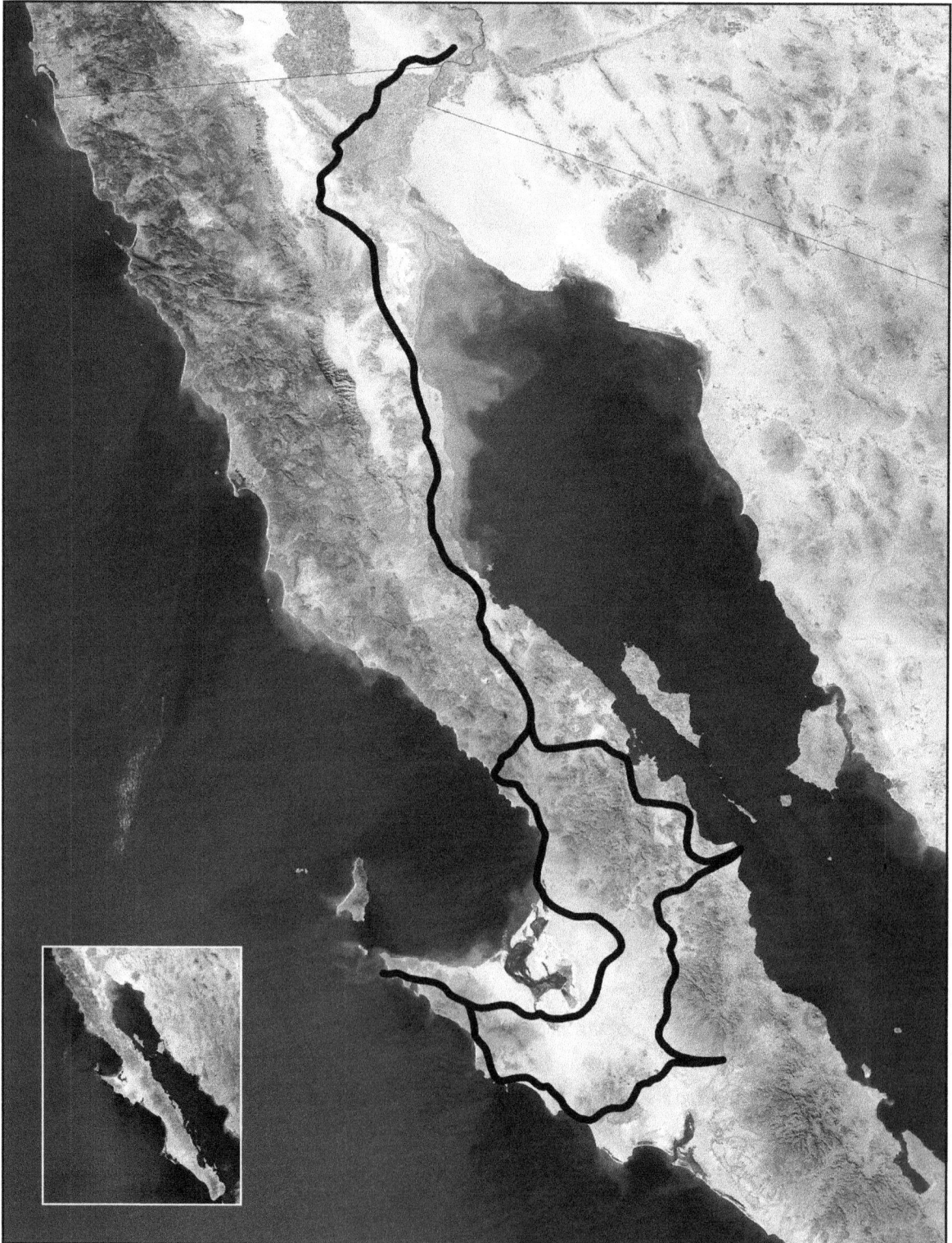

Dennis Hopper

buys Stovebolt a Margarita OR How to roll through a military checkpoint...

March 2008

"Team Ruptured Buzzard" in Coco's Corner. Left to right are "Stovebolt" (author), Berg Briggs, Lincoln Ramsey, Jay Cunnigan, Coco's niece and her son, Diego, and Joe Watsabaugh. Coco is seated in middle, down to one leg in his compound, and about ten days before he left for a Guerrero Negro hospital for scheduled surgery to remove his remaining leg. *(Photo by Coco's nephew)*

I crashed my KTM 640 Adventure in a sandwash on a Baja adventure, on the morning of Day 4 of a 10-day off-road ride, just West of San Francisquito, Baja California Norte. Dislocated left shoulder, busted up some ribs – same shoulder I had previously dislocated twice, same ribs two times. El Bummer-o.

I barely managed to get out of the dirt and back onto some pavement by the end of the afternoon, and by late day, I began to see some light at the end of a fairly fuzzy, pain-filled tunnel, in the form of a place to stay for the night, and get off the damned bike. Traffic was at a standstill at Checkpoint Charlie, and my peeps – 4 other rejects from Clown College, had preceded me through the line, after a long day of nursing me through unGodly washes and terrain as inhospitable as any I had seen before, save for Moab. I had hallucinated several times through the pain and dehydration of the day, after the crash, that although still strikingly beautiful, the area called to mind what it must be like to ride a motorcycle down the crack of Satan's ass after an all-night Buffalo Wing eating binge in Hell. I digress....

So, for those folks who haven't really ever gotten the dirt bike or dual-sporting bug, realize that a KTM 640 Adventure is a tall bike – seat height of over 37 inches. Okay, Stovebolt has a 29-inch inseam. Time for the cubicle nerd to erase the whiteout "X's" off his glasses and do some real math there... fully loaded with camping and survival gear, some fuel, water and a couple of pesos, the bike weighs approximately 1 each pant-load. Multiply that times a wounded shoulder that is worse than useless, and divide by 4 (the number of times I would have stopped to pee if I could have...) and it adds up to – pretty much a blivy. By the time I "tried" to stop for the good authority figure at Checkpoint Charlie, I was pretty much 6 pounds of sheeyat in a 5-lb bag, and warm.

So, thankful to think I was a mere few miles by pavement to a place I could permanently dismount and assess the damage and reconnoiter my situation, a small sense of the kind of relief you might get right after yarding on a big booger began to come over me. It was just enough to let my guard down, and I was about to mow the guard down. Guard down? Guard... down? WTF? GUARD!!! @#%!@#%!%#!!!!!

WAKE UP STOVEY! – YOU'RE HALLUCINATING! CHECK/CHECK/CHECK

I come sliding in to the military checkpoint with my head implanted into a rectal area with red Loctite... condition WHITE – oblivious to my surroundings, peripheral vision collapsed from too much effort spent and re-spent all day long, again and again trying to pilot that boat through a sea of deep sand with scorpions in it – cactus from the Devil's nether regions thrown in for good measure. I wasn't going fast, only second gear, when I came out of this Fog of War, and began processing real time visual data coming at me lighting fast through the dusty faceshield of my Arai XD. In a real sense, things got real easy all of a sudden, because my choices were so limited – there wasn't much I could physically do any more, I was just about completely locked up. Anybody who has been injured can relate to the phenomenon of compensating for the injured part of the body with other parts of your body. It took for me, my whole being to compensate for being injured like I was, and it just tapped me to near nothing. As I rolled in toward a line of parked cars, me going a little too fast to be graceful and way too fast to just roll to a stop in line – I would have hit the back of a parked delivery truck about five cars back from the STOP area for inspection – thus possibly causing undue attention to be drawn to me.... I pretty much just wheeled around the obstacle to the left, and while not having the speed to cause any serious concern, at least to what was left to my mind in that level of consciousness, I just leaned it over lowside and dropped the bike.

Stepping off wasn't as bad as you might think, I never actually fell onto the ground.... I ran, tripped, wobbled and grunted a little, but Stovey was a gymnast in High School and a diver in College... so I was tapping that remnant pretty

... the area called to mind what it must be like to ride a motorcycle down the crack of Satan's ass after an all-night Buffalo Wing eating binge in Hell.

hard right there, pretty much bangin' away on those old muscle memory cells... and sort of just skipped to a stop on my own two feet, about 3 feet from my sliding Pogo Punkin. (KTMs are all orange — I had completely blown my rear shock the day before after crashing my way up Calamajue Wash out of Coco's Corner. Ergo, "Pogo." There-go "Punkin."))

So I'm now standing about a car length away from the young soldier at the checkpoint, a fine young man in his teens, dressed in dusty BDU's and sporting his Hechler and Koch G3 at port arms, and who is now engaging me and closing our distance to approximately bad-breath plus 7 feet or so. I remain standing, turn and look down at my Punkin'.... My posse was gone ahead, nowhere in sight, and I recalled my Spanish language skills to comfort me. Ahh, yes — I can't speak Spanish worth a chit — now at least I can relax.

So, anyway, to draw this short story out even further before I get to the point, we had made a deal out on the trail after my tumble, and it was agreed (after a time or two when I fell down again and tried picking up my bike — I just couldn't do it by myself any more...) that I was not to even TRY to pick up my bike if I dropped it. Sort of like the snowmobiling deal if you get stuck (when not on the hill) in the deep — don't get a hernia or a heart attack or wreck your back — wait for help. So I pretty much just stood my ground, hovering over my behemoth, waiting for the cavalry to come over my hill, and pick up my bike for me. After all, I had done MY job, and nobody was hurt at the checkpoint — countless lives were saved, paperwork averted, catastrophe completely avoided on account of me being on top of my game and saving the public from certain harm, and laying my bike down in such a righteous act of self-sacrifice. Now where were my bike tenders at? Sabu — Sabu? Come hither bike boy.... I looked around, and everyone in stopped traffic was staring at me.

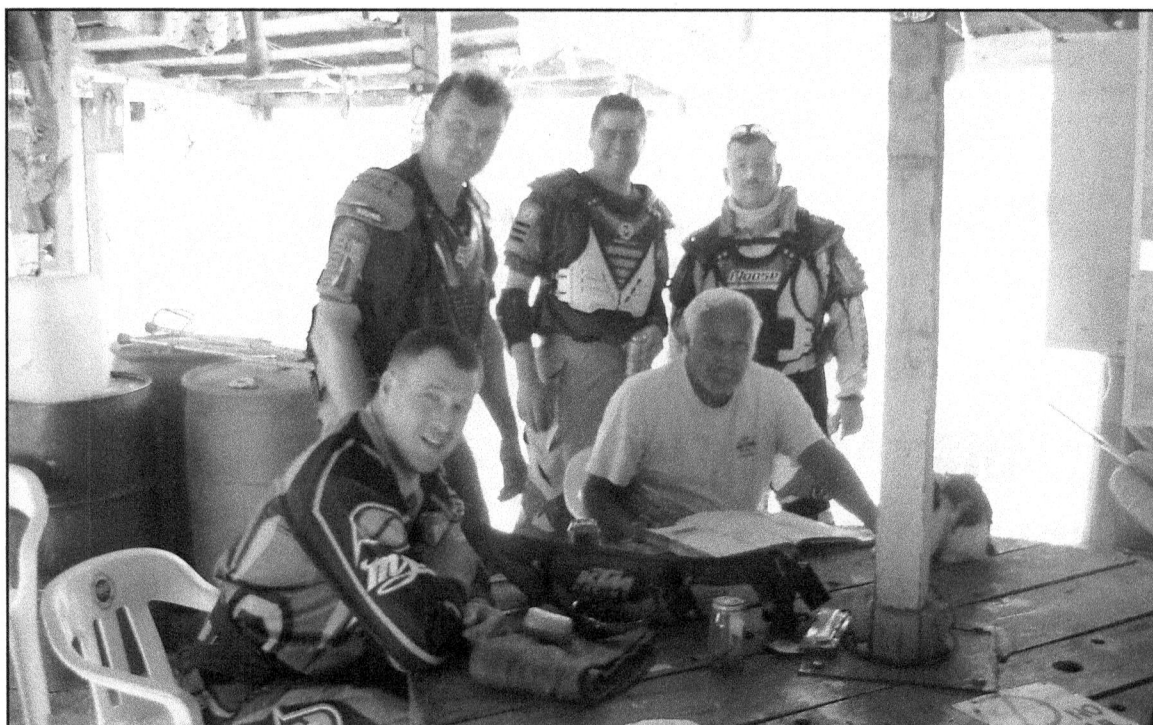

Coco's Corner, Calamajue Baja California Norte. Left to right are Jay, Joe, Berg, Stovebolt and seated in front of his guest book is Jorge Sandez, aka "Coco," with el gato by his side.
(Out of picture and photo credit to Lincoln Ramsey)

Yard sale in progress in Calamajue Wash, just outside of Coco's Corner, before hurting shoulder. And prior to my epiphany about Wolfman luggage. *(Berg Briggs photo)*

WTF...?

Well, sensing that the young lad sporting the G3 (the G3 is a military firearm chambered in a NATO caliber of 7.62mm, approx .308. It is made of stamped aluminum, steel and plastic, fires in semi-automatic and select-auto, comes with iron sights and has a sling and a loud, smoky end attached to it...) was not about to assist me, the driver of a delivery truck opened his door and exited his vehicle and came over to me. Without taking more than a second to make eye contact with me, as is the custom to acknowledge one another down in Baja, the man in his mid-thirties leaned down and pried that 400-plus pound bitch right off the searing Mexican pavement, and with one or two mighty heaves of that spindly stick figure of a physique, he got that bike upright and leaned into for all he was worth to prop it vertical – standing there smiling, holding it for me like a gentleman. Yes, like a true knight, he had helped one less fortunate than himself, and I was, and still am, grateful.

Soldier boy wasn't so amused.

At this point, like I had mentioned, my body was pretty locked up – stiff, sore, I could barely move. This information was actually still being processed as I reached across the cockpit of my KTM 640 Adventure Rally bike with my one good hand/arm/side and grasped a bar end, holding the bike upright by myself after my new Baja truck driver friend just handed it off with a sincere grin and gestures of compassion, and a final "thumbs up" to a sad, sad gringo. I flipped my tan crusted faceshield up and looked over at the checkpoint – I was being waved in ahead of other cars (now being passed over) to get me to the head of the line. Somehow, despite my best efforts, I had managed to call undue atten-

Things began rushing forward from the back of my mind, things like: 'where is my passport?' and 'can I remember where my insurance info is?' and 'did I bring my bazooka with me on this trip?'

tion to myself for one thing, and I was apparently, despite what I would have liked at the time, being given "EXPRESS" treatment. I had tried so hard to blend in too.

Being as wounded as I was — my self-assessment had caught up in real time, and I had processed the data — I was almost fooked.... I could either turn and run, fight, or cooperate. I eyeballed the only thing of interest to me at all at the moment, and that was the 4-inch concrete curb along the inside lane of the checkpoint, closest to my soon to be, new to me, friend within the Mexican Military establishment, and began heaving the bike for all I was worth over that scorching blacktop, toward the kid with the deadpan look on his face, now presenting the G3 at the Low Ready.

Since this whole thing transpired over the course of only less than a minute or so, let me accelerate. As I was on foot now, and walking (stumbling?) alongside my bike, approaching the "ALTO!" stop line — hanging on for dear life actually — it was all I could do to hold the bike up, because it was ALMOST all I could do just to hold me up by myself.... I stayed the course and kept eyeballing that curb. That curb would set me free, if I could only get to it. It stood alongside my stern looking young passport examiner, and I had to get through him first, before I could reach that 4-inch concrete salvation. Things began rushing forward from the back of my mind, things like; 'where is my passport?' and 'can I remember where my insurance info is?', and 'did I bring my bazooka with me on this trip?', and so forth. I gathered up what little intel I could before he stopped me before reaching the line with a gesture of "STOP" — hand held forward from his center of mass toward me, his feet squared off to me, and shoulder width apart. A real Dennis Rodman athletic stance, about half as high off the ground, and topped with a Kevlar pot instead of blond and blue nappy hair. Still, I understood and respected his command. This was it, another moment of truth in Baja, I had already had many and this trip was only on Day 4... hadn't even reach San Ignacio and been tried by the fire of the "bathroom dog" yet... here it comes... all I need is the curb. Got to get back on this bike... can't do it without a step up, and even that's not going to be easy. I want THAT CURB, and I want it next to the guard shack. I can lean the bike into the wall of the guard shack and use the curb to try to remount... if only... must get to the curb — and that wall would be so sweeeet. Dear God, please let... "Adonde Vas!"

"What?"

"Adonde Vas?"

"aaaaahhhh – Idaho. I mean, uh – Rice and Beans?"

Soldier boy is waving and I am beginning to unfold the map case on the bars of my roadbook holder in the cockpit, and begin "my cooperation" for all I'm worth. I noticed I had a hard time speaking – not just Spanish, but my mouth didn't seem to want to work – there was dust in it. My lips were a little dry and cracked and my tongue was a little swollen. Never mind I couldn't understand what this soldier was saying because my ears were slammed shut inside a form fitting Arai XD, that I didn't understand my own language at that point, let alone his – and that I didn't know if he was asking me where I was from, or where I was going. Either question way beyond the reach of my fried brain at that point, in any language – but good questions nonetheless.

Well, soldier boy gestured again, and stepped to the other side of my bike, in front of me. I had spoken enough "humanitarian" in my lifetime to begin recognizing a small flicker of compassion from a candle of kindness, and he seemed to be waving me off from the "project" I had started to get out my papers and surrender to whatever form of questioning

Moments after crashing and dislocating shoulder and crushing a few ribs outside of San Francisquito. *(Joe Watsabaugh photo)*

Rice and Beans, San Ignacio – fouled-up shoulder stuffed back in its hole, busted ribs stashed back in behind chest protector.

they might have wanted to do with me – it had not escaped my peripheral vision that two other vehicles – both with Mexican plates – were parked, stopped and being THOROUGHLY attended to by a small army of the well, Mexican Army – two lanes over and off to the side of the road. Some of the people involved in administering to the needs of the occupants of those vehicles now sequestered by many soldier boys didn't seem happy, from the facial expressions, movements, "luggage" and car parts that I saw....

"Passado...." "Passado...."

He was waving me through... is that what he's doing? What? I was not sure, but I couldn't believe my body was doing stuff without my mind's permission.... Even as I was questioning what the soldier wanted, in my mind I just wasn't certain... "JESUS IS THIS HOT!"... and all I could think of was trying to hold this bike up and get the nipple from my Camelbak into my mouth and not fall off the curb while leaning off from the wall with the bad shoulder....

Far off ahead were miles of hot pavement – not a car in sight, and the faint sound of several motorcycles.... One engine sound getting louder as the seconds ticked by, the heartbeat thumping ever louder inside this damned black helmet. I got the bike steadied, but with only one foot touching "ground" and that was my savior curb, and the other on a footpeg so high off the ground it'd never save me if I got the bike off center and lost my balance – she'd thud to the pavement and I'd be back to square one, hunting up that delivery driver to help me again; I needed to roll off right. No second chances. The starter began to light it, and I heard another bike nearby as mine roared back to life at the "STOP" line, and I looked up to see something wobbling toward me through a heat mirage, waving at me over the blacktop. One of my peeps had come back for me, and the military guys were just waving me through. One of them in the guard shack gave me a smile and a "thumbs up" while the frown seemed to have neutralized on the face of young soldier boy who had engaged me during my check. He was waving me through while another soldier held traffic from both lanes to maintain their standstill "until further notice" I think was the message. I got the bike rolling despite painful effort with the clutch side – anything including an eyelash being asked to move by my brain just hurt like hell, especially if it was on the left side of my body. I rolled forward toward an image embedded in the mirage, and kept shifting gears. It was about 4pm, BCS time, and what seemed like an eternity at the gates of hell was in reality only about a minute and a half. I had cleared Checkpoint Charlie, and was on vacation in Mexico. It was everything that I had dreamed....

We're not that far from our stop at RICE AND BEANS in San Ignacio, where food, water, shelter and parts are waiting for us. None of us knew what else was waiting there, but since I was about to get dumped by my posse, and left to tend to my wounds and reconnoiter my next step, I would have extra time there to figure it out. The four remaining long riders would have a quick bite and rehydrate, check to make sure I have what I need, a room, my bike and belongings secured – a plan... everything. Everything is fluid on a trip in Baja, and we were fluid at that point. We came into the oasis en masse, the guys having formed up on the side and waited for me catch them. It seemed that after Berg had wheelied out of the checkpoint, much to the delight of the attending military personnel – AND at their behest as it turns out – our posse was elevated in status to some form of instant local hero status, if for only a few fleeting moments. Probably why I was waved through without so much as a passport viewing – they know I was with "them!" So now, we were all back together, formation flying to a landing in the middle of a huge crowd of people and vehicles and traffic at the "resort" oasis that is Rice & Beans in San Ignacio, just outside of town to the north. What can all of this be? I can barely navigate....

Rice and Beans parking in San Ignacio – a central hub of off-road Baja racing activity for pre-runners.

There were RVs and dune buggys and trophy trucks and all manner of high speed-low drag desert conveyances all over this patch of sand they called a parking area, and people just scattered EVERYWHERE! There was a nice long veranda just loaded with people sitting at tables in chairs, talking, laughing, eating, drinking. Guys in Nomex suits walking around, back and forth from their trophy trucks who were down prerunning for the BAJA 250, all manner of hubbub and commotion.

I found the nearest wall and maneuvered toward it, noticing now nice the flower bed looked that was planted on the top, and crashed into it, plain and simple. Just like the wall at the Checkpoint guard shack, I angled into the side and just brushed in hard and chopped everything off, coming to simple slide-stop-thud against the wall. Leaning there against my bad shoulder and my feet still on the pegs, I just pushed my faceshield up, and waited for help – I wasn't going anywhere. A sense of relief came over me, and I realized that for a short time anyways, I might be safe here and I didn't have to try to ride anymore. Not until further notice. We were "here" wherever this was, and we had just rolled in from deep in the heart of nowhere, just outside the back of beyond....

...when last we left our intrepid hero, he was leaning against a wall, engine off on the Pogo Punkin' – feet on the pegs and slumping for all he was worth... the inside of his riding clothes was hotter than the hubs of hell and he was pretty much just leaning and blowing bubbles....

Captured whale

Steve and Steve – these guys are awesome! I can put readers in touch with them for some of the best motorcycle guiding adventures in Baja.... Author is in the middle, making new friends. *(Ricardo Cota photo)*

So I've got a good lean on the wall, enough to keep me up, and waiting for a hand to help stabilize the bike real solid so I can climb off this bike like a nancy boy, and slide to the ground under my own power, without all the extra help that gravity is just waiting to send at any second, and somebody comes over and grabs on and asks how I'm doing. Another guy comes and two or three people are anchoring my steed so it doesn't highside down the driveway when it gets righted, and give a couple hundred people a good show to go along with their dinner hour. I get off the bike, and get the helmet off and we're at Rice & Beans. Cool. The team owner on a Baja race crew comes over with a couple of guys and treats me like a celebrity – which of course I'm not, just a wayward gringo happy to stand up – and simply "hosts" me into position. He is taking my gear off me and instructing his crew where to put my bike and in general just making me feel like I'm going to be alright. My guys are making contact with the establishment, making sure that our tires are around somewhere for the return trip, and Ricardo the owner is handy and reassuring and says our stuff had arrived weeks ago in good order, and that he'll get me taken care of. So I've got a room, and my bike is parked right outside the door on the tile patio – I've gotten my gear off and had help getting an outer layer or two off – which was excruciating, but better now than later. I'm pretty much good to go. (I had reduced the dislocation immediately upon standing up right after the crash, small consolation but a big plus at that point nonetheless.) We're all sitting on the veranda for a few minutes, being "fluid," and the plan is for them to keep on riding, head south for a couple days, swing back through and be back at Rice and Beans for the tire changes and maintenance day planned for the return ride. If Stovebolt is

Dennis Hopper on the left and a tourist on the right.

still here, we'll figure it out from there. Time's a wasting, 'hasta luego' and 'vaya con dios' – off they go. I settle in and start licking my wounds, the lone rider down, but no longer puffing smoke and feeling like a dirt nap is just around the next bend in the river.

We had no working cell phones and no SAT phone. That was fine, don't really need them. So they wouldn't know if I was going to be around when they got back until they got back. The plan had been to service the bikes at Rice & Beans anyway, and we'd sent rear tires down there and planned on servicing the bikes there, calling it a midway mark for the trip. If I had to evacuate, with or without the bike, they'd know it when they came back from a few more days of riding on their return leg. I wasn't going anywhere farther south at that point. C'est la vie.

The next day I wake up – if you could call it that, didn't get much sleep, and the place is deserted. Literally. Last night the place looked like Mardi Gras, and the next morning there wasn't even a car in the parking lot. I walked down the veranda into the bar, and in about five minutes, somebody came around and reminded me how much I needed to learn Spanish. Oatmeal and cafe was inbound, and I started getting sorted out. There was a phone and internet – things were looking up. For now, I just needed to figure out how bad I was, and what, if anything, I might be capable of "doing" in a day or so on my own. My thoughts centered on self recovery, perhaps a lone-star hero ride on the slab on Mex 1 into Algodones, and crash and lean on somebody's wall so I could get off the bike and push it through Customs and throttle off into Yuma, and drop the bike on the sidewalk at the hotel. And take it from there. Just making things up as it played out. Where's the coffee? Hola Ricardo, pleasure seeing you, thanks for helping me... (glad you speak English.)

I entertain myself by eating ibuprofen and listening to an MP3, sitting at a table on the veranda and making contact with the outside world, and establishing a lifeline with my wife, Dorothy. She kept me alive and re-sync'd during this contemplative phase of my personal reconnoiter. Thank God I had her, wind beneath my wounded wings. Although she was ready to go right then and there to get in the Dodge with the dogs, and head south from Idaho and come and get me, I assured her that staying put for right now was the best thing, and that I appreciated the option. I was going to wait and see what a day or two would bring, and I knew if I could just handle the bike – if I could manage a way to mount and dismount on my own, or even with a little help – I could ride that thing out. That was my singular purpose, to be able to manage the Punkin' without dropping it. Tough enough on steady level ground, but the return trip as planned would put my wheels over anything but that kind of terrain, and I feared and respected what I would have to be able to do in order to try to take that on. As it was, I had to take a shower that first day in the room with my tee-shirt still on, because I couldn't get it off by myself. I finally got some help at the end of the day, and grabbed another shower, and continued that journey down the halls of pain in a Mexican shower stall. Nice tiles though.

So the place is a ghost town, and I'm sitting at a table, watching a Baja cat prowling for mice in the courtyard, all fresh in some relatively clean clothes while my laundry is hanging to dry on the motorcycle parked outside my room. There is absolutely nobody around save for the housekeepers and the bar guy, and once in awhile Ricardo comes by to say "Hi." What a great guy, Ricardo. Anyway, I'm sitting there, and reading maps like there is no tomorrow and playing with my GPS, running through different solo navigation options. Fuel was my main concern, and how far I could get before having to stop and refuel, and where I might land before dark to get hidden so the night creatures of the dark side wouldn't find me and rob me and kill me before I made the border. I would be on my own, so dropping the bike in the middle of nowhere – including stretches of slab where a friendly wasn't available to help me pick that bike back up – would be an issue. With a wounded wing, the 640 was heavier than a dead priest, and I needed to have a plan if I decided to solo out.

My thoughts centered on self recovery, perhaps a lone-star hero ride on the slab on Mex 1 into Algodones, and crash and lean on somebody's wall so I could get off the bike and push it through customs and throttle off into Yuma, and drop the bike on the sidewalk at the hotel.

I hear voices all of a sudden, and along comes this guy and a stunningly beautiful dark-haired woman walking down the veranda, and they take seats across from me. They are really going after it in this conversation between the two of them, and I make out that she is quite unhappy, and the fellow is being very polite and trying to console her for some reason. They are speaking English, but she has an accent, and as the barkeeper comes to greet them, he orders some things, and she orders several times, not getting what she wants from the available menu – and finally "settles" for something outrageous – I don't remember what, but they were "going to try to make it" whatever it was. We were in Baja, but she apparently wanted no part of that reality, and wanted to be somewhere else. I recognized her accent and the man said "Hello!" to me, brightly and offered his hand for a shake – which I was happy to have. An Anglo and a friendly in this ghost town was already another asset on my short list of things I had to work with at that moment. A very hearty howdy back atcha amigo! "I'm Steve," he said. "And this is Tasha." "Hi – I'm Dave, nice to see ya," I gave – and we traded faces. She looked up and just glared.

I tried this for size, "Prevyet, coch d'yla?" (Gave it the best Russian I had, for the hell of it....) "Prevyet, horoshor – nu pa Russky?" She continued to glare, from underneath her jet black hair toward me.

"Nyet," I told her; but I like to be able to say hello in a few different languages. "Hi, pleased to meet you." She just looked away and lit up a smoke.

Turns out, this fellow "Mike" owned a Baja motorcycle guiding business, and was serving as guide for a couple VIPs on a trip to Cabo – this lady was part of the entourage. There was another fellow along who came by and joined their party, a native New Yorker, and he was also part of the guiding service to the group. These guys started telling me stories every time they could break away from the guests they had in tow, and they were just cracking me up. The party was a lead element doing a reconnaissance in Baja for an upcoming Hollywood film. They told me names that were involved and what they were doing and pointed across the veranda to where a couple of gentlemen were sitting and talking, identifying them and so on and so forth. Longer story short, all the names were 'brand name' Hollywood heavy hitters, and among this scouting entourage was one fellow from Europe who was a director, and a VIP from a world famous museum. (I know who they are, but I'm not writing it down here....)

Anyway, the young lady was from Russia, and apparently not in her element. What her function was I will never know, but she turned out to be a real pip, and from what I gathered in my own mind from spending time in much animated conversation among the two guides over the next day and a half, something of a high-maintenance piece of work! The guides were hauling a trailer with BMW Dakars strapped on for the party to ride when and as they wanted, and doing their thing down there for a couple weeks. They were pretty candid with me, and it was clear they had the personalities and background to be doing what they were doing, very gregarious and experienced Baja people in the short of it. It was all very entertaining, and the sidetrack into the drama unfolding among these people was a rejuvenating distraction from my own problems, and the humor was pretty outrageous. It served me well, and those two guides really blew some wind into my sails. That, and when the original Easy Rider, Dennis Hopper, came by and introduced himself to me, ("Hi – I'm Dennis...") as I sat by myself at a table. He knew I had hurt my shoulder out riding, his guides had told him, and he came over to say hi, and hoped that I would be alright. Asked me if I needed anything. Sent me a drink. Later I sat and played with the two guides, and occasion-

Stovey northbound from Puertecitos on last day, en route to Yuma and hauling the mail all the way.... *(Lincoln Ramsey photo)*

ally "Tasha" (not her real name) and the entertainment value skyrocketed whenever she showed.

My post ends here, the how and why of when Dennis Hopper bought me a Margarita in San Ignacio, Baja California Sur. I made it back home a week later, without outside recovery efforts, under my own power. The ride back for me started a couple days later and took everything I had to give, and then just a little more every now and again. We rode beaches, two-track, sand washes; through the Cirio forests and over mountains from the Pacific side back again – over another 900 miles of off-road before I dismounted for the last time in Yuma. Outside of Laguna Manuela, I ran over a thresher shark in the dunes near the beach. No shit.

My posse came back and helped me do it; I couldn't have done the dirt sections without them, and it was hard. My shoulder and ribs were smacked up like the Skylab during reentry, and it hurt like almighty hell, all the way. It helped to Never Give Up. ■

Route of Legends of the Fall #1

Map of Nevada in the public domain obtained from the National Atlas. (Nationalatlas.gov)

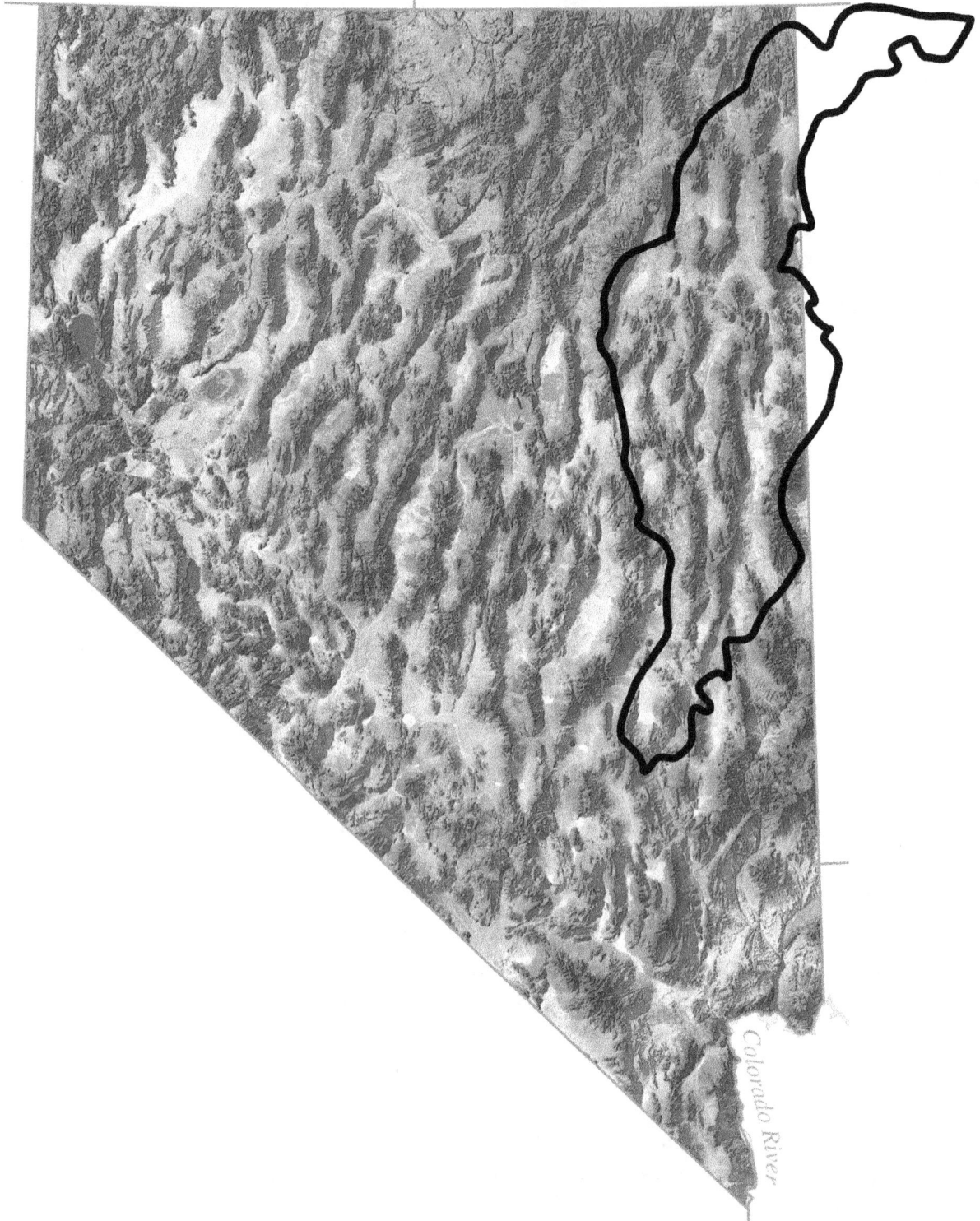

Colorado River

1st Annual

Legends of the Fall

Pre-Halloween Havoc Dual Sport Ride for No Wimps Tandem Bike Rally

October 2009

Day 1

"Forbidden Zone" landscapes abounding on the periphery of the Great Salt Lake.

Snowville, Utah / Bonneville Salt Flats

Keith and I had wandered around pretty hard en route to our rally point in Snowville, and had racked up more than just a few transit miles from Jackson Hole, Wyoming, on the way. We pulled my two-place utility trailer behind Keith's pickup truck down I-15 until we got to Malad, and had some grub at a diner there, figuring this might be our last "civilized" sit down for a while. After that, we felt pretty sure we were on our way over the scenic connections westbound into the Curlew National Grasslands, and then downbound into Snowville, right on the Idaho/Utah line, north of the Great Salt Lake. Well, it didn't work out as smoothly as either of us anticipated, and we SPOTcast our way over hill and dale for hours in those grasslands, looking for a good route and a decent place to land our heads before finally settling down alongside a lake for the night. Still, we found a warm meal at day's end via camp stoves, and a cold beer from the cooler. It was at least near the end of our liaison to Snowville, and an offload of our bikes the next morning.

Snowville had something we were looking for; a place to off-load our bikes and lock up the truck to abandon it for almost a week unattended. We found Delbert's campground on the west side of town to be a perfect location, and Delbert

Stovey getting ready to center-up on his loaner XR650 from Keith's stable. Thanks, Keith!
(Keith Briggs photo)

a perfect score as a helpful steward in our situation. His campground was completely empty at this time of year, but it was open for us and we could even use his shower house if and when the need arises — something that might come in pretty handy upon our return! We paid our camp fee, and got the bikes lit late morning, and gave that big empty horizon to the south a Clint Eastwood stare-down, and throttled off into the alkali flats. Rattlesnakes and cactus — here we come...

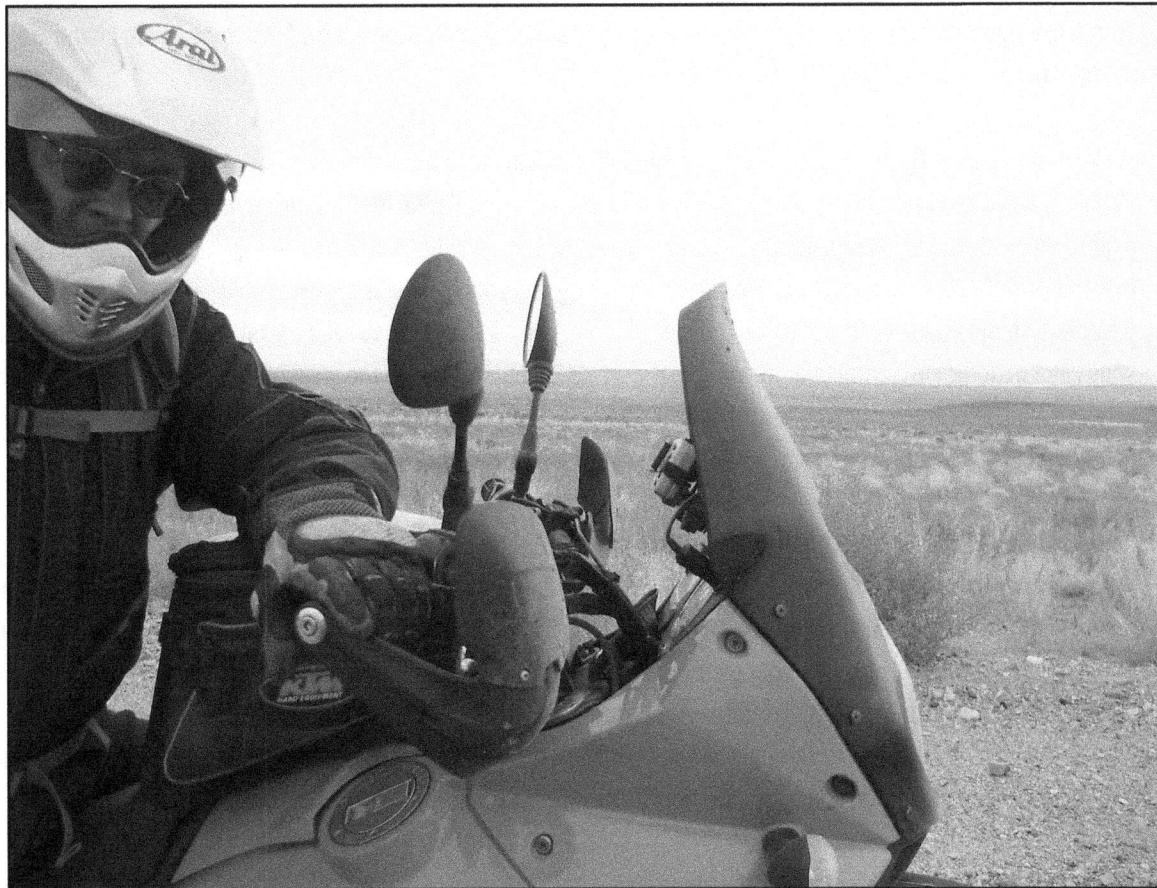

Keith Briggs scouting from the cockpit of his mighty KTM 950 Adventure.

Melancholy skies lent a captivating sullenness to the landscape; an eerie lighting overcast the apocalyptic environs we throttled through at a speed that no zombies could overtake.

We jumped on Locomotive Road and headed southwest towards Baker Springs, and made a right turn for due west — making it all the way to Kelton before we got lost and scared! Spying the vast expanses of salt and mud flats on the northern outskirts of the Great Salt Lake, we got the jits over losing our bearings on what turned into very obliterated two-track conditions, and decided to jump out from Kelton, heading back to the relative navigational safety (known as the "Pussy-ville Cut-off" really) and got back on Highway 30, and left the Promontory behind. Since the East and the West had long since been joined by that famous Golden Railroad Spike, I had every confidence we needn't hang around out here to try and keep things in order.

We knew we could make up some time if we hit the pavement and got around the quicksand potential and straightened out our routing by heading south again after a slabby bypass using Route 30. We bore down on the tanks and faced a grinding headwind under menacing skies and threatening rain showers that were coming at us from the southwest over the Pilot Mountain Range far in the distance — covering everything as far as the eyes could see in a dark and broody weather system forming up. It was all we could do, it seemed like at the time, to keep the bikes steering course into the winds and periodic gusts coming at us, with heavy crosswind bursts to keep the steering stabilizers stabbing. But we kept at it, and being "Day 1" we wanted to show our mettle back to Mother Nature, and not give in to feelings of building fragility on the opening vastness that we augered further and further into.

As we came up to Grouse Junction there was a line on our GPS screens showing the way off the slab, and back out into the desert two-tracks, leading toward Lucin, a Ghost Town whose ghosts had long since left for better grounds. Lucin is occupied by a sole inhabitant, a man named Ivo Zdarsky, a Czechoslovakian ex-pat who managed to flee from behind the Iron Curtain in 1984 in an ultralight glider that he built himself, and who now lives in solitude in a hangar he re-furbished at his own airport. We didn't trespass across this milestone property in the middle of nowhere, but I know if I ever get an invitation to visit, I'll certainly jump at the opportunity with this character. You have to admire this guy for his abilities, talent, determination and conviction. And also, his taste in aircraft and firearms.

Readers who may be interested in an article about Mr. Zdarsky and written by a hoplophobic softy from the East can find something further in the New York Times dated March 28th, 2012. If nothing else, the article illustrates the vast cultural

Navigate, or don't… pick a way and twist the handle. Compass be damned.

expanse between "East and West" that is still extant. Golden Spike be damned… or perhaps it was driven in a little too deeply and a little bit of Hell oozed up from the ground, and we are all forced to live in it in the form of such cacophonous disarray that is our "political diversity" we struggle with so fervently still. I digress…

After our brief passage through Lucin with Lucin Hill on our right, we throttled back up southbound on Grouse Creek Road along the eastern edges of the Pilot Range to the west, and continued down like the riders on the old Pony Express who ran these routes in the 1800s. We were mounted on modern iron though, and I like it better this way. Much better. Horses and ponies are for people who ride horses and ponies – not for adventure riders like me and Keith. Iron ponies made for dirt, that's for me. . . .

The Newfoundland Evaporation Basin to our left – a tidal flat from the Great Salt Lake – separated us from the restricted access Hill Air Force Range that borders just on the east, and we surged ever southward on a great gravel byway. Melancholy skies lent a captivating sullenness to the landscape; an eerie lighting overcast the apocalyptic environs we throttled through at a speed that no zombies could overtake. We stayed on this dirt road for hours and headed toward an ever heightening "island" of peaks that emerged on the southern horizon; the Silver Island Mountain Range that runs SW to NE on the northern outskirts of the Bonneville Salt Flats near Wendover. The skies continued to build broody. We continued to press on, sometimes hard, into the winds.

Stovey skitters a rear wheel into the impending storms ahead, and makes for Bonneville.
(Keith Briggs photo)

Keith had been here before, and he suggested this route which was all new territory for me on a bike, and I was thrilled to be running this express with him… and he knew of the Salt Flats Café toward the end of this day's trails. We made that stretch in plenty of time to have light left in the day for a pit stop at the café before trying to find a rock or a sage brush to hide underneath of for the night, come what may. The Mexican plate for dinner was excellent, and we watched a serious storm blow in as we looked through the café windows during our meal, replete with rain, snow, graupel and microbursts that heaved on the sides of semi-trailers parked in the lot. It was foreboding, but we were committed to the desert at this point, and would begin adventure lodging tonight!

The Salt Flats Café has served as a hub for socializing amongst many Land Speed Record (LSR) competitors over many years, and the place is decorated from wall to wall with hundreds of pictures, autographs, trophies and historic memorabilia revolving around the Bonneville Racetrack universe. I really enjoyed wandering around looking at these venerated heroes of the sport on the walls, and it called to mind my friend back in Bozeman, Dale Gullet. Dale and his Team Bozeman expend great efforts down here on his 600cc Yamaha LSR Warrior. Dale picked up the mantle after he lost his brother Cliff to the salt. Cliff was a land speed record holder on his streamliner, and sadly, he didn't survive a crash here very recently. May he rest in peace. And all the best to Team Bozeman/Team Bullit from now on, in memory of Cliff Gullett.

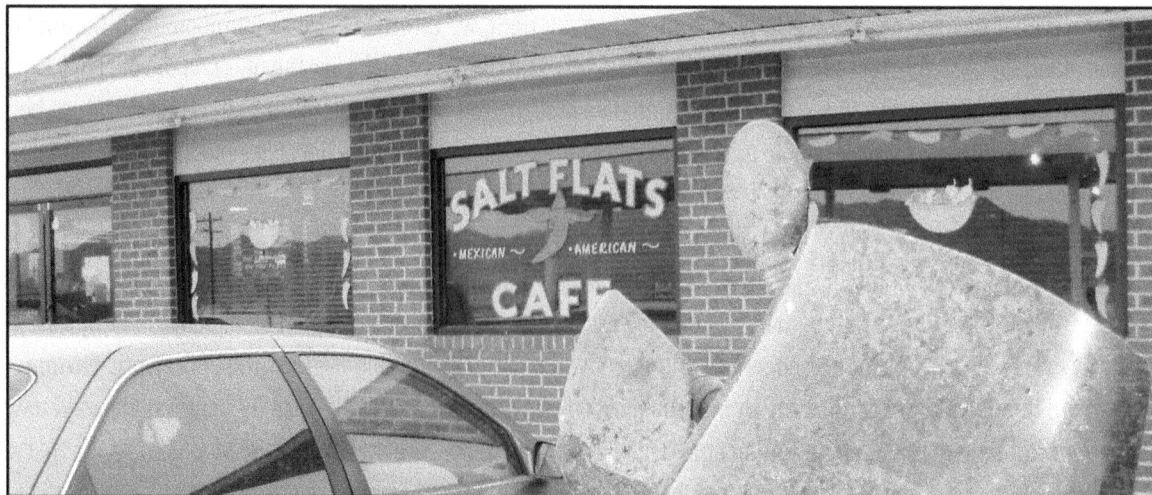

Salt Flats Café is a piece of Bonneville Speedway Americana.

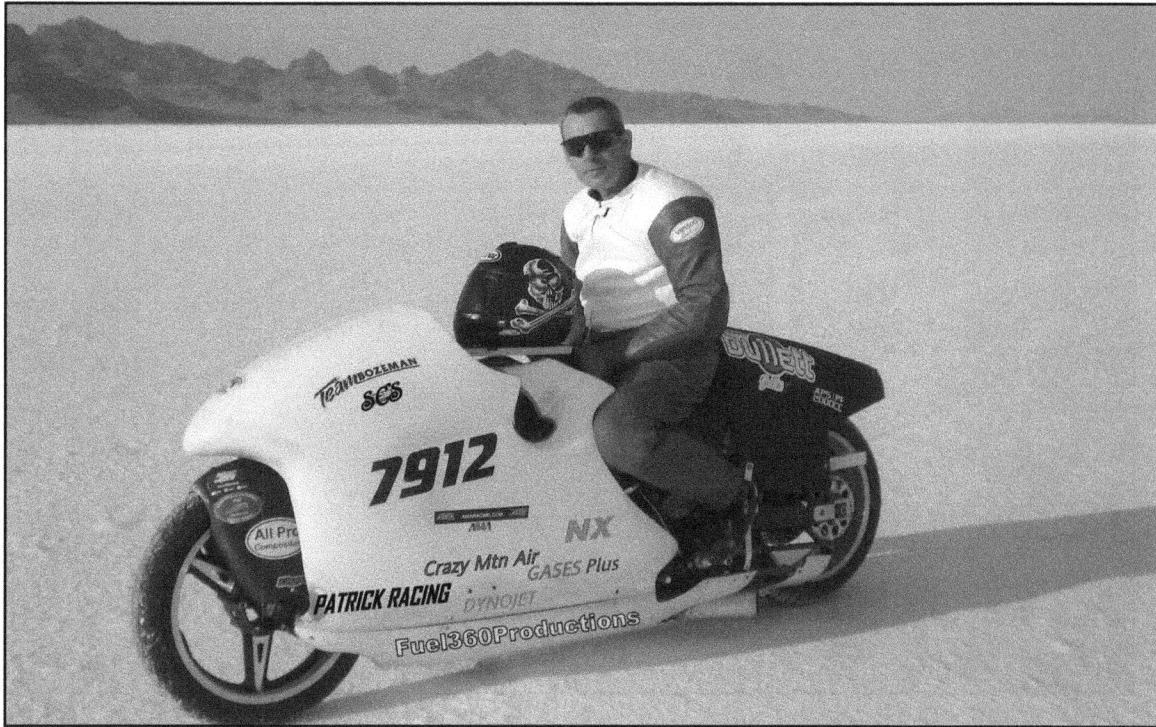

Dale Gullet on the flats. Time will tell. *(All photos this page courtesy of Team Bozeman)*

L: Salt Warrior Dale prepares to do battle with the flats on his Yamaha LSR Warrior; R: Team Bozeman

Dale heading through a time check at speed out on the salt.

No matter how many people are involved, how great the preparations, it's about to get very lonely out there. It's a different breed of man who can keep his vision separate from mirage while holding on with a chin bar on a fuel tank.

God's Speed, Dale... and no crosswinds to you, always.

"Let me tell you about this tent…" *(Keith Briggs photo)*

But as we emerged from the café, stuffed with rice and beans, burritos and ice water, we witnessed a sudden lull in the weather maelstrom. Stepping outside it was beginning to settle down, and we didn't even face raindrops on our faceshields or windscreens! The front had blasted on through, leaving us alone as we dined like adventure kings, and all we had to do was fuel up and head back the way we came in for a few short miles, and find a place to dig in and camp out for the night. Things were looking much better and cheerier! We even stashed a couple of cold tall-boy man-killers on our packs for the evening respite. Nice!

Keith has moments of genius, and his thoughts in preparation for finding a campsite included NOT fueling his big 950 Adventure at the café gas station before leaving. He was piloting a big bike, and we were headed for the hills – shopping for an off-road Shangri-La – and that means losing the gravel, finding two-track, maybe single track, and finally no-track. All in terrain that we could see and understand beforehand, that sidehills into the foothills of these Silver Island Mountains to the north of the Salt Flats. This means taking it easy with loading the bike down even further with the weight of full

Keith following camp setup priority checklist.

West end of the Bonneville Salt Flats

fuel cells on the big KTM twin. If he/we need to do any bike wrangling to get into our nesting place, why make it harder or impossible with that? Smart thinking, Keith! We'll be right back by here again in the morning and will catch fuel and maybe breakfast if the café side is open, and we'll be good to go.

Off we go into the wild grey yonder, but with little concern over being completely overwhelmed by Mother Nature's Wicked Winds of the West. A short 15-minute navigation around the western terminus of the Bonneville Salt Flats gets us right into the toes of these Silver Island foothills, and after a couple of side canyon forays to search for a level-enough bivouac, we find our private draw, and dismount and dig in. A couple of tent poles and an air mattress or two later, we've got some camp chairs out facing south, and rip the tops off of a couple of still-cold man-killers to wave goodbye to a great Day 1 on the trail. Darkness overtakes the bivy, and we're asleep and happy at a reasonable hour — well sheltered and without rain on our nylon castles; the stark, big empty of the Salt Flats our welcome mats.

Left: A KTM 950A, a Bibler, and a Keith flanking the speedway; Right: Utah stark-scapes…

The sun is up and the coffee is good!

Bonneville / Great Basin

Ah, dawn speaks and the deafening silence above the Salt Flats pushes a rested adventure rider forth from within this 40+ year-old Gerry tent that I inherited from my father. I may as well mention about it here, because I wouldn't let Keith have a day of rest from my remembrances associated with this tent – purchased by my Dad back in 1964, brand new from Bowcraft in New Jersey. Back then, this tent was the absolute shit for a mountaineering shelter, having been bred in the Gerry laboratories and sent off into the Himalayas inside the packed gear for the first successful American Everest Expedition, and Whitaker slept in one just like it. I have one of two my folks bought for us to backpack in, when I was 4 years old, long before John Denver started singing the "Rocky Mountain High" and before there were commercial enterprises like "Backpacker" and "Outside" magazines in print.

Hot coffee from the camp stove that Keith sold to me cheap before this trip was a great start as I packed up his Honda for the day, and we were off our plateau shelter in this canyon heading toward the Salt Flats Café early, a hot breakfast on our minds. Arriving before any kitchen people did though, we had to face being denied this sit-down breakfast like men, and I stowed my anticipation of some nice biscuits and gravy for later. A Cliff Bar it is then, and fuel for the bikes. Maybe a choke-and-puke in the city of West Wendover would provide calories for our cake-holes?

Sunrise hitting us below Tetzlaf Peak in the Silver Island Mountains on the north side of Bonneville

The ground is almost level enough to sleep on.

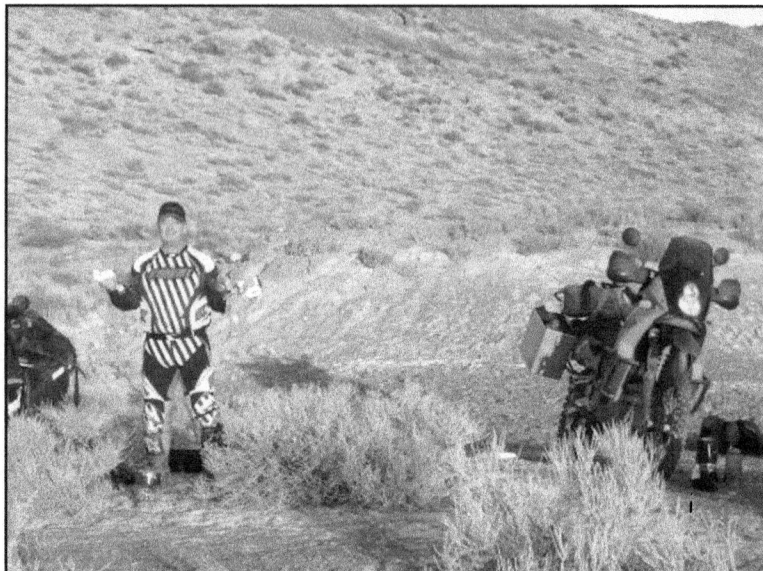

Paperwork at first light.
(Keith Briggs photo)

The USAF airbase at West Wendover sprawled a little to the south as we entered Nevada, and began the state line crisscross we would perform on occasion along this down-bound stretch of this ride. The Enola Gay was hangared here during atomic bomb run training prior to its fateful deployment during World War II. It would be great to stop in and tour the museum, but we decided to turn knobbies instead, and save it for another day. For today, we would run along the line in Utah, all the way to the Great Basin.

The Golden Arches beckoned us from the superslab en route to our connections to dirt through the gambling town of West Wendover, Nevada, and we pulled into Mickey D's for a quickie for the trail. Not the same as some shiny diner in the desert, but good enough. Coffee'd up and poop tubes filled, I was ready for a re-launch. The sun was giving some command presence to the day, so we left town and hooked a left on 93 Alternate to slab it south toward a turnoff back into the dirt on a left-hander towards Salt Springs and Blue Lake. Good traveling this morning on wide-open shots over gravel wash crossings, in between small hills and plateaus and over desolate flats.

The dirt road makes a jog straight south at Salt Springs and follows the Utah/Nevada state line, on the Utah side of things at this point. We were on the outskirts of restricted territory to the west of Wendover Air Force Base and the Dugway Proving Grounds where F-16 Fighting Falcons toured the airspace overhead, and we got to witness a couple of fighters on low-altitude maneuvers as we rode on through. I tried hard to look like dust, and not like a bright yellow jacket mounted on a bright red Honda. I don't think it worked though...

Another jog to the right along the Deep Creek drainage and past Elephant Knoll got us twisting past Dutch Mountain, on the Pony Express Trail proper and heading into Gold Hill. Gold Hill is inhabited still, but it is a place that exemplifies much of the remote desert outlands. Austere. Walled in and miles from anywhere. No Wal-Mart and no bowling alley. Lucky to get a prairie dog fart for entertainment amidst the run-down gold mine buildings and equipment that ring the small cirque hollowed up along this historic "express" way.

Keith up and making it happen in his "full battle rattle."

West end of the Speedway entrance from the café parking lot.

Above: Gold Hill

Right: A view back toward Gold Hill, from Canyon Station on the Pony Express.

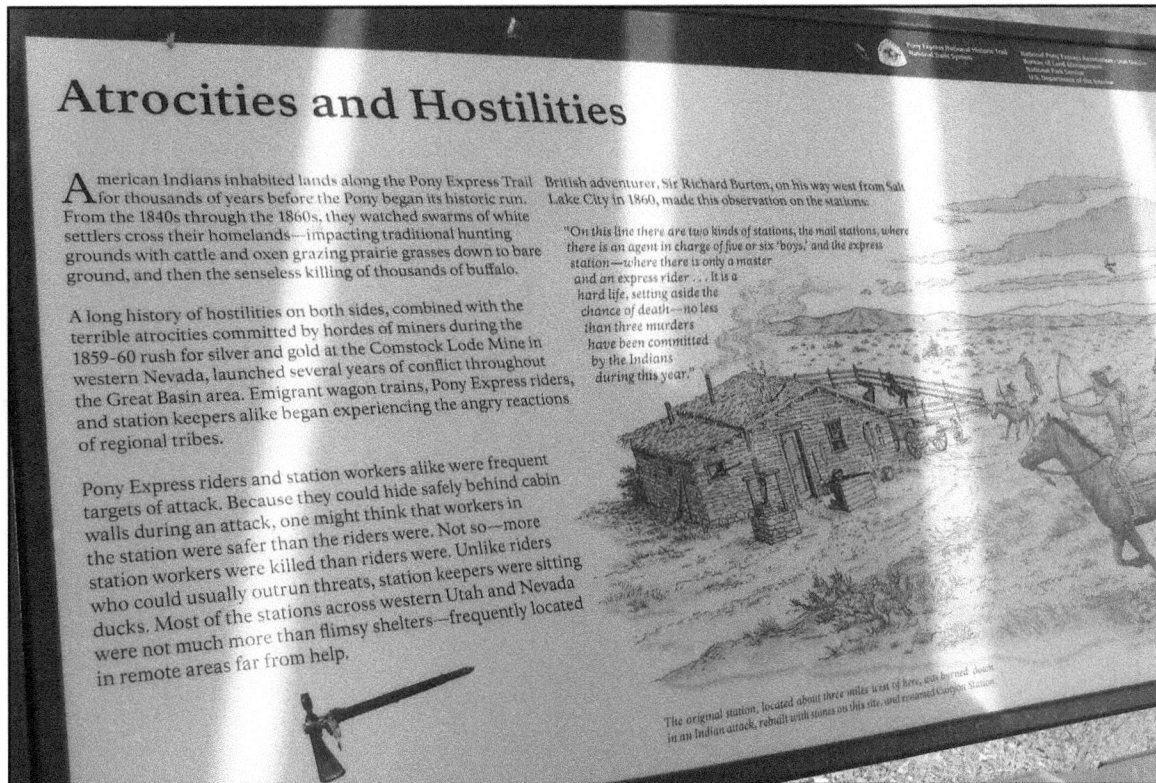

Atrocities and Hostilities

American Indians inhabited lands along the Pony Express Trail for thousands of years before the Pony began its historic run. From the 1840s through the 1860s, they watched swarms of white settlers cross their homelands—impacting traditional hunting grounds with cattle and oxen grazing prairie grasses down to bare ground, and then the senseless killing of thousands of buffalo.

A long history of hostilities on both sides, combined with the terrible atrocities committed by hordes of miners during the 1859-60 rush for silver and gold at the Comstock Lode Mine in western Nevada, launched several years of conflict throughout the Great Basin area. Emigrant wagon trains, Pony Express riders, and station keepers alike began experiencing the angry reactions of regional tribes.

Pony Express riders and station workers alike were frequent targets of attack. Because they could hide safely behind cabin walls during an attack, one might think that workers in the station were safer than the riders were. Not so—more station workers were killed than riders were. Unlike riders who could usually outrun threats, station keepers were sitting ducks. Most of the stations across western Utah and Nevada were not much more than flimsy shelters—frequently located in remote areas far from help.

British adventurer, Sir Richard Burton, on his way west from Salt Lake City in 1860, made this observation on the stations:

"On this line there are two kinds of stations, the mail stations, where there is an agent in charge of five or six 'boys,' and the express station—where there is only a master and an express rider . . . It is a hard life, setting aside the chance of death—no less than three murders have been committed by the Indians during this year."

The original station, located about three miles west of here, was burned down in an Indian attack, rebuilt with stones on this site, and renamed Canyon Station.

"Canyon Station Outpost" sign on the Pony Express Trail.

A slight chicane gets us through the bottom of Gold Hill and we course back into the hills through a pass in the Deep Creek Mountain Range. A pull off at a vista brings us to an old abandoned Pony Express station, long since forgotten or inhabited, but according to the historic marker information, the scene of a bloody Indian battle that left the original outriders and company perished. A redoubt was reconstructed on the site, and supported the Pony Express effort for some time afterwards, before falling to the technological mastery of the iron rails and telegraphs. From these wind-swept promontories in the Deep Creek hills we could view the vastness of the tough alkali flats and mountains far off in the distant east, the occasional Fighting Falcon roars the only sounds from off in the distance. We drop down from the foothills and into the crucible…

Headwinds are sweeping us as we brace our bars and tax the steering dampers, scanning vast open air over mirages into the Utah deserts, eyeing GPS screens pointing toward Callao. A right jog in the ranch spot of Callao keeps us strictly southbound and headed alongside the rainshadow (now that's funny!) on the eastern slopes of the Deep Creeks, and facing crosswind microbursts as we go. We're in the Snake Valley of western Utah, borderlands. Somewhere in between heaven and hell, a place you might well find an old sideboard out in the dust somewhere, with the place name of "Purgatory" scribed across it and left abandoned from having fallen off the back of a fleeing settlers wagon – the "last man out" who thought to bring the sign from an abandoned lonely outpost a hundred or more years ago as he tried to escape for a glass of water. Or one last look at a pretty woman before he died. We bore down on the tanks to shed some incoming wind blasts, and dust devils were visible on the valley floors in the distance, left and right. Looming. Moving. Dusting.

Canyon Station lookout

Redoubt at Canyon Station on the Pony Express in Utah. This is the second effort after having lost the original in a bloody battle three miles from this spot in an ongoing war with natives of this area during the mid 1800s.

I don't know where this happened, but somewhere between Partoun and Gandy we faced the tornadic blast from a single dust devil, and together we got hit only a few seconds apart by the same "devil." I had been leading this stretch on good dirt road, carrying plenty of speed on this Baja Blaster to force a hole in the wind, when a dust devil that I had been looking at for at least a minute or two suddenly got real big, and real close. Real fast. My eyes widened and my stomach tightened as this whirlwind gathered enormous steam at the last second before hooping from the desert floor of the Snake Valley and up onto the road right in front of me, heading north and straight at me. Miles of straight-line tracking on nothing more technical than a dirt road gave way to an immediate demand for some kind of skills, or at least some decision making. At least I thought to myself and then…

WHOOOOSSSHHHHHH……….. I slammed into this funnel cloud at speed – dunno how fast. I was carrying 80 mph during a lot of this transport, and that was my last read from the cockpit when I went in, but I remember throttling off real quick – I guess to let my microprocessor have a second for whatever it was going to be worth, and I remember the vortex sweeping into me almost head-on and slightly oblique from the left as it tracked into our road paths. When my mind clicked into a decision, I was laying my chinbar down onto the fuel tank and twisting my throttle wrist to the stop, giving all it had full-on. I prayed for a steering stabilization miracle from the Scotts damper, and punched into a dirty, swirling mass of dust and tumbleweeds.

Paying little attention to the puck-ered volcano I had just made in my riding pants, I swiveled my head around with the throttle shut off, speedo reading something close to 70 mph, and tried to get a look at Keith, who was right behind me just seconds ago.

I hoped I'd see him, and upright.

Deep Creek Mountain Range

The bike swapped ends back and forth twice, and it definitely felt "lighter" as I skittered through this pissed off wall of wind, but the track held straight and I didn't go down – it felt like a miracle. Paying little attention to the puckered volcano I had just made in my riding pants, I swiveled my head around with the throttle shut off, speedo reading something close to 70 mph, and tried to get a look at Keith, who was right behind me just seconds ago. I hoped I'd see him, and upright.

I watched just the tail end of Keith recovering from the impact of this mini-tornado on his big 950, and he didn't go down either! He punched that behemoth through the maelstrom, and rode that inertial mass from Austria right through the trailer park slayer like a torpedo through a coral reef! Damn – how did we make it? Better question – "how did it even happen?!" I mean, it's not like we have a lot to do out here, and we can't see a dust devil coming for about a hundred miles in most directions, sheeeshh! What kind of slacker could get hit by a dust devil in the middle of nowhere? My mind was reeling, as I reached back with a free throttle hand and pulled some extra slack out the seat of my pants, and made that area fit better.

Winds buffeted for a while, and it made my neck sore toward the end of a long day on the Pony Express Trail, but there were no more windy demons to contend with as the evening hours thought about coming in. We rolled past Gandy and through the Robinson ranch on the way toward "The Border." A few country road connections later, we were tracking straight into Baker, Nevada – home of the Great Basin National Park and Lehman Caves headquarters. And what would serve as our home for the night once we found fuel for the bikes and grabbed whatever we could find that might pass for a cold beer for around the campfire.

A phone pedestal? Seriously?

Just south of Baker is a USFS road that follows Snake Creek up into the Great Basin National Park, and has free primitive Forest Service campsites along its path. That's us! We're up Snake Creek and into the Humboldt National Forest on the boundary of Great Basin National Park for the night, and scouting for good sites in fading daylight. A superb site with picnic table, flat ground, alongside the Snake Creek and covered with Ponderosa, pinion and cottonwood – this will work tremendously, thanks! A few minutes unpacking and throwing out that Gerry tent that I need to remind Keith is over 40 years old now, and how it was the same tent they used on Mount Everest, and we've got a great Camp 2 established. Hot meals are prepping up and some cold beers are flowing around a growing glow in the firepit next to the picnic table.

Sure, it's mountain lion country, and it's also going to get colder up here than on the valley floors, but man, the Fall colors are out and we're traveling well and after all – we're not dead from getting head-on'd by a dust devil! Life is feeling pretty good as the stars come out and we scan for passing satellites overhead, a bag of chips to share with our conference under the desert skies. A great day in the Great Basin....

A scene from The Great Basin.

Numerous fantastic campsites are available up along Snake Creek. We took one.

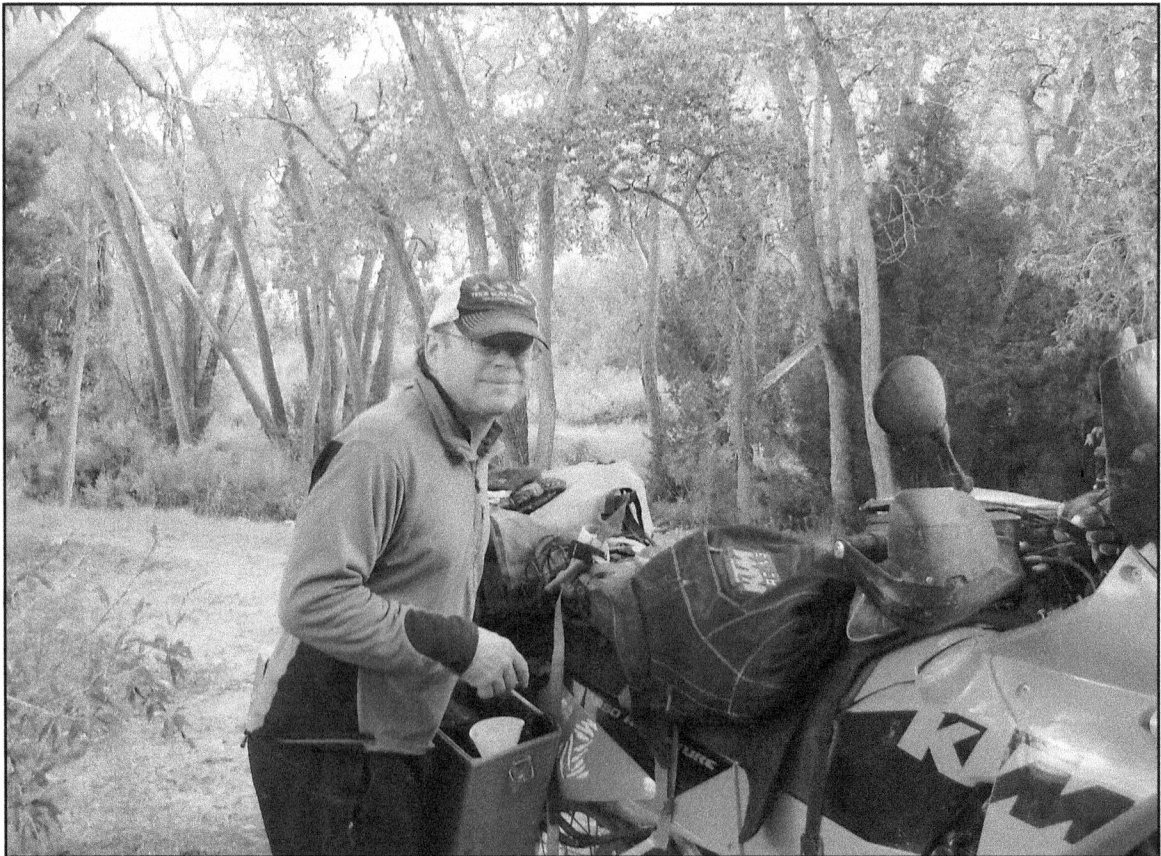

Camping along Snake Creek on the southern edge of Great Basin National Park boundary, not far from Baker, Utah.

View along Snake Creek beneath Pyramid Peak inside the Great Basin National Park.

Great Basin National Park / Area 51 (Mt. Irish)

Well, the weather has definitely turned for the better! A good clear day is waiting outside the blue Gerry nylon, and it's a bright breakthrough finding us at a good breakfast conference under Keith's juniper. We started this ride with no routing laid in, and just have our map data loaded on the GPS's and the usual hard copy Gazetteers. It was Keith's idea to lope down to the Bonneville Salt Flats, as he'd been by that way on his bike before several times, and listening to him talking about it made me feel like I definitely wanted to get some of that with him! So we just headed off pulling the trailer with the idea of wandering around a bit, and making it up as we went.

It was my idea to try and make it as far as Area 51, and turn around from there. Keith was pretty unconvinced we could go that far and back in the time we had, but I had it in my head that it was a "go." Easily. But my idea of a "go" and the pace I like to ride at is arguably mine, and not necessarily shared in earnest by the next guy. . . . So Keith was still a bit reluctant this morning at our Snake Creek campsite that we were within reasonable striking distance of such a far-off turn-around point. But, I presented my case on the picnic table, and persisted. I thought for sure it would be a reasonable one-day haul from where we sat just then to Ash Springs, Nevada – a place I knew we could refuel and find a place to pitch up afterwards, maybe into the hills surrounding Mt. Irish, which was close enough to the Area 51 vicinity to maybe give us something to look at during the night. Yeah, I

Food and fuel in Baker, Utah.

reckoned we could be enjoying a cold man-killer on some mountain top a mere few miles from the sky shows from Groom Lake, and I managed to persuade Keith to drop his guard and go for it. After all, it was only a few inches away on the map...

We made a dash downhill from the inside of the Great Basin National Park boundary crossing the Nevada line and back into Baker, Utah, for breakfast and gas. The map work I crammed into my head on short notice had us routing through Garrison, Utah, and hanging a right at Pruess Lake into the vastness of Hamlin Valley and toward Atlanta, Nevada. We danced our dance back and forth across the state lines again and again, and shot through some ranch tracts as we made bomb runs across the upper Hamlin Valley on BLM land. We had bluebird skies to rally under as we made for a pass between the Fortification and Wilson Creek Ranges, and came into the mining town of Atlanta. Being surrounded by big forests on high ground was a rush after the dry scab of all the valley floors we'd been violating for the past few days, and beautiful again in its own right. So much eye candy and diversity; traversing desert landscapes.

The dirt road through these sections of the Humboldt National Forest was perfect for good, easy and fast travel, so we did just that and had the throttles twisted. The Atlanta Road dead ends into a "T" at Pony Springs on Route 93, where we find a roadside rest area. That's a good place to stop and stretch a leg, and get a drink of water. Keith offers up his cell phone to me as my AT&T is useless here, and I make contact with the wife back home, and the check-in is appreciated by both of us. I hung up while watching the snow-capped peaks of Mt. Wilson and Granite Peak way off to the northeast from where we had just come from. We were on a stretch of slab known as the Mt. Wilson Scenic Byway. Take the slab south from here, and you go through Pioche, Caliente, Ash Springs and eventually end up in Las Vegas. Slab was not the idea though, even if we had to sample some from time to time.

The Atlanta Mine

Keith has a "Hero" upon his noggin, just in case.

Great dirt road from Atlanta south and west.

Our idea was to head south on 93 and get off into the bushes as soon as we could reasonably believe we had access across the mountain range to the west, and gain entry into the next big valley over. This desolate stretch in that valley ought to put us on the final leg into Ash Springs, and the turn-around point. All fine and good, in my head anyways! So after Keith was sure he couldn't get a good enough satellite signal to watch some SpeedVision, we took off and settled in to make friends with the searing heat that boiled off the pavement in miles of shaky mirage to the southern turnoff we hoped to find. I was looking for a way into Bristol Pass...

What seemed like a serious grind later, we got into a turnoff situation, and battled through some twisty dirt two-track leading west off the Route 93 pavement, and toward the hinterlands of the devil's playground named the Dry Lake Valley. You've got to be kidding me... they didn't even have enough energy to give this cauldron a better name. A few miles into it, and I begin to realize why. We crossed through Bristol Pass and left the psychological safety of the Bristol and Highland Ranges behind. Like ships leaving shore for the open sea, we began to resemble smaller and smaller boats the further we got from the mountainsides framing this huge sandy wasteland that seemed to stretch north and south into infinity.

Mid-day was giving way to later afternoon as we progressed into the middle flat of this frying pan, our riding jackets long since been stowed as we now sweated in earnest under a brutal sun, and even at 70-80 mph winds whistling through our pressure suits, and flattening our Camelbaks, it was still hotter than the hubs of hell. This was no place to nav-out, screw up and run out of fuel. My mind began to process...

Hours droned on and we passed by Coyote Wash, Dead Man's Wash, and "something poison" wash... Wow, the criss-crosses from all these two-tracks and old obliterated trackways were everywhere, and we just had to stay on the thickest piece of dirt that passed for a dirt road, and stick it straight south – waiting for mile after dust-cloud and silt-bomb-filled mile for some sign of the reconnection to Route 93 again, just northeast of Ash Springs. Not knowing firsthand any of the two-track or single track that runs all through this area handicapped me for want of a better navigational opportunity. I felt like a chicken and wanted more of a sure thing crossing this wasteland – I did NOT want to run out of fuel out here. I felt like a minnow in the middle of the South Pacific... only a whole lot drier. And thirstier. And more and more desperate for some sign of an exit from the Dry Lake Valley. Would it come? Would we make it to the highway? Would they ever find my corpse – or even think to look for me out here, weeks and months from now? Time + heat mirages + hallucinations from the wind-whipped, high-speed silt bed immersions gave way to mental meanderings I had become familiar with on other rides, but this was new country for me, and we were definitely putting on the miles. Ask Keith, he was feeling it, too, and he's a very experienced rider.

Keith installed a satellite dish on his KTM so we could pick up the Weather Channel and Cinemax soft porn.

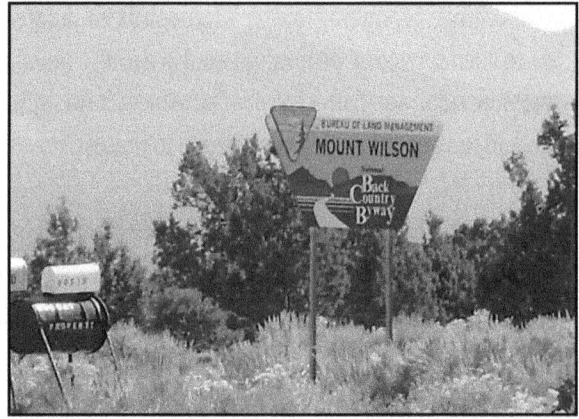

Left: Atlanta Road, the thready line we came out on through the mountains from Great Basin.
Right: Rallying along the Mt. Wilson Scenic Back Country Byway.

There's so much nothing out here in between Coyote Wash and Rattlesnake Spring. Well, maybe a few lost coyotes and rattlesnakes. And a couple of parched adventure riders.

Dry Lake Valley between Caliente and Ash Springs, Nevada

It didn't help that the highway we were hoping to bump back into lies in the middle of nowhere, and the peaks we could see to the south were so far away that it took hours for them to grow and grow into any appreciable bigger size as we neared them, ever so slowly it seemed. The Delamar Valley was just a new name for another vast stretch of nothing on the other side of Route 93, so even though we neared our slabby connection that would save us from a dusty death out on this hardpan, we never knew it until the last minute when the big mirages hit from the blacktop; right when we got on top of it! Finally — some slabby salvation to take us the rest of the way into Ash Springs! Right turn, Clyde...

A well west of the Bristol Range in Dry Lake Valley

...it was well into the 100s – but it felt to me with my Yankee blood drizzling through my sacked-out veins that I was riding right through the center of the Sun.

What was a nice consolation in terms of getting out of that roaster oven valley, and finding signs of civilization in the form of a highway, was paid for in spades with the blistering heat in the high 90s. But over top of this pavement, it was well into the 100s – but it felt to me with my Yankee blood drizzling through my sacked-out veins that I was riding right through the center of the Sun. God, only an hour maybe... gotta make it down this slab and dismount and find some shade, get a drink. Hope this motor holds together – the oil in the crankcase must be so hot and thin by now that it's practically useless. It feels as if I'm riding on top of a piece of molten aluminum, and this engine won't just seize up - it'll just glow brighter and brighter orange, melt through the frame, and leave a streak of lava behind my tumbling yard sale. I imagine these things as my neck strains into the wind I'm generating at this speed, and having fought cross-winds with my head above the plains for days now... I'm feeling fatigued. "How's Keith making out, I wonder to myself..." We burn and melt more rubber under these high-torque motors, heading into the turn towards the oasis at Ash Springs, and our salvation.

What seems like forever is really only a big pile of minutes, and we make that left-hand turn at the intersection of 375, the "Extraterrestrial Highway," and upshift gears one last time on the southernmost section of this leg; our turn-around point. Dead ahead; Ash Springs!

Shell station Shangri-La at Ash Springs, Nevada.

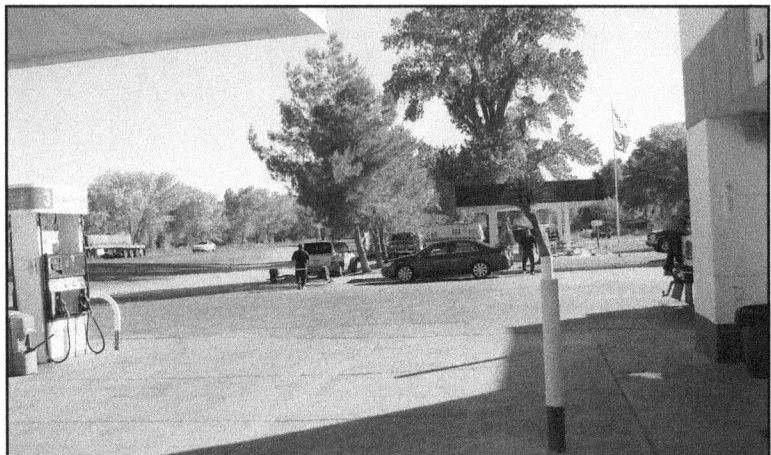

The Shell station is like the pearly gates as we wheel off this river of blacktop and slide in next to the fuel pumps. Damn, it's a lot hotter down here than in the Tetons! A refuel for the bikes and a park in the shade is called for, and that's just what we manage to do. My lips are dry and cracked, my water packs near empty. We make about an hour of it here at this oasis and get plenty of icy soft drinks, food and water back into our systems, and refill our Camelbaks and water bottles for the next leg out – northbound for home starts today. Late in the day, to be sure, and we won't get far, but that's not the idea. Let's just make it up into those hills around Mt. Irish to the north, toward Hiko, and find a place out in the forest to lay our heads; that's for me.

Keith is looking a little ragged and I worry that I pushed a little hard for more than should have gone on, more than a comfort zone amongst friends. Still, I did it – I pushed for it, sold it, and we committed to it. We are here, and we need to make a mile out of here to get back into the woods. A couple of cold man-killers ought to really help take the edge off in a couple hours when we're all done and laid out like condemned men on some dirt in a campsite, with the sun setting over our dirty, weary heads. Besides, this rest stop has taken some of the edge off from both of us, and if we keep going now, after a quick inspection of these cannonballs we've been steering through the cactus and sage mazes, we'll be alright again in a couple of hours. Come nightfall, we'll be done like dinner! Let's ride. . . .

We can't find a route into the forest at the Crystal Springs junction, even though our maps and GPS tell us there are trails into Mt. Irish from here. A couple of stabs following the nav lines on my window screen is getting me jack-shit, and we're bumping into hard fence with no gates. Private land. Sand washes. Nothing. Damnation! Back to slab, follow me to Hiko my friend, I'll get us off this day. . . stay with me Keith, I'm sorry bro'. "Tally Ho – Tally Ho – Tally Ho!" ("I see it – I see it – I see it!")

My gloved wrist is fused to soft rubber wrapped around the throttle of this 650cc Baja machine, and I order maximum fuel to course through this fuel system – the rear wheel barks and the bike rockets underneath my stiffened ass; I'm heading for the Mail Cabin Summit Road just to the north of Hiko, not far up this Highway 318. "C'mon KEITH! Let's do this thing!" We left Crystal Springs like men on a mission, and burned down the middle of those yellow stripes, and never looked back. Our camp was up ahead, somewhere, and we were going to find it and get off these bikes. Fatigue was talking to both of us, and we needed "OFF!"

A short while of slabbing it on 318 got us past the Key Pittman Wilderness Management Area, and through Hiko – a ghost town along the highway. Time is gathering more sand into the hourglass, and the day is long in the tooth. A few miles later and we're downshifting for a sharp left-hand exit from the last bit of civilization we'll see for many miles again, and onto another dirt zig-zag on the maps. A low sun is glaring straight into my eyes as we head in, westbound and upwards, and I'd hoped to be long settled into my Crazy Creek camp chair by this time. But we have more miles to get to the safety of a good piece of ground. "What would Johnny Campbell do? He'd be getting some fresh water at one of his pit stops outside of Catavina, and his crew would have just installed his twin-lens headlamps for the night legs of the Baja 1000. . . Johnny Campbell would take it on through the night, or Steve Hengeveld, his co-rider. They would take it. They would do it. I can make it. I can do it too. Are you still with me, Keith?"

Campsite not far from Mt. Irish, looking northward into the long and desolate valley route outta here, towards home on the return legs.

We'll find something good alongside the pass between the Mt. Irish and Seaman Mountain Ranges – and soon. Light is fading hard, and the sunset is upon us, and these boys' bones are hammered pretty flat at this point. I feel like I've been squeezed through the eye of a needle, and just want to get off the bike for 12 hours. 12 on and 12 off; that kinda works for me, but this was a hammer leg. I know my riding partner feels the same, and any discomfort he may have going right now is on me – I talked him into this marathon section. Will he forgive me? Is he even still back there, close behind me? God, there's just enough light left to do something with as we crest Murphy Gap... and – wait! Turn here now!

We find a side road track that leads a few hundred yards off the main dirt road, and there's a large circular dirt patch compacted on the mountainside and surrounded by about a million cedar – with a fire ring and even some firewood stacked nearby from the last inhabitants. Previous stargazers, campers, UFO nuts – who knows? We're here now, and we've got this grand place all to ourselves! Not a minute too soon either, because we're both shot from a long, hot, windy, silt-bed encrusted day of desert adventure and mayhem. Excelsior – home at last! It would have been easier to climb Mt. Everest, or swim across the Indian Ocean, it feels like. Speaking of Mt. Everest.... "Hey KEITH! Great ride, brother! Did I mention about this tent? This bad boy is over 40 years old, and they used the exact same ones on the 1998 American Everest Expedition... did you know that?... or was it 1963? '64? I can't remember, but anyway...."

Stovey working the camp setup checklist near Mt. Irish, and watching the skies over Area 51 as the sun gives up its last. It was a long, hot ride today. *(Keith Briggs photo)*

(The Milky Way above this 'Legends of the Fall' Camp 3 inspires my poem, "A Journey Under Starry Skies," which I penned after this raid. Reprinted toward the end of this book.) Meanwhile, Keith and I are set up and settled in good and hard. Food and beverages in hand and mouth, the stars are silly-assed bright, and we keep as long a vigil on the 'sky show' from Area 51 as we can, before yielding to the siren songs from inside our nylon castles and goose-down cocoons. Our engines may cool off by morning light, or they may not. Johnny Campbell and Steve Hengeveld might still be at it if this were the Baja 1000, and God Bless 'em for their abilities and might. But we're not long for the rest of this day, and we gave it our all. Two men at the mid-century mark having given as good a push through the barren sage and into the Chubasco blows. Farewell, "Day 3." Conk.

Left: Mt. Irish Range in the background of our southernmost camp on this raid.

Right: Keith settling in for a deserved rest around the fire ring after hammering some serious desert under a blistering sun all day. Maybe some aliens will bring us some ice, or even a frozen margarita? (It might be a long wait...)

Day 4

A nicely lit dawn-yawn somewhere between Mail Summit and Murphy Gap.

Mt. Irish / Ruby Lake NWR

"When gone am I, the last of the Jedi will you be…." "No – there is another…."

Huh? What?! Oh, God, I must have been dreaming…. "where am I?" My face is slathered in drool all covered in dust on one side, and my dream-state is beginning to perish along with any thought of staying down – I've got to piss like a Russian racehorse! I get up and crawl on my hands and knees through the doorway of my Gerry-rigged nylon castle, and out onto the welcome mat on the border territory of Mt. Irish; the few remaining stars fading like the last virgin in high school… a fleeting memory, and beautiful while it lasted. Time to stand up and whip out this light saber and deliver – I gotta jettison some water pressure from my loins. Dreamland meets desert-scape; it's an ethereal quandary as sub-consciousness does a full-contact mixed martial arts bout with the reality of my stark surroundings here in the high pinon flanks ringing these enormously blank desert floors. Day 4 has begun. There must be a Clif Bar and a smoke around here somewhere. Where is my instant coffee and thermo-tumbler? Keith, you awake?

Keith is alive, and he is also able to crawl under his own power, and makes the metamorphosis into Day 4 as well. We take stock – we're both okay, having had some food and water last night, and a night's rest. My Therm-a-rest did its

Cedars scattered to the north of the Mt. Irish Wilderness Area

job and kept me separated from the hardpan, so I did capture some REM sleep. My shoulders are always more stiff and sore from these ground lounges as compared to a Holiday Inn Express and having dislocated my left one three times before, I can really feel the shallow loft of a camp pad these days. Back in the day, a younger body counted lots of sheep while piled on top of these one-and-a-half-inch thick closed cell foam air mattresses, sleeping like a dead man on top of glaciers in the North Cascades, or in a hammock hanging off the sides of a granite cliff in Squamish, British Columbia. Jesus… that was a long time ago. 'When gone am I, the last of the Jedi…'

Stovey packed for battle, Day 4. *(Keith Briggs photo)*

Keith has a smile with or without a recent trail shower. Navigating silt and flats on the long start for 'home plate.'

Okay then, we're packing up well enough, and looking at the Gazetteer for advice, and I've got the GPS software humming alongside my other hard copy navigational brains, and together we figure we are smack in the middle of Nevada's finest hinterlands. We can either stay here, and die happy, or rally on and find our way out heading north. Snowville seems like a young man's dreams as I gather up the last of my gear, and push it all hard inside of this cool Giant Loop Great Basin that I borrowed from my good friend Berg back in Jackson Hole. His company is a dealership for Giant Loop Luggage, and he had a demo unit for me to take. Thanks, Berg! I'm packed, and so is Keith. Time to kick the tires and light the fires... there's a grim-looking valley off to the northwest with our names on it, and we've to return to civilization in a few days. Time for Stovey to try and find top dead center on this mighty Honda; the "Big Red Pig" of off-road desert demons.

After a few kicks like I really mean it, the "BRP" finds ignition and we're warmed up and ready to motor off. Keith and I are relatively rested at the start of this day as compared to how we ended it at day's end last night, but I can sure feel the difference between yesterday morning and today. Musta been a long day... and it feels as if there might be another one, or two, ahead of us. We drop into the Mail Cabin Summit dirt pipe and head off toward the desert floors – bidding a fond farewell to the comfort of these nice juniper sentries that surrounded us. It's off into the Garden Valley to the west of the Timpahute Range, which lies very near the small hamlet of Rachel, Nevada – right on the outskirts of Area 51. A beautiful sunny day is beaming straight at us, and we can't resist the urge to take part in it on our motorcycles, so we do.

We've got some navigational challenges going pretty quick and it's only an hour or so into this morning's ride when we've got some good looks at the mapping for answers to our questions. The veer to the right that commits us northbound across the long dimension of this Garden Valley seems a no-brainer, but soon after pacing across this diminishing track we find ourselves facing another option to run it either "straight up the middle" in a Hail Mary toward an end-zone we calculate as near Sunnyside, and the Wayne E. Kirch Wildlife Management Area; or to hug the valley wall to the west, alongside the Grant Range. Hmmm. . . . What looks like a good course up the middle gets a bit of investigation as Keith and I hump it into obliterated two-track, and silt beds. And badger holes. And even less evidence of humans having passed over this same ground in the past hundred years. And more silt and ruts. Hmmmmm. . . ..

Nevada is our most mountainous state, with over 300 recognized named ranges.

Our southernmost leg in our rear-view mirrors, it's off to the outskirts of nowhere, someplace on the border of the back of beyond once again. Throttles up, and away we go!

Hmmmm... time to reverse-ho. We get it turned around and gather back up on the two-track that hugs the valley wall to the west, and re-run this big Garden Valley. The sun climbs higher skyward, and I've seen this happen before — the days actually continue on until at some point, dawn has been so far vanquished that there is no such memory of it. Soon, there will be nothing but sun, heat and scorpions. Better have our navigation figured out before too long. Zombies will come.

After a bit of dirt road wrangling northbound, we find ourselves right about where we should be, and making good progress across the northern portions of the Garden Valley. There are some boundary issues around the Wildlife Management area, and some water to contend with in a marshy section, so we err on the side of the cautious adventurer and veer east toward Highway 318, to make our northbound connection to the mini-slab into Lund for fuel. We've got a plan, and it's unfolding in all of its Day 4 glory! Outstanding. Me likey. Keith and I hammer through a few sand washes and get up out of the Garden Valley, and grab that left-hand turn, and head north. Our southernmost leg in our rear-view mirrors, it's off to the outskirts of nowhere, someplace on the border of the back of beyond once again. Throttles up, and away we go!

The pavement on Highway 318 hasn't hit high temps yet and we jet up the eastern side of the White River Valley towards lunch and fuel at Lund with wind in our helmet vents that isn't so warm that it loses its cooling effect. If we've gotta eat some slab to make up for a lack of preplanning on our part, and making routes go up the White River Valley, then so be it. We'll make some dirty miles soon enough, when we leave civilization after lunch, and head for the Rubies.

Lund welcomes us at last, and we remove our helmets to expose some serious helmet hair and enter "Whipple's Country Store." Here we find a nice elderly lady slinging dead meat across a hot skillet for a living, and we take a booth after getting fuel. Food and service are high quality as compared to anything I could have been dreaming of, and my Dr. Pepper hits the spot with a hamburger and fries. We're ready for our version of the "Preston Cutoff" across Highway 6, and into Jakes Valley. We'll give it hell across two more big valleys this afternoon, and try for a spot to camp alongside or within the junipers scattered alongside the slopes of the Ruby Mountains, if they'll have us, and we find it. We leave the gentle confines of Whipple's Country Store, perhaps never to darken that doorway again, one never knows. So, the simple smiles and hearty handshakes to a local are all of what may remain if I die before I sleep. I make them the warmest smiles and firmest handshakes I have on board, and remount the Honda.

Nevada also has some seriously desolate never-ending valleys. You want a heat mirage, look no further than a hot Nevada desert floor.

They'll whip you up a good lunch at Whipple's in Lund, Nevada.

View from the 'scorched pavement cam' out of Lund.

Preston is off-piste from Highway 318, not too far south of Ely. We make a meander through Preston to connect some secondary and tertiary dirt roads alongside the Bald Mountain Wilderness, toward the eastern edges of the Shellback Wilderness. There are some great two-tracks up here, and we're giving the bikes their legs once again, but on some much more challenging high-speed terrain. We've got ruts, silt beds and rollers for miles through Jakes Valley, and we're having to stay on our game as we kick the throttles wicked up, and this is great fun! Finding our way across these washes – again with the "Dead Man's Wash" and "Poison something or another Wash" is great fun, silt beds notwithstanding. This section is a great blast for carrying speed – lose it at speed and you're done. Ride it at speed, and it's fun. No in between, just hammer it down and enjoy it; that's why we came out here in the first place.

A couple of brave cedar sentinels, toughing it out in the harsh.

A view north toward the Ruby Range. We make camp on the east side of the Rubys at Ruby Lake National Wildlife Refuge.

Getting out of Jakey's Valley took a few gated fence-line crossing maneuvers to accomplish, but we find our way across Highway 50, "The Loneliest Highway," and get our dirty connection on the north side into the Long Valley. And boy, is it a loooong valley – endless. We scamper up the eastern side on the edge of the Butte Mountains, and make good time on very smooth and easy high-speed groomers and travel this way for hours. There's a traverse across this Long Valley that crosses from the Butte Mountains northwest toward the Ruby Valley Pony Express Station at the base of the Rubys to the west of the Maverick Springs Range. That's where we're headed, and the miles tick away with Fall colors alive in the mountains, desert tans underneath our wheels. What a day this has been – another long one, but not nearly as long, hot or tiring as yesterday, and we had a mid-day food and fuel break, and travel was easy without debacle. Resting tonight will be welcome, as always, but I feel like there's still a little something left of me as we course alongside the mine entrances in the Ruby Valley that lead up into the hills. Tungsten, antimony, copper, gold, carbonite. . . . you name it, they've got a hole dug for it.

A short few miles in the shadows before evening falls, we locate a dirt pulloff from our already dirty road, and gather some steam for a short climb through the junipers to inspect the area for a place to erect our campsite. Just before a spooky little hamlet called "Shantytown" we find this redoubt, and call it good, even though we have to fight the steepness of the slope to pitch in good and proper, but we do and there's a couple of small patches around for each of us to call level and raise tents on a bed of soft pine needles. I get established here with a juniper motel, and Keith finds a spot he likes, and we're in once again – home sweet home!

Our respite overlooks the Ruby Lake National Wildlife Refuge, and it's 'bird central' out there. Sandhill cranes, ducks, geese and everything with a feather is holing up here, and it's quite lovely. I'm happy by the fire Keith has made up for us, and another night of holding court under the stars is upon us. What a journey it continues to be, with more miles yet to go before it's over. But this is our last night out on the trail. Tomorrow, we'll likely find Snowville, and camp there at the end of a marathon sprint through the last of Nevada, and a lick of Idaho, and a sniff of Utah. For now it's a good, good night. And the night comes, and it is indeed, good.

Southern terminus of the Ruby Range near the Chase Mines.

Pinion Inn Express above Ruby Lake National Wildlife Refuge marshlands (aka "Dump Camp").

Mochachino and a Luna Bar makes breakfast a lot of fun!

Ruby Lake NWR / Snowville

Almost a little frost on my tent walls this morning – hell, no "almost" about it. . . but it doesn't feel so cold. I slept warm and cozy in my bag, and the duff was so thick underneath me I didn't need a Therm-a-Rest. Wonderful! I've got a freshly unwrapped "Luna Bar" going for breakfast along with my hot mochachino, so things are not only in order but there is great majesty to the start of Day 5 according to Stovey. We don't have any specific goals for the day, and we even have options, and don't have to end it today either if we want to keep it going for another day and night out. But we gathered ourselves in for a reconnoiter, and we came up with this – "let's get to Wells and find that truck stop, and see how well they manage to feed our sorry asses, and head north onto the California Trail from there. . . ." Sounded like a premium plan to both of us, and we let the gavel fall right on it. Packing and stowage commenced at a leisurely pace, knowing there might be some waitress up on the interstate already waiting for us – to pour me some water and hot coffee while I scour the buffet for everything they have, and eat it.

The Fall colors are more in evidence here alongside these gem-like mountainsides, with the aspen and scrub oaks giving up their jobs, and getting ready to go dormant for the winter. Chlorophyl, xanthophylls and such gasping ghost breaths through living leaves and leaving colorful farewells on branches dotting the hills for miles all around, reflecting in the

Cliffs illuminated by dawn sun in the Ruby Range.

morning sunshine. Frosts of snow are gathering in dusty depths way up high. All sentinels bearing witness to our efforts on this legendary ride, as they die. Bikers with twisted throttles, leaves dead and dying – inspiring future dreams as this ride begins its last day, and the leaves give it their all before their colors perish from this earth. Pictures to last a lifetime etching themselves across the convulsions of Stovey's hard drive as we pack out, head down the slope from camp, juniper berries tumbling off seats and luggage over the bumpy trail back down to the main gravel road along the Ruby Lake. "Goodby geese and cranes, seeya. . . ."

A juniper berry's view from our fire pit, Camp 4.

"Shanty Town." Literally, it's marked as such on the maps.

We get those motors warmed up and start a slow steady cruise north on the Ruby Valley Road past Shanty Town. What kind of place "Shanty Town" might be is anybody's guess at this point, and I can only conjecture that it's a morphed settlement from an old mining genesis. It's definitely occupied and modern vehicles are parked in front of homes; a rope swing hanging from a tree here, a dog barking in a yard there. A few hundred yards later, and we're past the entire settlement – another interesting story rolled past without explanation. Left to our imagination, we roll on by and continue ahead under bluebird skies, making for that buffet in Wells…

Cliffs just as hard as rocks. There's a "Fall bite" in the air as we rider farther north, towards home.

Granite cliffs exposed in the northern part of the Ruby Range.

The maps show ranches, mines and even something named "Ruby Valley Indian Allotments." What sort of real estate that is a man can speculate, but I'm guessing it's not prime ground with much commercial value to a white man – otherwise, why would it have been "allotted?" Alas, the fate of a conquered First Nations people. The tribes of this country won't take any solace from the fact that I personally honor and respect them for their native cultures and tribal ways. There is no consolation for having been decimated and subjugated; lands taken, languages gone, cultures influenced, generations defiled with contamination from "Whitey." I don't have any First Nations friends, and never have. Even though I grew up as a kid not far from a reservation, I never got to know any people who lived there, or had any friends and acquaintances who were First Nations people. So, I press on by this spot on the map in the Ruby's; "Whitey" on a Big Red Honda with a Luna Bar melting in his grumble box.

Our right turn is approaching and we'll leave this gravel road with a connection onto 229, a short paver that'll give way to the slab on Route 93, "The Great Basin Highway" that we've done some business with off and on already on this ride. Knowing that you have to take the good with the bad in life helps me digest the fact that I've got to point this Baja capable machine down the pavement again, but I know that after a sit-down meal in civilization, I'll get to burn another full tank of gas on the California Trail, and run some dirt twisties through several different mountain ranges in the borderlands of Idaho, Nevada and Utah this afternoon. The terrain promises to be enjoyable and adventuresome, not to mention, new to me! So I'm still grinning underneath my battle gear as we motor off the dirt and hit the highways into Wells. "Take 'er easy, Ruby Valley. I hope to pass your way again."

Stovey shoots a shoulder cam view of Keith, who is snapping a still whilst staying at the ready with a Hero Cam on his head. Where's a Bigfoot or a UFO? We're ready...

Snow is capping the peaks and ridge tops where "dustings" are paving the way for more serious winter layers of snow.

Stovey can't remember what a hot shower feels like sometimes. *(Keith Briggs photo)*

Northeastern view across the top of the Ruby Valley, heading into Wells – the Spruce Mountains in the background

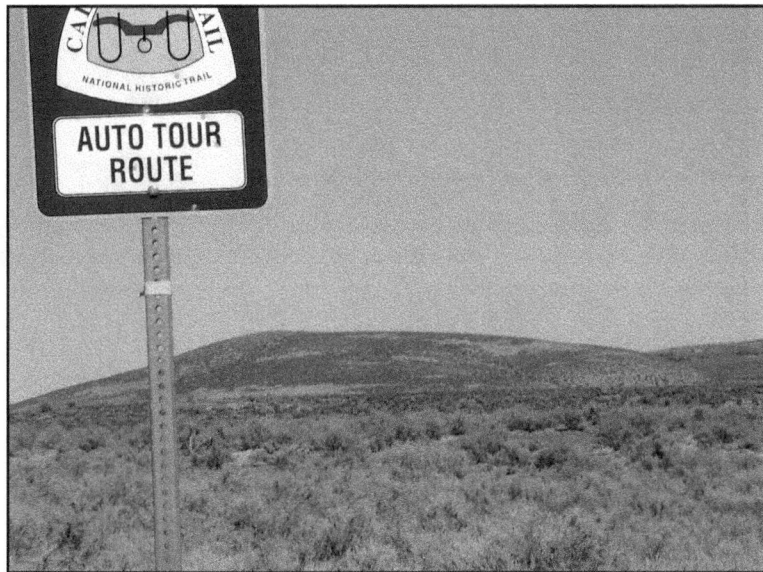

One of my least favorite photographic compositions. Ever.

Two or three mountain ranges over to our right is the track we laid a few days ago on our down-bound legs out of Wendover, but I can't see them from the saddle, just imagine it in place somewhere on the jigsaw puzzle I have in my mind. All the ground from here to there is still unexplored by Stovey, and I take mental snapshots all the time as I go, putting them onto that "hard drive" I have in there somewhere. I hope that if and when the right times come in some future moments out on another trail, that I might conjure them, and they might help a few useful pieces of a puzzle together, for navigating. Or, perhaps it'll be just another <CONTROL>, <ALT>, <DELETE> moment for me, who knows? Where's that "Flying' J" truck stop anyway?

Another rolling dismount at the pumps and the sidestand is down, high grade octane pumping away into this giant Acerbis Rally tank. Keith and I are about to relish a cornucopia of delectable culinary treasure, for about $7.95 apiece. Endless coffee, bacon and eggs, hash browns, biscuits and gravy.... whatever a lucky adventure rider could dream of, and probably more! I let myself be ambushed by the whole experience and settle into a nice booth and let the comfort of a covered building with lights on inside and the smells of fresh hot food enter my pores. There wasn't much I could do for the helmet hair I was presenting to the general public, but I performed one community service in the form of a good hands and face washing before sitting down. Man, that feels good, too! Coffee and water are being laid in by the nice waitress as I begin the approach to my grazing strafe upon the buffet. Plates are too small, gonna take a few trips back here, so I'll recon the area of operations on this first pass as I go... it'll save time later to not have to fly over the whole thing just to find a bucket of gravy, or some syrup. Details, details...

It almost takes a wrecker to hoist my fat ass back out this booth, but I managed to get un-wedged from in between the table and the back of the seat, and my pack, helmet, fanny pack and bar-pak gathered back up into my warm, semi-clean paws for a push through the door. Heading for the bikes were two well-fed, happy men! That was a stop worth aiming for and I note that it's usually always a good call to make for a civilized stop every now and again. I get a lot of mileage out of a stop like this, and feel like I can go for days and days right afterwards. Sometimes I can. A lot of times I do. Grateful for the good meal and warmth on a chillier clear Fall day farther north than the devil's cauldrons below us, we gear up and take our saddles for the northerly latitudes on the California Trail.

Nearing the end of our trail...
for this trip. *(Keith Briggs photo)*

A last big slab blast on Route 93 northbound from Wells will take us to Wilkins and the right turn-off onto the old California Trail Backcountry Byway. Thankfully, the pavement isn't a marathon, but it takes a while, and I'm feeling about through with it. If I don't see another foot of slab for the rest of my life it would suit me right down to the ground. I'm not a road rider – never have been. No appeal in it for me, and fifty feet of travel on it only serves to reinforce why that is for me. It just sucks. Gimme some dirt, and lots of it, if I have my first pick of terrain.

Another pioneer trail is beaming a squiggle across my GPS screen as we follow along to punch through these valleys ringed by mountains in the extreme northeast of Nevada, and it's a pleasure to let the scenery in as we ride on. Our trail ahead will have us passing through valleys along Rock Spring Creek and in the shadows of the Delano Mountains covering more mines to the east, and still more ranches and abandoned town sites from days gone by. A byway with silent hulks of ramshackle huts from old settlements built by pioneers with no chance of stopping in at a Flyin' J truck stop for a buffet feast. Whatever they ate they had to hunt down and strangle into a cookpot, and grow in a field plowed by some aging nag that might also have ended up in the same soot-covered pot after a lifetime of toiling under a plow yoke. Different life and harder times than I have ever had to endure, previous employments for jerkoff bosses notwithstanding. People from my generation in this country have not known these kinds of odds, in large measure. Rolling by ghost towns and decrepit home sites from abandoned pioneer settlements gives me perspective, and I hope I never lose touch with what I have to be grateful for. More fuel for the pumper carb in this Honda, and I straighten out a few more twisties through the forests... sweet adventure land. I am immersed on a Fall afternoon in valleys and foothills on the California Trail. "Catch me if you can!" Whitey is on a rampage...

There are a couple dozen side road and two-track turn-offs alongside this route and we encounter a map-maze of opportunity to get lost "out there" right now, or on future excursions. It would be easy to sidetrack up any one of them and explore in more detail the micro-adventures that lead to still further off-road challenges and premium campsites. More nights under the same stars await here, to be sure, and it's like this on every ride – going by chance after chance to shut it down, and change the big picture – to go out on a two-track or a single track and head in. Commit to something else. Make another ride happen. Make another connection to some farther valley. Crest a rocky pass and make another

CALIFORNIA TRAIL — ROCK SPRINGS
"WE PASSED ON OVER A ... BARREN ROAD ... TO THE ROCK SPRINGS. ...
THE SPRINGS RISES ON THE RIGHT FROM UNDER A LEDGE OF ROCK AT
THE POINT OF A MOUNTAIN RIDGE. ... IT IS GENERALLY CROWDED WITH
FOOTMEN, HORSES, CATTLE & WAGONS." – A. R. BURBANK, AUG 7, 1849
GUIDEBOOK AVAILABLE
TRAILS WEST INC. P. O. BOX 12045 RENO NV 89510
2000   C-20

A quotation from A.R. Burbank marks Rock Springs along this section of the California Trail in extreme northeast Nevada.

valley view appear across the faceshield of my helmet. I should be so lucky as to get out again, and make these kinds of decisions in life. Dual sport adventures and off-road riding hold the world for me, and I hope I'm around for a lot more of both. I miss my dog, Captain. I wonder what my wife is doing? There's a really cool-looking spring on the side hill right there! Here's another left turn... "Where's Keith?" Streams of consciousness from my brainpan on Day 5.

Rock Springs. Pretty cool place along the California Trail, northeastern Nevada.

Keith doing a leg stretch before we commit to a solid afternoon in the saddles through mountains in three states on our way back to the truck in Snowville, Utah.

Goose Creek Road is our yellow brick road this afternoon, and putting its course in the middle of our GPS track is the goal as we fight some dusty road particles that continue to argue with the surfaces of our faceshields. In late afternoon lighting, the glare is a safety and navigational challenge as we have to continually wipe off the dust and flip up a shield suddenly to get a clear view of an approaching corner, oncoming hunting party in a truck hauling a trailer full of ATVs or take a quick look down at a GPS screen. Hours are ticking away on us, as we approach the witching hours – when the lighting changes for the worse as far as navigation and safe sight lines goes, and fatigue sets in – and another day is getting long in the tooth. A few more stretches, twisties and settlements to go, and we'll be through all these valleys to the south of City of Rocks in Idaho. It'll be a three-state day by the time we're through...

Somewhere in here is our right turn from the Goose Creek Road onto another dirt groomer that follows south along Grouse Creek, and we leave Nevada for Utah. We're making big zig-zags now on connections around these mountains, and head through some pretty country still beaming with good Fall color on the way toward Lynn. Another left angles us northeast through the Grouse Creek Mountains. If we turned the other way, we would shoot straight back down to where we headed south from Route 30 into Lucin, and made our descent through the flats along the Pilot Range, heading towards Bonneville. A few short miles in the opposite direction, and we could start this ride all over, and do it again! "Throttle back Stovey.... you're homeward bound on the last leg." More mental shenanigans – it's easy to digress!

We exit the western shadows of the Grouse Creek Mountains along our dirt pathway, and have the sun more or less at our backs now, thank God for that. We're rolling by the Raft River heading north, and enter Idaho in late afternoon, passing by several small town settlements like Yost and Standrod. The Raft River Mountains are on our right as we head across the northern edge of these sweet peaks in extreme northwest Utah. Strevell, Idaho, is coming up on my GPS, and we'll lose the dirt roads we've been riding on all afternoon for good as we turn onto Route 42 for Snowville, a sunset at our back. I've had a great trip, and I'll

I'm thinking we're going to enjoy a hot shower at this point... commando wipes will only carry you so far...

Left: Back at Home Plate for a shower and a good meal. Keith and I will spend this last night out camped at the truck in Snowville – miles of memories freshly brewed.
Right: "Grime" ambassador. Fully qualified. *(Keith Briggs photo)*

end it soon in slab formation with Keith on his big 950 Twin in a short time. I'm glad he got me into this ride with his inspirational banter about Bonneville, and the backroads and byways he'd taken in the past. I only hope he's still talking to me when it's all said and done and we're back in civilization. We had some long day pushes to be sure, and a couple of them made for sustained life outside of comfort zones for both of us, and to each his own and everybody's mileage varies on this. I don't mind a bit of rough, and I know Keith is as hearty a fellow and capable riding companion as one is likely to encounter, experienced too. I just hope we didn't cause any permanent harm to our riding experience by going all out on the high-mileage days! Time will tell...

Headlights are on for safety, not for visibility – it's not dark out but the evening hours are upon us. The paver we're on is losing its grip on us as Snowville emerges from the horizon, and the vast flatness of the Great Salt Lake shimmers twilight glows to our right. The final downshifts are happening as we turn back into the empty campground that Delbert let us park our rig in for the past week, and save for one RV, the place is one empty campsite after another until we find our parked pickup and trailer, just where we left it about six days ago. I'm thinking we're going to enjoy a hot shower at this point as we made no opportunity during the ride, and I'm a pretty ripe apple. Commando wipes will only carry you so far, and I know I've hurled myself way past the breach where this is concerned, and I want a hot shower and something to eat. And a cold beer. I'll be looking for some contact bars on my cell phone, and I miss my wife. And my dogs. And this ride. I miss it already, where did it go? It's gone, already! Gone but not forgotten, shadows and dust. Images in my mind and smiles on our faces, 1134 miles under our wheels, and not one flat tire. I'll buy that.... ■

"Thanks for the ride, Keith!"
(Keith Briggs photo)

Route of the Adventure Rider Montana 1000

Map of Montana in the public domain obtained from the National Atlas. (Nationalatlas.gov)

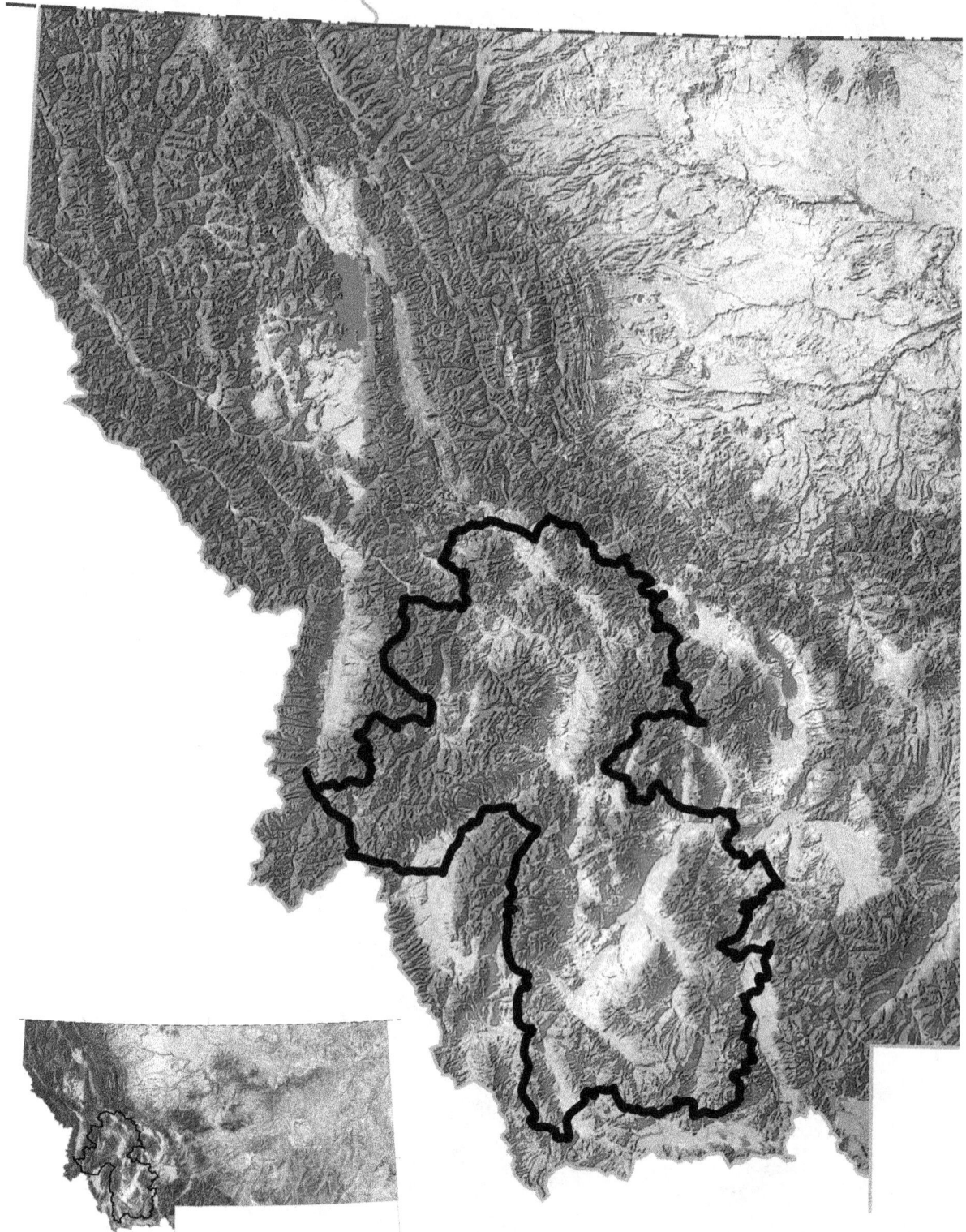

The Adventure Rider

Montana 1000

July 2010

Mike and his son, Conrad. Stovey leaning on "Casper the Friendly Punkin."

The Adventure Rider Montana 1000 is in the can — another great ride is a memory, and one for the books. I signed up for the ride in February on the forum, and knew I just wanted to go. The KTM 640 Adventure was still in the stable, as was the 300 EX/C, but I decided back then I wanted to sell them both while they were still in good shape, and convert that into cash for a single brand new rally raider — that's how "Casper the Friendly Punkin" was born. Armed with my new 450 XC-W Six Days, I set out for Darby, Montana, to do some raiding on dirt roads in the hill country of Southwest Montana.

Having the opportunity to visit my grade school and high school friend Mike and his family along the way to the rally point was a good thing, and a wonderful experience. I met Mike's wife and son and I was asked to spend the night in their beautiful remote home they had built near the Continental Divide. Thanks Mike, Jane and Conrad for your hospitality and warmth! A week after I arrived at Mike's, I would end the rally on Day Six on an alternate to the primary route that I conjured, taking me to within about 10 miles of his place once again, more or less as the crow flies.

Day One of the Rally proper got us off to a good start from Darby, right from the fairgrounds south of town where they had just finished the first half of the annual Logger Days. An hour after our morning departure from the riders' meeting there would be chainsaws re-fired for the rest of the competitions and we left that junk show behind by about 10 a.m. I decided I wanted no part of dirt road dust from what could have been 80–200 riders in front of me, so I was the first to leave and solved that issue right off. I stopped somewhere along the way to Skalkaho Pass and took a few pictures, and after about 15 minutes, I heard

Jane and Conrad

riders trailing up from behind, and let them pass as I got more pictures. Soon after remounting, I passed all five again and was out of the dust for the rest of the day. I found fuel and a couple of 'man-killers' at the convenience in Drummond, and by 3 p.m. I was on my way to Garnet for camp and end of the day. By 4 p.m., I had located a recovering roadcut with pines jumping back up through the middle of the road, and pitched in. Five bars on my AT&T got me through to my wife, I had camp in, and two relatively cold 24-ounce Hard Ice Tea's on standby for the night. The view from the roadcut – which made for a landing strip of about 12 to 14 or so campers in all by the time the last riders settled in – was outstanding. 165 miles under the wheels.

Skalkaho Pass in the Sapphire Range

Day 2

View from Camp 1 on the ADVRider Montana 1000, 2010

Garnet / Marysville / Delmoe Lake   265 Miles

Day 2 began at 0500 and I lollygagged about with two cups of steaming orange mocha cappuccino going as I broke camp – quietly. I broke camp with throttles open by 7:03 a.m., continuing solo. There were more than a dozen adventurers dozing nearby. I passed a group camped in the trail by pushing the bike cold through the tangle of tents and bikes, then out away from everybody toward the dirt road, and lit Casper up once again. He fired and purred, then he roared slowly on and on as I began to cruise on a warm 4-stroke from Austria; a fabulous dream machine begging for technical track and a good whacking on the loud handle... but this was a cushy ride to make miles, see some country and meet new people having some fun. I made a fuel stop after making pavement, and inquired about a café for breakfast. Thirteen miles ahead in Ovando was the "Stray Bullet Café" – perfect. I rolled in alone and as I sat to order, Marcin dismounted his bike outside, filled the door frame then joined me. "Huzar" had ridden in to the rally from the Seattle metro area, and he and I ate together exchanging pleasantries. He's a very witty and fine fellow; a Polish National here in the States for the past couple decades. He's also a computer genius with a degree from Princeton. He was on a big Suzuki V-Strom and liking his ride as well. I petted the beautiful Shepherd (looked like he had some Tervuren in him) before idling off and heading east to Lincoln. More fuel and a right hand turn got me back onto the dirt toward Marysville, the rally point for the day. I made a photo stop and let some riders past as I took in the view and snapped some pictures, then made tracks and passed a few riders back, and made Marysville by 12 noon.

Sanitation is paramount in grizzly bear country, so "MasterChief" is practicing camp sanitation and personal safety by disposing of his trash. Underneath a co-rider's tent.

"Mikrow" at Camp 1

My new best friend...

Stray Bullet Café in Ovando, Montana

Above: Near Lincoln, Montana

Left: Fellow adventure rider south of Lincoln, en route to Marysville

Marysville, Montana

Parts of Marysville had seen better days. Inside the old saloon.

Looking south from near Mullan Pass, 12 miles north of Highway 12 and still north of Comet

Marysville's one horse up and left long ago, so I bolted for Day 3 on the spot, deciding to try some of the more challenging navigation on the rally in the afternoon, and see what I would find out about the alleged road closures dooming the primary route as planned going through and past the Rimini mines. As it happened, I made good time with nobody's dust ahead, and navigated on the fly with the Garmin 60CSx in my custom cradle I had made myself. The road closure was there, but I routed around and stayed legal on good dirt into Cataract Basin and some glorious views. Penetrating further into the late afternoon, I made the ghost town of Comet and found bad tracks in my GPS, but good directions on my paper. So, after wangling around that extinct mining community, I set off down the High Ore Road toward Boulder, and made the Frontage Road in good time.

Downtown Comet, Montana

I fueled again in Boulder after backtracking for it, to load up for a final rally that would bring me all the way down along the Boulder River, along Lowland Creek and towards Butte from Walkerville past Sheepshead Mountain. The sun began to drop to the west as I made the north side of Butte – hometown of Robert Craig Knievel for those who keep track. I had made some bigger miles today and was beginning to feel it, and would have poured a basketful of wolverines down the front of my pants on a bet to secure a shower. After checking a few motels for exorbitant prices, I grabbed a trayful of Arby's glick and used the bars on my Sony Walkman cell phone to holler at my wife. She had been following pretty attentively along this day on the live feed from the SPOTcast, and was wondering when the heck I was going to go down by 8 p.m. at this point and the cell call. I still needed fuel but vowed I would make the Delmoe Lake rally point that marked the end of Day 3 on our route. I grabbed gas and a liter of water and stuffed it in my pack, and hauled out of town to reconnect with the route on Continental Drive, and remake the route connection south of Butte. Whoever laid in these tracks was in good humor, because I was leaving dirt road for two-track, then two-track for single-track.

There along the interstate I found a wire fence keeping me from the slab to the exit less than a mile away, and try as I could I could not find the way according to the GPS route laid in. There were two-track ATV trails scattered all around up in the hills and running underneath power lines, going in every direction. Clearly it was a well-used recreation area, but I just couldn't connect the dots or breach the fence to I-90. So, I ended up blowing almost a half hour trying to connect the dots before I bailed out and turned around for a sure thing as I know my way around Butte in general terms. It was back down the hilly two-tracks and into the outskirts of town on backroads for me. I made for the nearest I-90 on-ramp, and jumped on. The sun was a red rubber ball, quickly sinking to the west...

88

One of the United State's largest Superfund toxic cleanup sites – the mine in Butte.

The sun was almost gone by the time I made the Interstate 90 on-ramp and headed east for one exit, getting off at the top of the hill, Our Lady of the Rockies watching me the whole way until I disappeared at the Homestake exit, right past the fence along the highway I was handlebar close to 40 minutes before, and having no luck punching a hole in the wire to make a leap out onto I-90. Just as well....

I found the nearest Forest Service fire ring as the sun was setting, and was glad to spot it. That ring for me meant weight management, and as I dismounted at dusk, the flurry that ensued had my bike drained of oil for both the engine and

Butte, Montana

Our Lady of the Rockies, watching over Butte

transmission, pouring it out over the leftover coals and logs in the fire ring, still boiling hot. Filters and oil changed, the mosquitoes continued to ravage and swarm as I gave the fire one match and incinerated some of the pesky rascals, along with my trash and empty oil containers. I had the cell phone hung up with Dorothy and the tent up with mattress and bag inside by five minutes to 10 p.m. 265 miles today – I'd killed two rally days off in one, and my plan for "Day 3" was a down day – by Delmoe Lake. And my bike maintenance was mostly done!

With the evening meal having been devoured at Arby's and the oil change behind me as well, there was little left to do but enjoy a few minutes under a wild Montana sky with the Milky Way in attendance, and a few incinerated mosquito corpses for ambience. The riding was easy, but the navigation was rewarding and I had covered a fair bit of ground during the day, giving myself a good challenge. It felt really good to cover all that ground that was new to me, and see those high mountain valleys with blooming wildflowers in perfect weather. The heat of the day kept me after the water in my Camelbaks, and I had established some Monkey Butt on top of that typically plank-like KTM saddle. With the lake just down the road and down the hill, I could almost smell the water! A good lake or a creek bath and a full rest day tomorrow would be really nice, and the weather so far was fantastic. Nothing to do but drift off and let another dawn greet me whenever I managed a roll-out, and not worry about a single thing.

Life feels pretty good, and this ride is showing some great mountain eye candy to this frisky adventure rider. I hope all is well with the rest of the rally raiders on the trails out there, wherever they may be. Many should be in or near Marysville, but that was just not enough riding for me today, to stop there. Some of the guys on big bikes would appreciate the shorter ride miles no doubt, but Casper the Friendly Punkin, my dream bike white KTM, was feeling his legs and wanted more than a stop at the scheduled end of "Day 2" had in store. My bike had performed flawlessly – a wild ride and a perfect fit for me, and no disappointment for the investment made converting two motorcycle sales into this one excellent match for Stovey.

Happy, lucky and a little stinky, I finally drift off to sleep on top of a Therm-a-rest mattress; pissed off relatives of the dead mosquitos I had eliminated in my small conflagration trying to get at me from outside my nylon castle.

Day 3

Dawn at the Homestake exit, my Camp 2. I had all day to make it less than 10 miles from here and set up a new camp, take a bath and do nothing but air out freshly stream-washed riding duds.

Delmoe Lake Rest Day!   10 miles

Day 3 – a "down day" at Delmoe Lake. Good campsite along the route and away from the pay campground. Just want more water, no bears and some rest for the route tomorrow. I got all of the above. Changed air filter and lubed chain.

A little background on the monument, "Our Lady of the Rockies" that stands watch over the city of Butte is interesting. With donations from benefactors and the time of volunteers and a Sikorsky Sky Crane from the Nevada Air National Guard, "The Lady" was completed in December of 1985 after six years of construction. She stands today atop the Continental Divide as a monument to women, and is a lighted memorial at night. She reminds us of how powerful the force of our wives and mothers is in all of our lives, perhaps much more so in a rough and tumble western mining town such as Butte. I've seen her day and night, and it is a sight to behold, glowing on her watch at night especially. A mining town can use such a guardian, I think...

The Berkeley Pit is a giant copper open pit mine on the north side of town, and one of the largest Superfund hazmat sites in the country. Groundwater continues to fill the mine, and with the high ph (negative logarithm of the hydrogen

Eureka Solitaire one-man tent; or "maxi-bivy?" Not a freestanding unit and cheaply made, it is none-theless a pretty compact and inexpensive utilitarian way to get light-duty shelter. If it explodes or melts in rough weather, you're out a night's sleep and about $65. I think of it as a giant bivy sack rather than a 4-season mountain survival in all conditions setup, and it's worked for me for several seasons already. I wish they made a more "bombproof" version, and freestanding would be a plus.

ion concentration...) very acidic water in the pit, it leaches the surrounding heavy metals from the rock and soils. The resulting soup is a toxic liquid full of arsenic, cadmium and sulfuric acid. A flock of migrating geese landed on the water surface in 1995, took a drink, and burned up from the inside out. Not good. As it is, the pit is a ticking time bomb with a race to mitigate the disastrous effects of the toxicity with the surrounding aquifer. As the groundwater in the pit rises, the water level gets closer to a level at which it will intermix freely with surrounding groundwaters, and then it's a "superflush" into the aquifer and downstream of the Silver Bow Creek and thence the Clark Fork River.

Meanwhile, the labcoat geeks are figuring out ways that certain bacteria actually metabolize some of these heavy metals for a living, and maybe there's a way to get them to come onto the job and eat up the toxic soup in the pit. Who knew? As it sits, it ain't a good place to put your pet duck, or go bobbing for cutthroat. It will be years before it can be pronounced anything close to safe, but they only have until an estimated time around the year 2020 when the bomb goes off from rising groundwater in the pit hitting a critical intermix elevation level. Yikes. Reminds me of the Love Canal situation and Hooker Chemical back in Niagara Falls, New York – the original Superfund Site. I remember touring that site as part of a research project in college, and seeing the aftermath of the struggles people had to face from the toxic pollution. And here I am, in the Montana Rockies, far away in place and time from coming up with a report on the "Socio-Economic Considerations of Hazardous Waste Remediation in New York State." I am old, and far, far away...

A bee buzzes past, on his way to somewhere.

Clothes closet, drying rack, kitchen table top, work bench, office desk, food pantry, navigation library, water depot… everything but a place to sit.

In 2007 they had a blue-green algal bloom that caused a little stir when somebody witnessed some cows take a couple sips from the lake, walk a few steps and drop dead right in front of them.

Left: Walk-in area below the dam at Delmoe Lake. It's non-motorized here, but you can park right alongside the road in a pulloff, and yard your gear off the bike and camp for free outside of the developed campground, which lies above the dam and around the other side of the lake.

Right: A vacation day amidst the beetle-kills in Montana.

My GPS is reading just over 6100 feet here and it's another gorgeous day in the Rocky Mountains. Perfect for doing absolutely nothing. Not even read a book. Just a creek soak, listen to some flitting birds and buzzing bees. I can take it. I swear.

Delmoe Lake is a popular boating and cutthroat trout fishing destination, (it's stocked) and Butte is only a few miles down the interstate making it easy for a large number of people to get to in short order. Especially for such a beautiful getaway. The lake was created by the construction of a dam on the Big Pipestone Creek, and I'm camped along the outlet below this dam.

In 2007 they had a blue-green algal bloom that caused a little stir when somebody witnessed some cows take a couple sips from the lake, walk a few steps and drop dead right in front of them. I guess I'm going to be stuck finding a deep hole in the creek just below the dam for a cold wash off, and try to keep from drinking too much of the cyano-toxins if I can help it. If I can't, then I'll do my best to get out of the water and beach myself during my last gasps, and do my part to keep the water free of my corpse. That's how I roll.... Anyway, there's fresh water from hand pumps up at the $8/ night State-run campground, and I can run up there to refill my Camelbaks and get camp cooking water, rather than risk giardia and cyano-toxin death. I'm a cheery bastard!

I think I'll spend the rest of this rest day lying in the shade and ogling my dream bike and massaging my throttle wrist. (I should be wearing a wrist brace because there's something not quite right about it. The right wrist ain't in near as good a shape as Casper the Friendly Punkin!)

Day 4

"Stinky," "Huzar" and "Stovebolt" in Whitehall, Montana, on a bluebird morning, Day 4.

Delmoe Lake / Gravelly Range / Lucky Dog

Day 4 — I got up at 5 and lounged with three cups of steaming orange mocha cappuccino again, and bolted toward Pipestone and the breakfast café awaiting rally raiders at Whitehall. There I ended my solo adventures and traded that for some company with fellow riders, Rod and Cal. We ate breakfast together and enjoyed a good one, and sat leisurely getting to know one another as other riders slowly drifted in. They asked if I wanted to ride together and I gladly accepted their company, and off we rode toward the Tobacco Root Mountains, and the old mine town of Pony. We made a good ride of it on excellent dirt roads, watching pelicans fly overhead on our way past the Indiana University Geology Field Station. Once past Pony, I remarked to the men that there was a hot springs in Norris that I'd never been to, but had driven by many times — and that today might be the day to actually go in and start scraping some barnacles off our hides. (I had made a giant score yesterday on my down day at Delmoe Lake, and had two major mountain stream visits with Dr. Bronner's Peppermint Soap — complete with all laundry — so I was pretty flush.) But the hot springs sounded pretty damned good, and we made a pact to give it a try!

Meet and greet with the natives.

Looking northeast from the Tobacco Roots towards Bozeman, a little haze in the air. Fire season brings eternal smoke from California, Oregon, Nevada, Utah, Idaho and Montana.

"Stinky" rolling up on his BMW.

I had been in close proximity to my "local" area of operations since Butte, and was familiar with the southern portion of the rally route, so I made mention of a few local landmarks to the fellas as we rode here and there. We blasted out of the Tobacco Roots and on into Norris, only to discover that the hot springs was closed. Damnation! We refueled and continued west back into the Tobacco Root on the primary route toward a GPS connection that would allegedly lead us in a loop out to McAllister. The GPS tracksetter was a graduate from Clown College, and we got a bit tangled up high and fence-locked on a non-motorized boundary, giving Rod some extra pucker on the escaping return ride over slippery grass with bald tires on a huge BMW. The guy was magnificent the way he skied that sled down outa there — zero adhesion on his contact patch — just wishful thinking and some big seeds. Way to go Rod!

Above: Cal and Rod pondering what could possibly be better than this?

Right: All kinds of bikes and all kinds of riders attended the first ever MT1K 2010 ADV rally.

The cells rolling in were so ominous and the lightning such a real threat, we made a decision to un-ass the area...

We made it out of there after navigating one other possible routing solution and turned away from the sun, and rode on into Ennis for a reconnoiter, food, fuel, water and last provisions for the 20-mile exit from town and on to the end-of-day rally point on the top of the Gravelly Range. We met a couple guys hiding in the shade at a fuel stop in Ennis, and became a group of five for the remainder. Mike and Pete had been riding the rally together, and after sharing some commentary there, they hooked up and gelled into a solid pack of wild men, out to taste Montana in the dirt.

After a grocery stop to load the tin panniers some of the lads were sporting with ice and refreshing beverage for camp, we hightailed it south on the Varney Road to make dirt connections to the top of the range, and a rally point at "Crockett Lake" in building storm clouds. We made the rally point after braving some gusts of wind, hail and a torrent of Big Sky rain, and I for one sniffed ozone at least twice for the proximity to the lightning being hurled at us. Unbeknownst to us, lightning was playing hell with climbing parties in the Tetons at the same time, and "Art'y" was getting called in 'danger close' all the way around. The cells rolling in were so ominous and the lightning such a real threat, we made a decision to un-ass the area and just get back out of the hills, and follow the lunatic to his cabin in Island Park to take shelter. We just needed to hang on for dear life through whatever got thrown at us for an hour and 20 minutes or so of high speed pavement — easier said than done, but all of us knew what that might entail. We voted, and off we went after gearing up for battle on the slab at speed and wind and rain and lightning — but less lightning than we were facing up here.

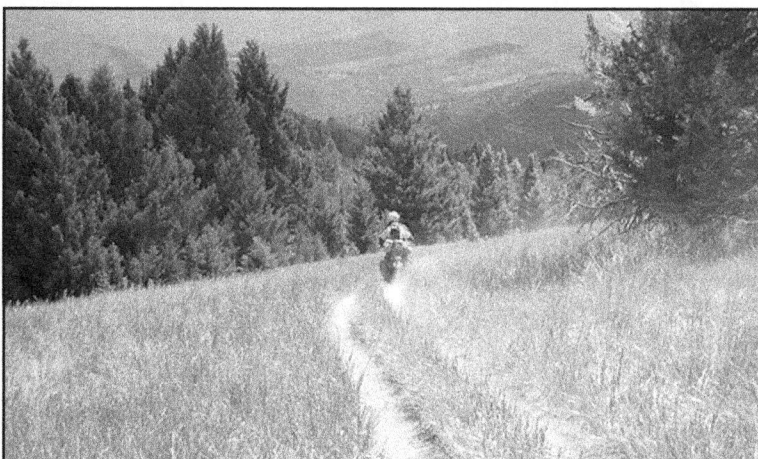

MasterChief railing some two-track on his Husky.

Scouring the USFS facilities for a way to find emergency shelter from lethal lightning bolts after diving off a slippery ridge in the Gravelly Range. The supercell that roared over top of us here on this raid continued east, and later threw life-killing lightning down on climbing parties in the Tetons. We knew we needed cover as fast as we could find it, and would have taken shelter in these primitive Forest Service buildings if we could have gained entry. No dice...

We made the cabin after a great meal stop, and actually outran the nasty thunderheads that shook the top half of the Gravelly Range all afternoon and evening. We feasted like condemned men, and by 10 p.m., we had secured hot showers, a good meal and had already consumed some man-killers by the blue glow of the "On Any Sunday" DVD, and even lit up the "Enduro at Erzberg" for good measure. By midnight, all the adventurers were secured in bags or bunks, and we laughed ourselves to sleep at the "Lucky Dog."

Supercell building from the southwest and heading right toward us.

Day 5

The Lucky Dog Cabin was a welcomed port in last night's storm. We were rewarded with a beautiful sunny morning for our ridgeline escape efforts.

Lucky Dog / Tendoys

By dawn's early light Rod had broken his camp and was packed up and ready to go. A few of us stragglers caught up to him at the café and we had a great big breakfast, got fuel and wandered off pavement toward Sawtelle Peak and the north side of the Centennial Range, and a reconnection with our previously abandoned primary route at the toe of the Gravellys. Our reconnect path took us through some silt beds that had Rod battling to get his big GS through, and had he not brought substantial off-road skills to the table, he would not have made it across the sand flats as far as he did before making a sound Adventure Rider decision and turning around. He had to manhandle his big bike back up on his own after crashing, but he got it righted despite tweaking his back. He made the right decision and stopped the folly while he was still capable and uninjured and continued back out on an alternate route under his own power, after coming to within a mile of the end of the treachery. We rejoined him at a fuel and meal stop in Dell, Montana, along the interstate later, and he was raring to rejoin us.

The original front rim off the 640 Adventure that was destroyed in Baja now adorns the entrance gate to the "Lucky Dog Cabin."

Getting hurt is unwelcome, but it's also a very real eventuality. A fellow did crash hard enough to hurt his shoulder, somewhere out on this ride. (I found out later it was a guy I had met briefly on a previous trip in Baja, and I hope he's okay. Good luck and take care "Jonz.") After reloading with food, water and a fresh load of cold 24-ounce man-killers for camp, we set out toward the end-of-day rally point at the southern part of the Tendoy Mountains. As we neared that destination, Rod had to pull the plug on the journey and make a rendezvous with his wife that was off our primary route, so we said goodbye to a good rider and stalwart companion, and off he went. He shot a text to Mike later on, to let us know he made it back out to civilization okay, and that we were on our own to finish the rally. And then we were four.

"MasterChief" wants to know 'where the grizzlies are, and which way they're headed...' He intends to head the other way.

Cal glancing back for any signs of Rod… way back there in the silt beds as we waited for a spell for him, just before going back to find him.

"Wait! Cal!.. take your bike with you, man!"

Left: Sage, subalpine fir and spruce motel at Camp 5.

Right: Cal's nest in Camp 5 south of Clark Reservoir in the Tendoys.

Mike lit up his WR250 and led the way toward a campsite farther along the tracks than the rally point indicated for the final night rendezvous for all riders en masse, because the track-laying monkey was laughing at us again, and there was nobody there. We found it hard to believe that we were the lead element in the entire gang of fools, but in any case, a better campsite was bound to present itself, so we rode through some good remaining daylight, heading north toward the Clark Reservoir to claim a patch of solitude wherein we could camp in peace under tree cover in the sage, and enjoy the coldy goodness of our recently packed man-killers. (I got hard lemonade x2, and they were good!)

We had navigated along some two-track up into a draw and found a great little spot with enough flat ground to pitch tents and tell stories under the 'Wild Montana Skies.' I enjoyed myself perfectly, and the company of my new friends kept me happy through dinnertime and beyond. Holding court that night under the starry heavens, I thought of my good fortune to be doing such a great ride, seeing such wild Montana country, and traveling at such a satisfying pace. Doing it all on an exceptional bike with some really fantastic people really made me a happy adventure rider — THIS is the way to appreciate summer! I drifted off on night five, feeling I was a lucky, lucky man indeed… not only for the riding, but to be living right in the heart of all this country.

Tomorrow is the last day of riding for us, and it ought prove both scenic and entertaining with an interesting route laid in for more valley and mountain pass travel, and excursions along the Lewis and Clarke Trail and parts of the Continental Divide. Having let the steam out of my riding boots and settling in to the cozy embrace of a goose down sleeping bag, there was little else to do but let the Sandman take over once again. He beat me to death at once, and Day 5 was nothing more than a helmet full of memories. Good ones…

Day 6

Mikrow and MasterChief getting morning coffees at the ready. We scored a beautiful perch higher off the valley floor, on a plateau hugging the foothills to the west of the Tendoy Mountains. Spruce and sage got the decorating done for us around our living rooms, last night out.

Tendoys / Darby

Alpenglow on the peaks to our west along the ridges of the Continental Divide punctuate a glorious dawning to Day 6 as we kicked back in camp for a couple hours and I finished the last of my cappuccino while packing for the last day of the rally. The old ghost town of Bannack lies northwest of the Clark Reservoir, and it's been restored for tourism. Under the clear skies of another bluebird day, we'll make tracks toward the northern terminus of a loop that will take us through Polaris and the Grasshopper Valley to the east of the Pioneer Mountains.

Throttles go blipping in the weeds as we light these trusty bikes and warm the engines. Scanning for bits of trash to keep our site cleaner than we find it yields a pristine area to launch from and there's no reason for further delay… it's time to join the Lewis and Clark National Historic Trail for a short zig-zag up ahead, and head through more Nez Perce country in and around the Trail of Tears in our travels today. What Chief Joseph could have accomplished with a herd of these bikes as his warhorses is a mind-staggering thought, and there may well be an entirely different monument on the map up north in place of the "Big Hole National Battlefield" just east of Lost Trail Pass.

Even though it's hard to pass by a place on the map marked "Bloody Dick Creek" we opt to do so — in case the place happens to be aptly named.

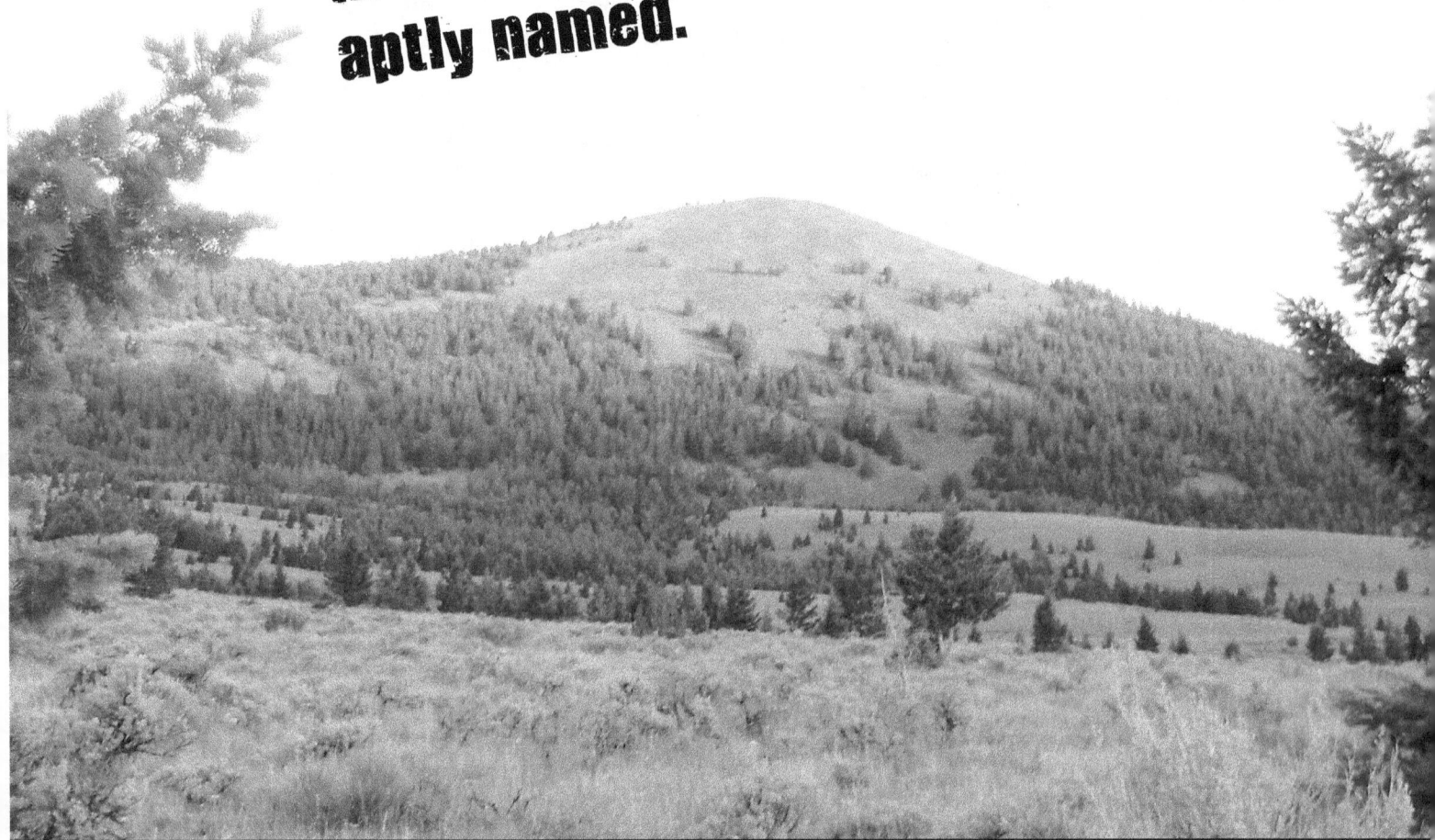

Tendoy dawn-scape.

With the divide on our left and the Tendoy crest on our right, we gather steam on gravel road through these mountains, watching the eagles above soaring in search of breakfast. Since the Bannack townsite is a nicely refurbished ghost town and a rally point of interest en route, we head there for a first stop to take a look around. Even though it's hard to pass by a place on the map marked "Bloody Dick Creek" we opt to do so — in case the place happens to be aptly named. No time to tarry near a place like that, I'm thinking, and we leave it off to our west as we make a dirt road connection in Grant, and head north through ranch land and BLM tracts toward Bannack.

It's hard to pry a guitar from some Canadian's hands. When you see something like this, it makes you appreciate every note around a campfire!

Bannack

"Mikrow" is in Montana, while the "MasterChief" has traveled on ahead over Big Hole Pass and into Idaho.

There are scores of parked adventure bikes in the parking lot as we roll in, with plenty of MT1K Adv'ers having gotten here before us. Where everybody camped last night is anybody's guess, as there was nobody at the "Camp 5 Rally Point" when we cruised by late yesterday afternoon. They found somewhere to lay their heads and a couple dozen bikes parked attest to a good number of folks still going strong at this stage of the rally. Our stop is brief and we have a look around, and opt to keep riding after only a short helmets-off respite for a gander at the restored mining buildings and main street. A dirt street lined with restored tumble-downs; ghosts whispering through the cracked shacks with maybe a speck of gold dust that hadn't made it into the miner's leather pouch... now sealed beneath a repaired floorboard and entombed along with memories and hardships, forever.

A brief section of pavement brings us on a short northwestward swing to the turnoff into the Grasshopper Valley. A mild right turn gets us all heading in, and we're looking forward to a decent breakfast stop somewhere if we find one. We do, and we'll score some fuel here as well, in the vicinity of the Magna mines, Maverick Mountain ski area and the Elkhorn Hot Springs.

Having our last breakfast of the rally at the Grasshopper Inn was great, and the place is well worth stopping in for future adventures – so noted! Checking out the aircraft propeller and historic memorabilia on the walls was a trip in itself, and both the food and service rate high on Stovey's scale of adventure accommodation, but it grew time to depart and head for the northernmost point on this loop, Wise River. Riding past gorgeous meadows and stands of Ponderosa Pine along the way gave us something nice to do while waiting in construction traffic and suffering behind the pilot cars we were forced to deal with. The "State Flower of Montana," the road cone, was

Pete, aka "MasterChief"

Cal

Mike, Cal, Pete and Rod

Marcin, aka "Huzar"

Mike and Cal at the restored ghost town outside Clark Reservoir.

rearing its ugly head here in abundance to confound the needles on our pleasure meters, but you gotta take the bad with the good. So there…

Wise River was small, quaint and picturesque, and we yarded on the handlebars there to turn southwest toward the Big Hole Valley along the river of the same name. A pretty cool loop along this "Wise River – Polaris National Scenic Byway."

We made Wisdom for last gas, and topped off for what we thought might be a good alternate to the primary route and a good way for our group of four to end the rally. Having been through a section of the Big Hole Valley on a previous trip that ran over dirt Forest Service roads, I knew a route that would get us off the pavement and onto the dirt tracks, taking us over the Continental Divide at Big Hole Pass above Gibbonsville, Idaho.

A locked gate at a ranch failed to stop our crew, and Cal throttled his mighty 690 through a nasty little creek crossing like he was on a mission. Pete blasted through the same obstacle on his big Husky, and we all thumbed our noses at the ignorant cattle guard that places the rider at risk with the grate running parallel to the wheels, rather than perpendicular to them. It would be a real joke if it weren't so dangerous.

We finished the day with a run over the Divide and down through "Banjo Village" and not a single one of us was abducted by local headhunters. That's a good thing in my book. We made Darby and the end of the rally by 4:30 p.m. under

Greg at West Fest in Darby, Montana

a blistering sun. We were bushed, but settled in under the shade of "Gentleman Mike's" van and proceeded to relax and wind down. My personal GPS page 4 data from the ride read:

Total miles = 1,063.72
Max Speed = 90.4 mph
Moving Time = 28 hrs 42 min
Moving Average = 37.1 mph
Stopped = 16 hours
Overall Average = 23.4 mph

Everybody else's data would vary, of course. It was a good and successful journey. No bears found me – and we rode through and camped in bear country. Today's newspaper carried the story of a bear attack that occurred in the wee hours yesterday morning in a campground at Soda Butte, in the Gallatin National Forest near Yellowstone. Three people got munched, and one of them perished at the scene that covered over a quarter of a mile. The lightning storm that scattered us from the top of the Gravelly Range moved through the area and wiped out three or four climbing parties on the Grand Teton, creating the need for the largest and most complex rescue on the Grand since the 1960s. People were injured and some lost their lives. All we smelled was ozone, and we made it through our route and out from underneath of the same supercell with much better luck. Lucky Dogs at the Lucky Dog Cabin.

My posse on this ride were great riders and great guys; good men to "ride the river with" (with apologies to Bill Jordan). I learned things from each of them and I tip my hat to each of you in turn; Rod and Cal, Pete and Mike. Thanks to Pete, I am now embarking on new sojourns ensconced in the knowledge that "I might be here, or I might be 19 feet away..." and perhaps that is the way it should be. Mike, we will meet again. Cal, nice work out there; you are a better rider than you give yourself credit for. Rod, "salute."

Greg and author after Stovebolt's "de-noobing"

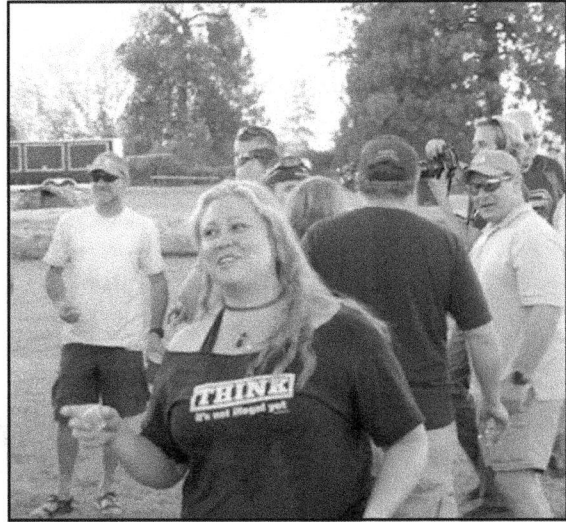

More ADVRider diplomats at West Fest

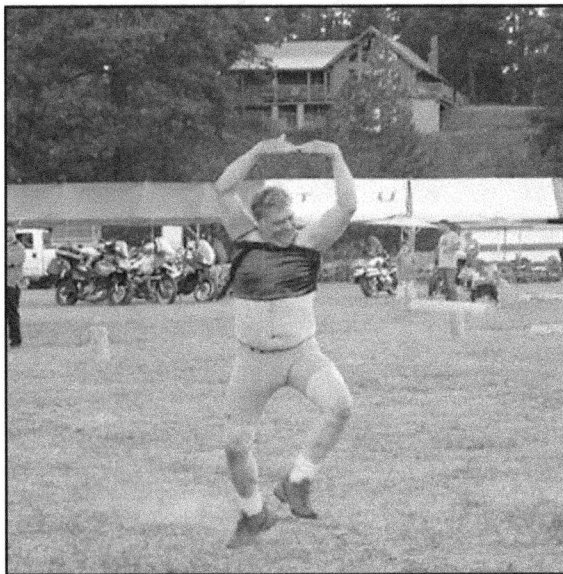

"Putts" keeping things serious at West Fest

Freshly "de-noobed" Stovey

Thank you to all the great people on the Adventure Rider Forum and especially to those who volunteered and coordinated efforts to put a rally route together. It was in the making for almost a year, and it went off smoothly thanks to the efforts of a lot of guys working together for each other. Adventure Riders are the greatest! FYYFF's.... ■

Rally on....

Stovebolt
Team Ruptured Buzzard
"Never Give Up"

Route of Legends of the Fall #2

Map of Nevada in the public domain obtained from the National Atlas. (Nationalatlas.gov)

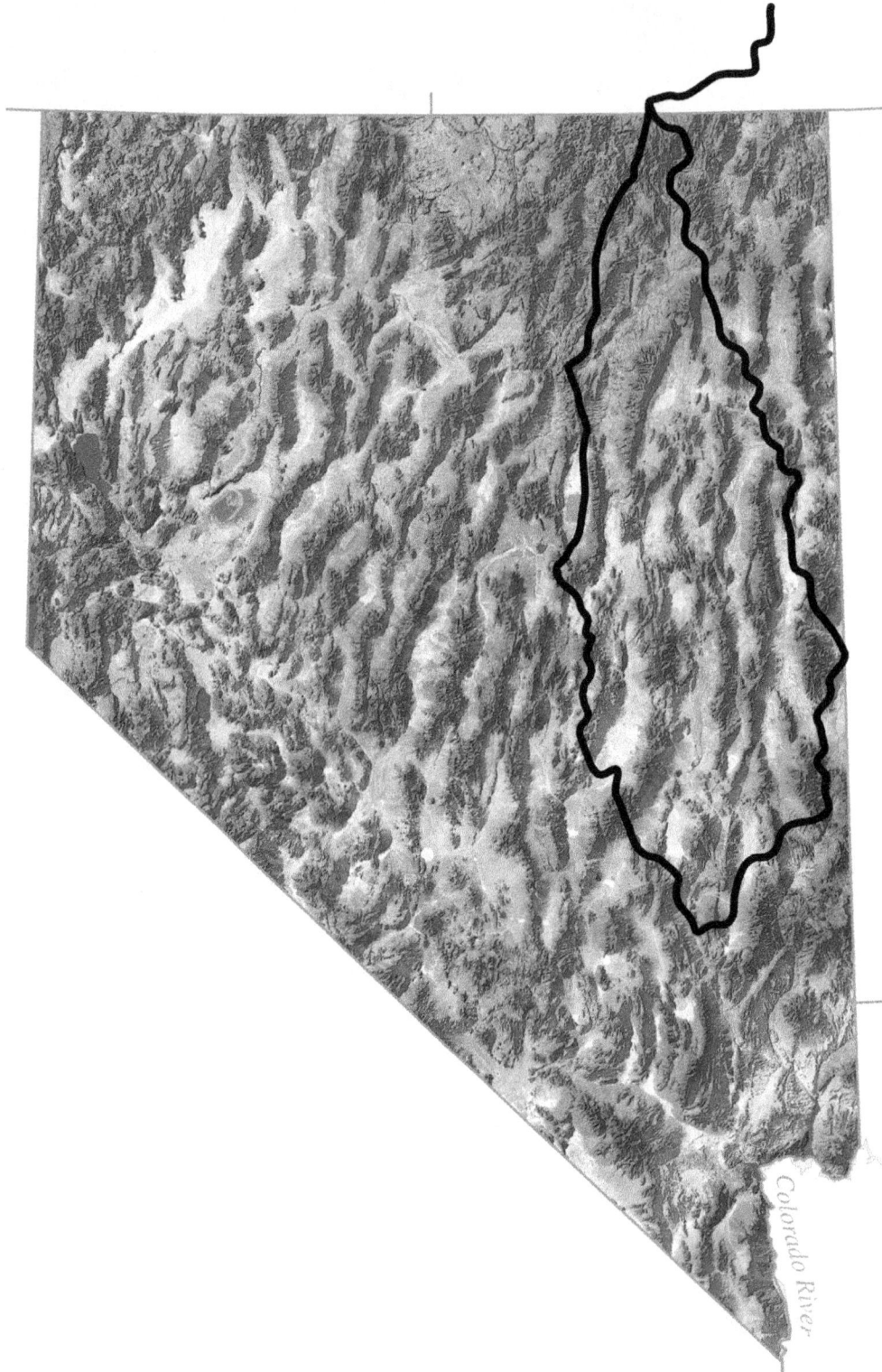

Colorado River

2nd Annual

Legends
of the Fall

Trans-Nevada
Whorehouse Hare & Hound
Dual Sport to Area 51 for
No Wimps Rally Raid

October 2010

Prologue

Flash back you movie buffs… CADDYSHACK starring Bill Murray. Scene is when and where Bill Murray is caddy-ing the priest in the rain, and the priest is having the game of his life. You know, where he drives the ball onto the green, and it goes two feet long, stops – circles back and then 'sinks it' in the cup. Just one unstoppable lucky play after another. (Then he gets struck by lightning, and dies….)

That was my ride, only no rain and I didn't get struck by lightning. In a word, it was magnificent!

There had been a few riders interested in the journey this year and we had, at one time, six people going. But, as things progressed toward the departure time, we lost all but us two same guys who rode it last year. And so it was that Keith (950transalp) and I were the only ones left to carry the flag to the top of the hill, and ride this monster ride – the 2nd Annual Legends of the Fall, Trans-Nevada Whore House Hare & Hound Dual Sport to Area 51 for No Wimps Rally Raid. If nothing else, we had a name for i….

I was mounted on Casper the Friendly Punkin, my new 2010 KTM 450 XCW Six Days machine. Keith would be on his 2001 Honda XR650R. Both bikes were reasonably well equipped, maintained and prepped for a ride across the remote hinterlands of Nevada, and ready to cross mountain range after mountain range; desert after desert – for about a week straight.

GPS routes were laid in, all nine of them, and transferred to Keith's Garmin Quest and my own 60CSx – mine residing in a way coolio hand-built "Buzz-Bomb" cradle manufactured by Rogue Dog Communications for TEAM RUPTURED BUZZARD in Idaho. BarPack was loaded with navigation paper, spare batteries to run all external cockpit instrumentation and my rubber thumb 'windshield wiper' just in case. St. Peter in a dump truck already, time to ride… Area 51, here we come.

St. Peter in a dump truck already, time to ride…

Area 51, here we come.

Keith and I stop near Murphy Hot Springs; Jarbidge just down the twisty gravel from this rest stop.

Twin Falls, Idaho / Jarbidge, Nevada

We loaded up the small two-place bike trailer in Victor, Idaho, and set sail southwest toward Twin Falls, Idaho, where we had arranged with Jeff at J&C Motorsports to park our rig for the week. (A sincere thanks goes to Jeff for this mighty fine favor – it was a real help my friend!) After a pit stop in Idaho Falls for Starbucks and a donut, and a spark plug for the fanny pack, we continued on under bluebird skies across the high-speed cage pavement. Arrived at Twin to our rally point jump-off, and met Jeff. Unloaded, geared up and jumped off at mid-day, heading for the Sinclair station across the street for a fuel up. This last-stop landmark became significant a couple hours later, right Keith?

Ahh, there we go, bag off... now, where is that pesky gas cap? No – really, where is the damned gas cap?

Off we go, southbound on Blue Lakes Road toward Rogerson, Idaho, where we were to make a right turn for Three Creek Road, past Murphy Hot Springs and into Jarbidge Canyon for the night. Keith's bike failed to relight with pleasure on a couple of occasions inbound to Jarbidge, but we didn't make too much of it. . . . Perhaps it was sensing some Nevada air and was taking time to get readjusted. Maybe it knew beforehand some of what it was about to be asked to ride over and through, I dunno.

A few coughs and sputters later and we were in Jarbidge proper for dinner and a campground, replete with cold beer to settle in to our first campsites for the journey. Ahhh, life is good. Back at camp after dinner, and no Keith. Hell, he was right behind me at the Trading Post, I wonder what could have happened? Too early in the trip to lose a guy to a bear or a mountain lion. . . . Huh, I'll give him a few minutes before I go back to scan for his corpse. A little time goes by, and then some more, and finally the thump-thump-thump of the XR650 comes more loudly and distinctly into the earshot of my wind-whistled noggin. F-shizzle, here he is – nice, now I don't have to drink a beer alone. Beautiful sunset is in progress, and all seems right with the world according to Stovey.

Keith is grimacing, however, and there is a lack of joy upon his freshly-fed visage. "What-ho?" thinks I, and make an inquiry about his apparent lack of joy.

"Bikey-no-starty" is the reply, and he is given over to another cursory examination of the dilemma, looking here and looking there, and there's some immediate sign of trouble in the air bubbles gurgling backwards through the fuel line under the petcock. Hmmmmpph… what's that all about? Why is the bike gurgling fuel and air bubbles upstream through the fuel system? I'm thinking, "perhaps there is a stoppage at the gas cap vent hose" or something, and Keith is saying how he thinks the fuel is charging right past the whole works and filling his cylinder with gas.... Let's take a look, shall we? Off comes the tank bag for an examination of that damned gas cap, for starters. Ahh, there we go, bag off... now where is that pesky gas cap? No – really; where is the damned gas cap? Can't really start looking for trouble with it until we find it... nothing under the tank bag but a big hole where the cap might oughta be... Hmmmmph. No gas cap. But, a really, really tight-ass seal on the tank with the tank bag. Kind causing a big giant vacuum in the fuel system; so tight it wouldn't even leak gas to give any indication of a missing cap, just a vapor lock it was so tight. Well, half of the problem was solved – we found the problem. The other half would be fixing it, short of riding 100 miles back to where we just came from to the Sinclair Station on Addison Street in Twin Falls.

Day 2

Dawn on Bear Creek – Jarbidge, Nevada. *(Keith Briggs photo)*

Jarbidge / Cissillini Canyon

We arose in camp along the river and found a beautiful morning waiting outside our bivys.

Keith's bike needed a gas cap, and our bodies wanted some fuel, so we idled into Jarbidge after packing up and found ourselves back at the Outdoor Inn for breakfast/brunch. It turned into "brunch" because we lollygagged around with the natives who were friendly and helpful in the extreme! They were all so pleasant and nice – it was a real treat to be around them.

Big Agnes with a load of hot air proves to be no match for Stovey.

Keith's area of operations.

This would be our stopgap solution. Many thanks to the pit crew at The Outside Inn...

The local heroes sallied forth and rallied behind Keith with all manner of helpful strategies and equipment; everything from old plastic peanut butter jar lids to a custom-fitted Mason jar lid fitted with a vent setup. The mason jar lid did the trick! And it ended up working like a charm. For 1,270 miles.

South Jarbidge Canyon

Near Bear Creek Pass, outside of Jarbidge, Nevada

We said our goodbyes after a fine breakfast, and headed south outta town after a refuel at the 24/7 credit card pump serving the small community of Jarbidge, along the Jarbidge-Charleston Road.

We made our way through a beautiful canyon being careful to avoid oncoming hunter traffic, and on up to the Bear Creek Pass at approximately 8,400 to 8,500 feet ASL.

The riding was great for dirt roads, and the scenery was outstanding as we rolled through tunnels of shimmering ("quaking" maybe?) aspen; their leafy yellow branches arcing over the passages of our once-again legendary ride. Me likey. Casper just roared and purred.

View from near Bear Creek Pass

Legendary Fall landscapes

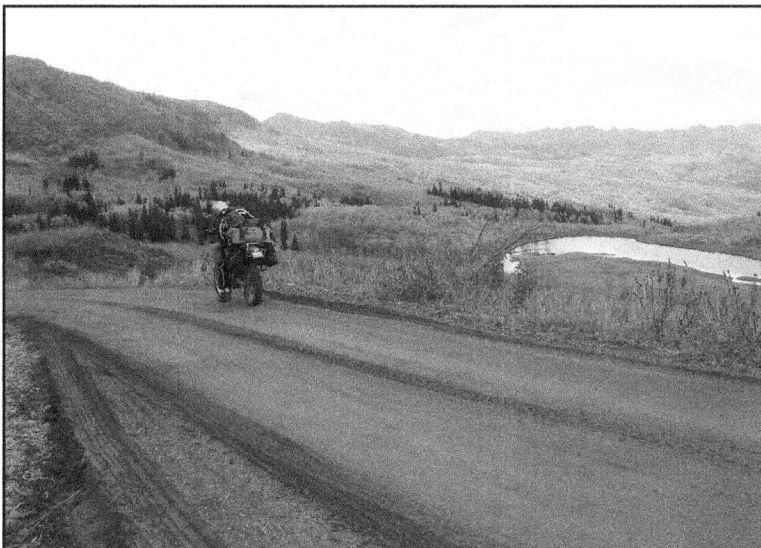

Cresting Bear Creek Pass, southern deserts await…

A cool sip along an ancient stage route.

We broke out into some Palouse as we dropped down from the Jarbidge Mountains and made our right turn on the route, and within a couple of miles I managed to miss a turn to take us southbound through the hills directly north of and into Elko. So we proceeded onward toward Highway 225, confident I could rejoin the route farther on, and pick up some time we left in Jarbidge retrofitting a gas cap and having a leisurely breakfast. After slabbing it for a few miles southward on 225, we jumped off and headed back into the bush, making a stab at another dirt run into Elko from the north. We lost some time over a navigational difference of opinion, but it didn't do any harm – we recalculated on the fly and put ourselves through a bunch of ranch fences on and through washes and two-tracks to I-80, about 20 miles east of Elko later in the afternoon. The riding and scenery continued to be awfully good as we purred and pawed through gullies, valleys,

Downtown Charleston, at rush-hour..... (Best keep ambling along, as there were signs of occupancy. I thought I could hear banjo music... not a time to tarry.)

124

Legendary Fall landscapes

ditches, rivers and fences. We made the interstate after a bit and hit Elko for fuel, water sleeves and a couple of cold man-killers for the trail, and left town on the next magenta line called up on the GPS, heading out shortly after 5 p.m. and a phone contact with my wife, Dorothy. My evening plop zone was reconnoitered to be in the vicinity of the Bullion Mine in the Pinon Range, southwest of Elko. So we needed to make time to get Casper bedded down before I might have to face the folly of calling upon the dismal rays of the stock headlight ("forward-looking-infra-DEAD"). We snicked a few gears as we followed my route and made two-tracks in short order. I let the loud cannon roar, made 85 mph once or twice once we got back into the bushes, and before sunset we had a camp in up Cissillini Canyon near the Bullion Mine. It was beautiful; camp was level, aspen-sheltered and isolated. The cold man-killers didn't hurt either. Stovey was in "happy-ville."

Tomorrow would be another great day, and Keith had a nice incline to roll his Honda down for a bump-start if he wanted to take the edge off his knee. If the lions didn't get us, or a satellite fall out of the sky onto our heads, we remained golden yet again. We would cross these hills toward Railroad Pass, and be in Eureka tomorrow afternoon – a point where we needed to take on serious fuel and begin the first committed leg of the raid. Until then, we were still on Easy Street – so easy even a caveman could do it… "All is well, safely rest… God is nigh."

Camped near the top of Cissillini Canyon.

125

Day 3

Riding south beneath the spine of the Pinon Range.

Cissillini   / Pancakes

Dawn broke like a glass rod snapping, and the early rays found me recently un-entombed from a delicious slumber ensconced within my zero-degree Gore-tex Feathered Friend with so-many ounces of 900-fill Polish down. When the dawn-whip cracks, I can often crack back when I'm on these rides... looking forward to those steamy, delicious blends of instant orange mochachinos – freshly brewed and warming to my aging paws. I like two or three of those bastards around me while I break my camps and prepare for the daily fools parade down the paths to nowhere. Works for me all over the place – this morning was no different, and I found pleasure in every stuffsack packed, and each sip from three full thermo-tumblers. The ride ahead looked good on paper and from the air ('Thank You' Google Earth) and the papers had already been exchanged in the Bar Pack, new route toggled to "navigate" the night before. No satellites fell upon my helmet-haired head during the night, and not a mountain lion to be found in my shorts – I looked. My checklist was complete, and I was ready to roll. "You ready, Keith?"

"Yep!"

Off we went, down the canyon from underneath of the "Raven's Nest" 8,710-foot pinnacle that shielded us from the north, and off through a couple of ranch gates to rejoin the route, and get back on "that purple line." It was no trick following my route, it was easy enough especially for someone who studied the route ahead of time, and spent a goodly amount of eyeballing the paper, software and Google Earth views. We had navigation to perform at junctions with all manner of obliterated two-tracks here and there, but it was pretty straightforward stuff. We paraded through BLM and ranch tracts for miles, making good our threat to rally and raid like legends in our own minds – each brainpan collecting images to last a lifetime through our glasses and faceshields. "Picturesque" doesn't exactly hit the nail on the head, but already my mind was searching for modifiers and superlatives – it was just outstanding riding and scenery.... Dry mountain mile after mile.

Pinion Range landscapes

Lava scar on a drumlin alongside our two-track

No, it's not a hunchback – it's Keith stretching his hamhocks before leaving the Pinons.

Looking west across the Diamond Valley into "The Devil's Cauldron." This dust devils' spawning ground lies to the east of Sulphur Spring Mountain Range in the background.

We were southbound to a place called Railroad Pass, and approaching the Pinon Range exit that would take us through and past the Red Rock Ranch, and down into the Diamond Valley on the north end of Eureka. The Diamond Mountains began to emerge from the south, and the Diamond Valley alkali flats would greet us on our right as we popped down for a dirt road cruise into Eureka. I remembered last year when Keith and I were shit-stormed by a powerful dust devil on the Pony Express Trail between Partoun and Gandy, Utah. It took the bars nearly out of our hands and made puckers in our 'brown pants' – leaving both of us spun at 65 to 70 mph along a gravel road, and with new respect for the 'wicked witches of the West' after it passed. The same devil got us both, within seconds, but neither of us went down for the dirt nap. As we came down out of the Pinon Mountains, I saw those alkali flats, and knew it was a spawning ground for those dust devils... and I respected it for the crucible that it was. I thought to myself, "...I will serve as no dust for the Devil's pestle and mortar this day..." and rallied onward and downward toward the alkali – both hands gripping Casper as we motored together over an altogether abandoned two-track with baseballs, cactus and cobble in 1st and 2nd gears.

Keith and I met the Diamond Valley floor through a couple miles of deep and powdery silt beds, filling 6-inch trenches that served as either side of the two-track. Hmmmmph. At least there were no baby heads rolling around in the bottom of that silt - that would have sucked. "Glad I'm on a dirt bike. Hope Keith is alright on his bigger XR650 behind me...." He was, and we made good the transition from "technical two-track" to a real dirt road. I heard that loud cannon roaring once again, and 6th gear put me into a meteoric trajectory toward a right turn onto our connection at Railroad Pass, and down-bound to Eureka.

Fisheye lens from the Hero Cam on Keith's helmet. *(Keith Briggs photo)*

Passing the Diamond Mountains to our left, and the 'Devil's Crucible' to our right, I was able to witness the dust storms producing as many as six dust devils at a time as we roared down the valley toward the still actively mining community of Eureka, where rough men toil daily in a vast expanse of molybdenum mines. God bless each and every one of those crusty, hard-working, brave bastards. Soon, we will sit in one of your cafés and buy some fuel from your local depot… and ride through your mines.

We made town and gathered in fuel for the bikes and food for our grumble-boxes, stuffing each to within an inch of torso-bursting capacity. I poured in an extra gallon of fuel between water bottles that were emptied into my two Camelbaks and sleeved into Wolfman Water Bottle Holsters strapped to my Giant Loop, and inside my daypack. Keith found a big-ass jug to serve his purposes in the local mercantile, and we motored away under dark skies with sucker holes in them, and raindrops aplenty smacking my Arai XD faceshield. A new magenta line bleeped forth on my cockpit TV set, and I knew with active mining going on, the data vs. real ground might undergo a disparity, and navigation around and into the mountains to the west and south of Eureka might present challenges. We made good though, and we passed through the Mountain Boy and Fish Creek Ranges on ABSOLUTELY STELLAR new and old/abandoned mining paths! What a trail we blazed through the pinon and cedars, "tunneling" our way through helmet-smacking branches from junipers oh-so-ready to peel us off the bikes, or strip an unwary Hero-cam from a helmet mount. Keith was back there somewhere, riding like a champion, and refusing to give that helmet cam away to the demons lurking in the hidden passageway we were forging. Coming down through those last bits of mountain "two-track" (it was VERY single-track for a lot of it) we now had a clear view of "home" and the Pancake Range to the southeast. A mad late-day dash across the Little Smoky Valley would find us with the last desert underneath our wheels for the day, and into the shelter of a mountain hideaway for the night; a place where we might find comfortable lodging alongside our route, and under-neath some nice juniper boughs.... So close, and a mere hour or so away from the viewpoint near the Fish Creek Ranch we approached from the northwest.

I asked Keith how he was doing – and it was all "thumbs-up" from my riding partner, giving a grin as we rocketed off towards much easier ground to cover before settling in for the night – ready to make camp; and did I mention we got away from Eureka with a fresh load of cold man-killers? We did, and they were going to be sore-needed come tent-pitching time, and when I pulled out that Crazy Creek to plop my fat ass down into. Throttle systems were still intact on each bike, as it turned out, and oinking a mere quarter-twist to my 450 XCW gave amazingly rapid results yet again.... Keith would have to fend for himself in my dust for a moment, as I gave Casper some legs and we hauled the mail down across that final valley for the day. I could "smell the barn" like an old horse coming back from pasture, and it was a thrill to light that bike up in 6th and laser beam my way from GPS connection to GPS connection. It was straight as grizzly's dick for miles, and a rather wicked speed approaching Shuttle Escape Velocity and the point of no return was achieved and maintained. (I was thinking how my dust trail would likely be visible if SPOT or Google Earth was focusing during those moments.) And the moments roared by quickly as we entered the northern terminus of the Pancakes, and home for the night.

Pancake camp scene

Camp 3 under the junipers in the Pancake Range.

After a short bit of two-track high-speed meandering along that little purple line on my TV, we came to rest at long last in a really cool little valley in the shadow of Moody Mountain to the north of Brown Summit which lies to the east of Duckwater. It was a beautiful hole-up to be sure, and we dismounted under sunset-filled skies, the rainwater having long since disappeared. We even managed a nice enviro-campfire under stars so bright it could make your brain bleed after a day in the bright dust trails of Day 3. A quick oil change gave Casper a late afternoon orgasm, and the noodles and chicken with a cold man-killer nearly gave me one. Another legendary day, glorious in its way-too-generous offerings for tainted souls like us. I went to bed again, a truly, truly happy man.

Keith found fresh kitty tracks a short drop-a-steamer distance from where we laid our helmet-haired heads. I hoped he was a friendly kitty, a stupid retard of a kitty, or simply blind with no nostrils... I would be too tired to fight, and too happy to care if a pounce was on his mind. Goodnight, Keith. Goodnight "John-Boy." Goodnight Kitty....

Anthill could be used as a sundial, I think.

132

Day 4

Casper and Camp Stovey

Pancake / Lunar Crater / Nyala Wadi / Ash Springs

This morning was crisp — frost everywhere. Bike seat and instruments were all covered in frosty mini-feathers, but even though it was obviously sub-freezing, it hadn't been that much colder or been that way for long. The water in my Camelbaks wasn't frozen — just liquid and waiting for me to fire up my stove and brew some orange Mochachinos. If I'd had a Pop-Tart I could have been in training for the Olympics… and a bright Sun from the east told me I was in the right place, and having the time of my life.

... I had to choke my motor this morning and run it like it was the last tank of fuel I'd ever have – and in fact, that might possibly even come true if I pooched things hard enough.

The bikes were ornery this morning, both requiring a little more oomph from the operator to get things lit. I even kicked mine to keep from running the battery down, and she fired up nicely after a few strokes from the Alpinestars Tech 6. (Bastards quit making these boots in favor of the new breed of plastic hybrids... DAMNATION! Best boots I've ever owned. You reading this ALPINESTARS?) After we were packed up and the bikes lit off and warmed up, we faced south and knew we were on the pivot leg of the journey – at day's end, we would rest at the southernmost point on this ride, hopefully in Ash Springs. I was loose and focused, because I also knew I had to stay on my game to keep from losing track, and blowing our fuel somewhere and causing us to lie stranded in some God-forsaken valley... scorpion food, or worse. Well, time to jet. Clear left – clear right, clear prop... throttles up.

The dirt we were on in the Pancake Mountains was great too, and there were twisties everywhere. Often there were berms you could rail, but I had to choke my motor this morning and run it like it was the last tank of fuel I'd ever have... and in fact, that might possibly even come true if I pooched things hard enough. So I leaned back and enjoyed a nice ride out of the mountains and through a small pass joining Brown Truck Summit Trail, and onto the desert floor on the west side of the Pancakes. We needed to follow dirt tracks south to Black Rock Summit on Highway 6, and jump out of the Big Springs Valley we were in, and fall off into the Lunar Crater – where would face "The Wall."

As it happened, like Wolfgang Amadeus Mozart – who was also proud of his work... I was told I had "too many notes..." and my route got cancelled by Garmin. Of course, I knew ahead of time I needed to check each of them for complete translations, knowing there is a memory limit. But I blew it off, and figured if something happened, I needed to be able to navigate completely without a GPS at all, and thus I was pretty much prepared to see my magical purple line come to a complete stop out here underneath the disappearing shadows of Portuguese Mountain. "Too many via points," Captain Garmin said, and right in the middle of my ride, he threw out my route, snickering at my folly I do believe. My critical issue was fuel (and time) because I needed to keep moving in the right direction, no mistakes. Time spent going in the wrong direction meant fuel disappearing that I couldn't get back, short of the kind of luck you simply don't think about – you can't. It doesn't exist – you need to hit the nail on the head sometimes.

Camp Keith. Zen-stance to will the XR650's engine to start by sheer adventure rider mind control.

Heading south through the Pancakes toward Brown Truck Summit Road.

Perfect traction through the pinion two-tracks. "Disneyland for adventure riders."

So, a few minutes with the kickstand down to double-check my bearings and landmarks with my paper maps, and I was confident I knew where we were, exactly. I also felt I had to keep focused and stay the course because the dirt road was an obliterated two-track at this point, and there were crisscrossed same-sames intersecting with us and running all through the place. There are many tracks into the Devil's cauldrons! We just needed the one that would take us out of this one, and into the next.... So, we relit and motored down alongside the base of the Pancakes on the west side of the range, continuing south and toward our connection on the highway near Black Rock Summit. I left the GPS on "Navigate" for entertainment value… it would always read, "Head North to Road." I thought of how funny it is that some folks will take a message like that literally, even under the same circumstances, and wheel off a cliff someplace, calling their attorneys with their last dying breaths over a Blackberry, rapidly losing its signal as their "Tom-Tom" blinked "…heading into a chasm…" at them. Still funny.

Nearing Black Rock Summit

Pancakes

Casper packing an Original Giant Loop. CycoActive BarPack out for a peek at the paper during lunch break north of Lunar Crater.

Keith, just north of Black Rock Summit.

Stovey sets out for the Lunar Crater connection. *(Keith Briggs photo)*

Wild mustangs near Portuguese Mountain.

Being a student of navigation, well, a former student... now more or less a reject from Clown College, I was comfortable on this leg, even without my purple line. With the "TV" now in use as electronic paper, and my rolling thunder beneath me, we just thumped along that desert floor. At a point farther south but above the Black Rock Summit, I gave us a right turn instead of a left – a left that would have kept us exactly on my route. My choice of the right was based on the data I had in my head and it was actually a great choice – it probably saved us a little fuel. But, when we reached the highway at Black Rock Summit, old Stovey's 'Nav Center' tricked him into thinking we were hitting the nail on the same old head I had programmed on my route, and not on the "new and improved" nail on the head I had just developed. So, without much ado at the pavement crossing, and almost while staring at my landmark features within the Lunar Crater we were to travel directly into, I made the decision to make a right turn. Thinking I was at a place literally a few hundred yards east of where we were, we were actually a few hundred yards downstream, and needed a left, and then a quick right. Ahhhh... "too many notes" in my head for my own good. When we made our turn off the highway a few minutes later, and headed south at the sign for "Lunar Crater – this-a-way..." I felt like I had us on track, yet something still didn't feel quite right. Throttle in and settle, the paper and TV set on the handlebars are in good agreement, and... Uh-oh! What's that?

Heading through Lunar Crater National Monument.

A sign alongside the road is reading "Easy Chair Crater – This-a-way" and pointing to my left. That smelled right away like a pantload I ought to be digging into right away, since I knew that at this point the Easy Chair Crater needed to be on my right hand side. Sure enough, the landmark feature we were scoping called "The Wall" was easily viewable in the distance (not too far away) to the east, across this crater floor. All this data processing while rolling and down-snicking – no stinking mapwork required at this point for my light bulb to go back on. (I like to think that it stays on, just shines in the wrong direction sometimes... times like these for example.)

"Backside" of The Wall.

I was concerned about being mistaken for a cow, and mutilated by some unseen cosmic force from above. But, I digress...

Anyway, 13 miles off-route meant 13 miles back to get en route, ruling out the shortcut to The Wall. Having sorted this wrong turn out and re-engaging our objective on the right course, we proceeded to continue taking in the magnificent scenery in and around this monumental crater. My pictures suck and my camera was basically half Tango Uniform the entire trip – sometimes just not working at all. But, it was a breathtaking spot with lots to look at and glide through as we made our way up a gradual grade toward a passage through a landmark feature guarding the Lunar Crater on the east side of the Lunar Lake, known as and marked on the map as, "The Wall."

The back side drop through The Wall was instantaneously recognizable – we were apparently in Moab. Holy crap! Nice view, but better stay focused as we pilot these whales down the steep rocky cobbles and slickrock that will empty us, eventually, into the Railroad Valley… and the Nyala Wadi. But man alive, what cool stuff! I knew as my enjoyment meter started to peg with the addition of a little rocky single track that Keith might have to summon enough effort and chutzpah to navigate his heavier and tippier XR over this same ground, and that I should be mindful of this and find places to stop to get off and assist if needed. I was waiting at a flat spot below these massive rock pillars when Keith rounded the corner on top of the passage through The Wall, and made his right curving arc towards the "Moab Imper-sonator." His descent would not be as smooth and smiley as mine was....

Anyway, to make the short story short, he waddled down the hill, then high-sided. Full somersault on all the sharp and pointy things... and then he bounced back up. He wasn't far away, and he was up and had his bike back upright before I was able to get to him. So we had that going for us.... A quick relight for the XR and we were back underway, quarter steam ahead, and down through more tumbly slickrock and cobbles. At the bottom of this passage and after we made the valley floor, we came by a butte with a unique rock formation at its base. It was clearly a man-made object, and roughly 80 feet across or so – perfectly circular. It was some kind of a wall, approximately 5 to 6 feet high and made of tightly stacked flat rocks all similar to each other in size, shape and color. Tan, black and golden brown, the henge was a real surprise, and begged for a picture. (This feature is actually viewable on Google Earth.) But between my camera sucking and Keith off ahead, I just kept motoring to get back in front so I could keep the course through Nyala Wadi and up into the last navigational challenge of this, our most seriously committed leg. We were approaching mid-afternoon as we got onto the Railroad Valley floor on the west side under The Wall (that place was sooo cool!) We needed to make some miles, and stay off the throttles if we were going to make it. Already fuel was at the forefront of both of our minds. Well that, and of course I was concerned about being mistaken for a cow, and mutilated by some unseen cosmic force from above. But, I digress.... Probably should sip a little more brain juice outa this Camelbak.

Nyala.

A few more zigs and zags in 6th gear brought us around the giant triangle of a connection we needed to nav through to get us across the valley and into the only vestige of modern civilization in these parts – a small smudge on the maps named Nyala Wash. Having scoured the area on Google Earth, I knew there wasn't much here to be expected by way of comfort or salvation, but it was en route and we would soon see what this "smudge" was all about. As it turned out, that took all of about 45 seconds to shop through, and that was on foot going back and forth twice. Once we made it through a stubborn ranch gate that forced me to unfurl my tool pack for a crescent wrench to disengage the chain keeper that was keeping us trapped inside this cauldron; like being in that stone henge without any door, we entered the vicinity of habitation. Signs of life and farmed irrigation pivots were sparse, but we rode through them and came upon a small "ranch outpost" that was the Nyala Wadi.

Nyala consists of a half-dozen or so mobile homes stacked side by side and a couple of shacks, along with a bigger Morton building type of a shop, and about 20 or 30 empty red gas cans scattered on the desert floor. Near as we could tell, the place was a candidate for Hollywood location scouts for any B-movie you could think of involving teenagers disappearing one after the other, all night long on the big screen of a drive-in theater. We dismounted after having passed through the only gate, then decided we might try for fuel and water, while we were here. (And on the "other" side of the gate – just in case. . .) Keith had managed to cook off his bike while letting it sit idle, being distracted at the gate chain mechanical debacle just previous to our unannounced arrival to Nyala, and we thought if we could score fuel and/or water, we might hedge our bet a little, and make better our chances to get through the Cherry Creek Pass ahead – and find a friendlier passage across the Garden and Coal valleys on the other side of the Quinn Wilderness en route to Hiko, and the highway to Ash Springs. God, we still had a long way to go, and limited fuel and daylight to make it happen.

Fleeing from "Leatherface." Outbound from Nyala Wadi. Will we make it through to Cherry Creek Pass?

So we gathered up our nutsacks and walked back through the gate into Nyala, hoping for the best. We found a young man there, the only live warm body we saw, and he agreed to fill water bottles, but could offer no fuel. He said they had run out, and one of the guys had taken all the fuel cans somewhere back out to go get some. ("Back Out" to where?) We thanked him openly for the water, and went back through the gate after the long walk downtown, and I remember thinking to myself that we could die any number of slow deaths out here in this hamlet, or while trying to run away from it while being chased through the wash by a maniac with a chainsaw in his hands. I needed another sip from my Camelbak, to get back on track and stay focused.

We remounted after giving the XR a drink of water, and took off again, setting sail north toward a right turn that would take us back into some mountains, and over a pass into the next, and final, big valley crossing on this leg. The "keeper" crossing on a big keeper valley, the Garden Valley, which lies North of Rachel and Area 51. Off we went, and a glance in my Highway Dirtbikes rearviews revealed dust, Keith and no saw-wielding maniacs. It was still a good day!

Ash Springs as viewed from bordering BLM land, the oasis and hot springs hiding in the cottonwoods.

The Cherry Creek Pass was stunningly beautiful and the dirt was fantastic. The water truck had been out all over Nevada the week before we left for this trip, and the roads and tracks were in such awesome condition it was simply unbelievable! Groomers and twisties and berms. It was tough at this point to not just twist that handle and rail it – but fuel was going to be critical. Short of digging an oil well and refining it ourselves, we were dicked. Plan B was cannibalism, so I was conscious of not flat-tracking like Dave Aldana, and just letting Casper sip along. I kept an eye on my TV and the rearviews for Keith, and stayed frosty and focused, and kept enjoying the ride. Who knows? It might be my last; I'll be damned if I ain't going to have fun!

We made the pass up and down and I decided to let Casper coast for a few miles on the downhill side to conserve fuel. I was on my game and navigating on the fly, panning and zooming in the cockpit while I had easy trails to divide my attentions. Keith's headlight was still on in my rearviews, and I was bumming to think that his motor was still running when he had a chance to coast like I was doing, but at that point it only strengthened my resolve about "Plan B." If it came to that, I was determined to just eat him, and this would be useful if I flinched at taking that all-important first bite. "You should be coasting with the engine off, Keith!" I remember thinking to myself.... Rally on.

The Garden Valley greeted us with a locked ranch gate where we wanted to keep going, and Keith made time to reflect at that juncture, while I simply said, "... follow me – I can get us around..." and made tracks on an alternate. We got our bearings well enough through a section of "many road jumble" and faced the front fenders into the wind, and across that endless valley of no return, toward Mt. Irish. Having successfully found our ways onto the Mail Summit Road, we knew we were home free on the navigational aspect of things, and the only thoughts were that we were going to get low on fuel. I was still confident we had plenty to make the main slab at Hiko, though, and was a joyful bastard inside

144

my helmet as the sagebrush, cactus and occasional cow skull whistled by. It was 5 p.m. and it would all be over within an hour — we'd be at camp, or out of gas one way or the other. I thought how that stark truth spun an entirely clear perspective on things, and pressed on at 55 to 60mph atop my Friendly Punkin.

A flag came into view on my TV, and I recognized the immediate surroundings as we came by the site of last year's "2009 Legends of the Fall, Pre-Halloween Havoc Dual Sport Ride For No Wimps Tandem Bike Rally" — http://www.spotadventures.com/trip/view?trip_id=180528. We were getting close enough to really feel it now, and the critical fuel "tension" was palpable — it was as though Keith and I could read each other's minds! What in the hell could either of us be thinking about that would be more important. It was funny, because you could almost see the words floating back and forth between his helmet and mine, in mid air — like those little "thought bubbles" in a cartoon. "Got gas?"

Mail Summit Road brought us in, and we made the slab under our own power, finally! What a long crossing those last couple valleys were, coming in toward and past Mt. Irish to the north of Rachel and Crystal Springs. We made the highway, and had a home free run down into Ash Springs! We rallied on under a very late-day sun, and a warm wind.

We motored down the pavement, through Hiko (no phone, no lights, no motor car — not a single luxury) and into Crystal Springs to pick up the intersection of Highway 93. What, less than a dozen miles or so to Ash Springs? Hot damn! As we cruised those last few miles into the stable, and our camp and respite, I thought about the huge miles and vast array of images that got jammed into my skull this day. This fuel leg had us passing by and through so many stunning landscapes — rock, sand and one mountainous feature after another for hundreds of miles… it was dreamy. It was tremendous. And it was all mine — to savor forever. What a blast! Aaahh, the Shell station is right here — right where we left it last year! Cool… check the rearviews, and Keith is right here with me the whole way — no doubt feeling the joy of a day well ending, and great things accomplished on a motorcycle — it wasn't all easy, and we stayed hard at it all day. And… ppphhhttt….   thump, grrrrr,,………. Pppphhhhhhttt……..

WTF?

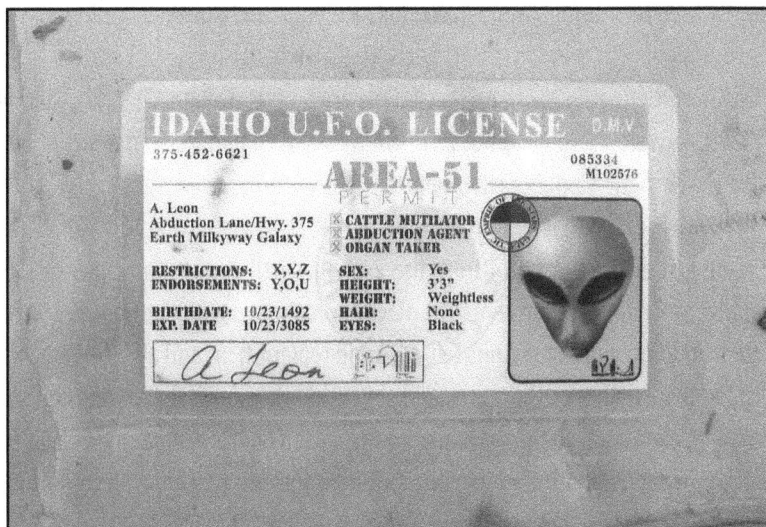

My license displayed on a SAM splint.

Casper slumbering beneath a crescent moon, in full view of all things "Area 51."

About 5 seconds before I would have begun braking and downshifting for the right turn off Highway 93 into the Shell station parking lot, I flamed out. "You have GOT to be shitting me...." I didn't catch it in time to get it onto reserve safely – I had a semi with a double pup right on my ass and instinct just kicked in and had me pulled over as I waved Keith by me, smiling inside my helmet at what just happened. The petcock turned after the truck and Keith got by me, and Keith was looking over his shoulder at me as I had the choke on and the bike refired. My smile turned into little giggles, and I blinkered my way back onto the slab, and didn't even make 4th gear before having to brake, signal and downshift for my exit.

As I pulled into the station and swung a leg off while the bike was still moving, the laughter was echoing inside my Arai, and I just couldn't believe it! I had the helmet off, my dry lips cackling this no-doubt maniacal cackle, and I was grabbing Keith by his shoulders and laughing and yelling, "I ran out of gas – I ran out of fucking gas! Can you believe it?!" And he was laughing as we stood there in front of "civilians" parked at the pumps who were apparently just staring at us – knowing Area 51 was just over the hill from where they decided to stop and get gas in their cars; they must have been convinced that they had stopped in the wrong place, at the wrong time. "I don't know what these nuts are going to want with us, but I'm pretty sure I know where they came from... quick, take a picture and call The Enquirer...."

I just propped the kickstand down, and with my helmet in my hand I raised my arms up in a sign of "Victory," and like Maximus I remember thinking with my eyes skyward; "... are you not ENTERTAINED?!" If I'd had a sword in my hand I'd have flung it into the audience, and walked back to my gladiator chambers....

So it happens, "gladiatorial chambers" were just across the street from the 24-hour Shell station/convenience store, and on BLM land where we would be momentarily pitching our tents – a place approximately 200 foot paces from the city park hot springs. That's right; fuel, food, lodging and hot springs to bathe and replenish in, and all within walking distance from where the leg of my kickstand rested. And, as the sun would set within the hour, we had ringside seats to whatever show might be on the skychannel over the Pahranagat Range to the west. Food, a soak, and a Crazy Creek chair facing Nellis with a cold man-killer in my lap would round out this 248-mile fuel leg pretty nicely. If lightning struck, it would not have been a life wasted, from just this one day alone. The game of my life? You bet.

146

Hot Springs city park in Ash Springs by daylight. A real oasis for the adventure rider.

Ash Springs / Pioche / Baker

Time to pee.... I get up in the dark and find a thirsty prickly pear. My ICO tells me it's 5:30 in the morning. Hell, may as well stay up and grab me a nice sunrise. After my leisurely recharge last night, and the flying circus we got to witness over the Groom Lake vicinity with military formations, countermeasures and one particularly fast moving aircraft the likes of which neither Keith nor I had EVER witnessed, and the nice dip in the hot springs and food and all.... I was already a pretty happy camper. But, I thought I would sprinkle a little sugar on top and go for the big one.... I walked over to the Shell station and commissioned myself a cup of freshly blended mocha jojo and grabbed a nutritious athlete recharger in the form of a donut, and wandered on over to the hot springs for an early morning riser.

I found Keith there already, steaming around in the dark with some trucker. I hoped they weren't capturing a special quiet moment under the stars, but either way I was cannonballing my way into Day 5 of this Raid, coffee in one hand, my yeehah in the other. The springs were great, and we got a nice long soak again – me with my mochajojo poolside; and called it a nice way to start the day! This place was built for Stovey – walking distance to and from your camp (BLM, free). Springs under the shade in the day and starry views in the dark (free). Dumpster nearby to offload your refuse (free). Super access to 24-hour convenience store and fuel. It was an adventure rider's heaven, I swear. But, after scraping all the barnacles off from the journey through every desolate valley, trench and wadi that Satan ever manufactured, and convinced that we'd frightened off more tourists at that truck stop to shut the entire community right down to the ground for about a week, I figured we might as well start the SPOTcast and get underway. There were bound to be a few more trails to run and berms to rail, and we were just the superheroes to do it! (More on this coming up....)

Abandoned mines above Pioche.

Keith and I were fueled up and resleeved with water and some morning body fuel and coffees. Camp was packed and the new purple line was blazing away on another route toggled to "navigate" on TV. Time here was well spent, but too short. I neither saw no Aliens, nor felt no probings but met some nice people and thoroughly enjoyed a starlit evening with some cold man-killers, and watched a good show with my friend as we sat fat and happy at the end of a long day. Now, after spring soak number two, it was time to rally on, and make for Pioche through the desert across the Delamar Valley. But first, a short cruise through "Hell's Half Acre" just to the south of Ash Springs. "Kick 'em and snick 'em...." We're off on the northbound return legs toward home, and the beginning of a long Day 5!

"Hell's Half Acre" is on the maps, and it was a really stunning cruise (short) through some good dirt road alongside and through shallow canyon country to where we intersected the next dirt road and headed more northerly through the Delamar toward Caliente and Pioche. Caliente was not on the agenda this trip, but we ran a nice bypass on through some great rollers back toward the Highland Range over Bennett Pass. We had a great run meandering alongside the Comet Road and into and out of lots of washed-out two-track and some single-track in the Silver State OHV Trail System, and on into Pioche, up over Zero Pass. We made good time and under perfect skies again we rolled into town for a nice lunch and fuel stop in this once-thriving silver mining town. The mines played out and were shut down in 1975, and when I asked the nice lady at the café what people did in Pioche (pronounced PEE-Oh-She according to the locals) she replied, "Nothin."

Zero Pass near Treasure Mountain, above Pioche, Nevada.

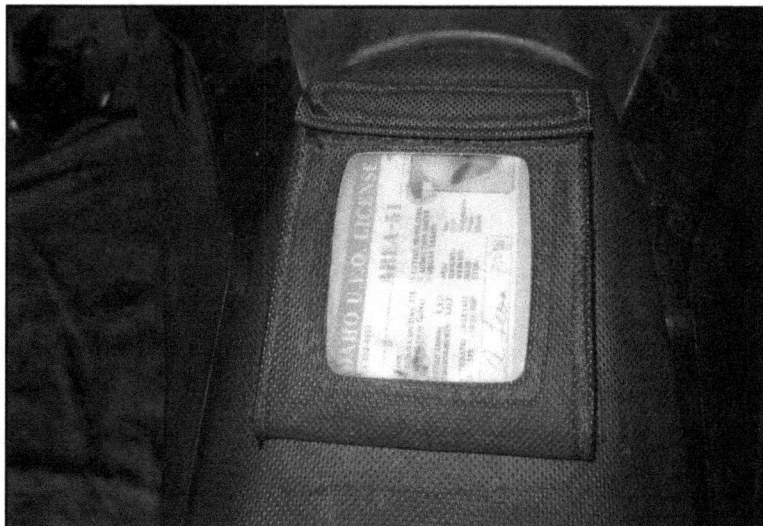

Credentials at the ready.

... with all the crash armor and riding pants and boots, and my face that must have looked like a ripped sneaker, it may have appeared like Halloween had come early.

A nice lunch with plenty of water to drink would hit the spot, and the only market left in town was right next door, so while lunch was being burned according to my request, I walked over to buy a few liters of water to sleeve up and save for fuel bottles later. Once we made Baker at the end of the day, I was going to want to have another salvo of auxiliary fuel on board, stashed in my pack and into Wolfman Water Bottle Holsters for a calculated "iffy" rattle northward from there to Wells, by my route. So, I wandered into that store on a mission, and the lady at the counter just stared at me then smiled. Another lady filed into line with her meagerly-filled cart, and she was smiling, too – and the first lady at the register asked, "...are YOU a SUPERHERO?" and started giggling. The other lady was starting to giggle, too – they had me bracketed, and so I just smiled back at both of them and said, "Why Yes – Yes I am! Can I sign something for ya?" We all cracked up just standing there in the market in the middle of Pioche on a nice day in October. My Six-Six-One pressure suit was still a-dangling off me like a cheap suit, but with all the crash armor and riding pants and boots, and my face that must have looked like a ripped sneaker, it may have appeared like Halloween had come early. It was a funny moment, and I was grinning broadly as I beamed back through the doorway as I left; "I'll send my sidekick in – in just a few moments, I sense that he too will need water. It's what we run on!" We were all still giggling as I walked back out the door, and went on my way down the sidewalk to finish off a nicely charred burger. We 'superheroes' run on them, too. (For more on what "Team Ruptured Buzzard" eats, visit my website for details here: http://bustedcompass.com/Ruptured_Raids.php#buzzard_food – and feel free to peruse the rest of my site, should you be locked in a bathroom with a laptop at some point in your life.)

Anyway, we met a little 3-year-old boy, "Kaden" at the local gas station, and he wanted to see my motorcycle. Being a Superhero, I told him he could come outside and see it if it was alright with his Mom, and she was smiling and nodding her head. There was still nothing to do in Pioche at that time, so it seemed like a good idea, and we all three wandered back over to where Casper sat waiting for me, and we got that little boy up on top of the seat as soft as a rusty girder, and he was thrilled to death. Even got to beep the horn and everything. "Bye-Bye, Kaden," be well my young friend. We must be off, to patrol the desert and keep it free from fiends and boogeymen. Adieu!

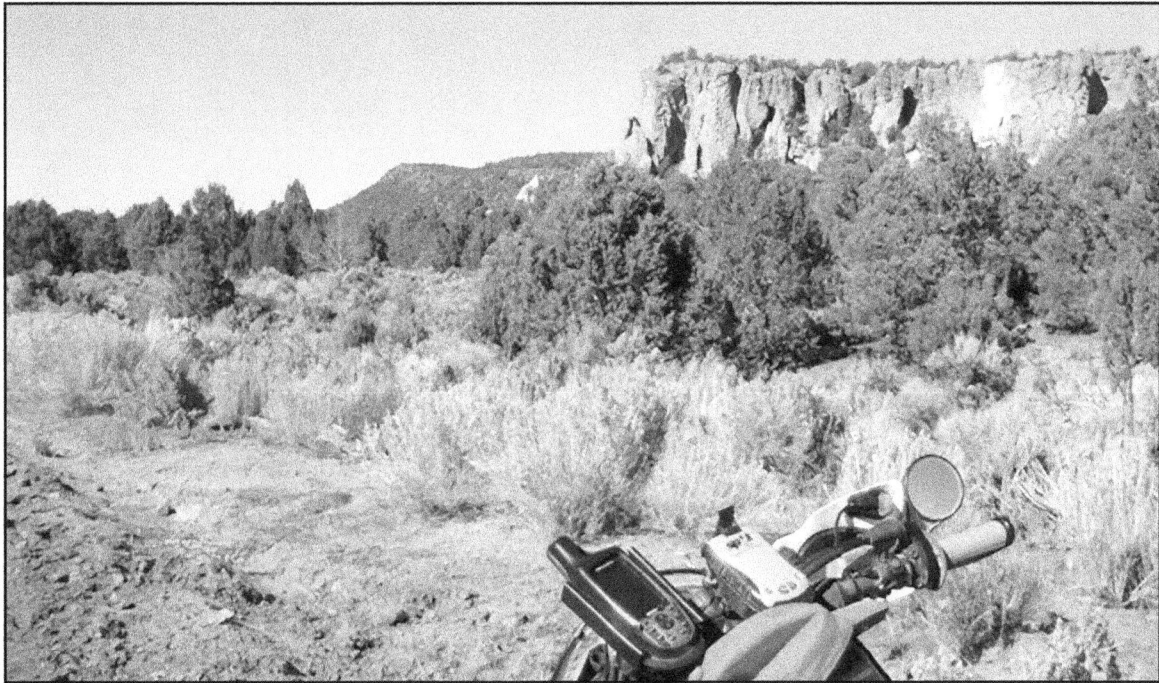

Heading north between the Wilson Creek Range and the White Rock Mountains.

Favorite mount of the author; 2010 KTM 450 XC-W Six Days. One mean Ruptured Buzzard Rally Raider.

Keith riding sweep in Spring Valley.

The route out of Pioche led us onto some slab for a short time, until we got off onto some dirt roads leading away from the things of man. We spent the rest of the afternoon loping through foothills on great dirt roads to the north and east of Pioche, heading up Camp Valley toward the mining town of Atlanta where we passed through last Fall. We would skirt to the east of Atlanta on this run, cutting through the Wilson Creek Range and staying to the east side of those mountains and through the endless expanse of Hamlin Valley. The Granite Peak (elevation 11,218 ft.) was visible for almost a million miles from the south, as we headed north toward it, and the Great Basin National Park. (The "Great Basin" per se is a huge land area, encompassing a big part of Nevada, Utah, Idaho and Oregon. They make it a National Park within a small part of that all-encompassing land mass, with a visitor center in Baker, Nevada — which lies north of Garrison, Utah, right on the state line smack dab in the middle of nowhere.)

We wicked it up in the late afternoon, knowing that we had a great campsite waiting for us up ahead and I for one was looking forward to another great starlit night around a campfire and a cold man-killer. Our thought earlier in the day was, if we made it to Baker with no trouble, and didn't get any vultures or anything tangled up in our Superhero capes, we would go for the same campsite we held last year up Snake Creek to the south and west of Baker. After a short stop in town for water and cold ones, and a bag of chips for the road, we waved "Hi and Goodbye" to a passing solo Adventure Rider on a new KTM 990 who was pulling out of a café across the street from the only store in Baker, and headed back out of town. The sun still had a few good rays left in it when we made camp, and I used them to air a sleeping bag and my riding clothes from the day. Keith took "his spot" from last year, and I claimed the same spot I had previously as well. This time, Casper took the place of the bike I was on for last year's "Legend" – my partner Keith's very own XR650 that he was riding today. Son of a gun flat gave me his motorcycle to ride, because my 640A had a water pump go Tango Uniform on me two days before we left, and I had no time to fix it. We simply performed a "New York Reload" and threw the bad one down, and picked up a fresh one, worrying about fixing the bad one later. His XR was a good bike for the ride we did last year, and it was a better bike for this year's route than Keith's other bike, a bigger KTM 950 Adventure. Still, this route took us over and through some more difficult ground than last year's ride, to be sure. And Keith did well to jockey and course that XR through it. My hat is off to you Keith, and a sturdy nod in your direction for all you did to keep yourself aloft on a sometimes very challenging set of tracks! Good man. Salute. Shut up and give me my beer then....

Heading north through the Hamlin Valley toward Great Basin National Park.

Big, big valleys...

Back up high in "cat country" again, we spent a little bit around the campfire after I made another quick oil change for Casper, to keep him purring and happy, even if a mountain lion should get me in the night. At least this way, if somebody came to repatriate my corpse, my bike would be ready for come what may. That's how I roll. ;-)

I set another "Mark" on my GPS, for "LOF2 – Camp 5," and enjoyed another good evening of dinner, campfire and Colorado Cool Aid. The Big Agnes mattress was going to do its magic once again, and I reflected on the day's journeys – rocky canyons, groomed dirt (did I forget to mention the motor grader in front of us when we made the left turn out of Hell's Half Acre through the Delamar?) and some single track and high-speed rollers. The compressions were so huge coming into the Highland Range south of Pioche that I had to drop a gear a few times for fear of a catastrophic collapse of everything I held dear. We G'd the bikes out for miles along that section that was straight as a grizzly's dick, but full of both fun and trouble for the unwary. Good times... Good times... We had good food, kept hydrated and had no mishaps. I got to be a superhero to a couple of ladies who could use a good laugh, and knew how to use one. And I got to be a little more of one again to a 3-year-old kid, holed up in a mining town gas station with stars in his eyes when he saw two motorcycles rolling by. All this after having my morning cappuccino poolside in a hot springs with pea gravel on the floor that was so soothing to aching feet. Precious gems in another perfect day sent straight through from above.

When in the hell was the first shoe going to drop!? A nervous man would have been dying of the jits at about this point, but I was just happy to take it all in, and count my lucky stars. Thankful for my good fortune and for all the good things that led me to be able to make this ride, I drifted off again in my downy cocoon, content in another Nevada canyon, juniper scents on the breeze.

Day 6

Looking back down toward the Mount Moriah Wilderness.

Baker / Currie Hills

Sure, I had a sinus headache last night, and I had to get up to take some Tylenol to try and get ahead of the beating crush behind my face. But, there we were a long way from home with miles to go before we slept again, and the pills would help take the edge off. They did, and after packing up and saying goodbye to our Snake Creek campout once again, we glided down out of the canyon beneath Wheeler Peak, and on into Baker for fuel.

We opted for gas and go this morning, and jumped onto the little purple line heading northwest out of Baker, and into the Snake Range of the Mount Moriah Wilderness on dirt roads. The route looked good, but I wasn't sure if my purple line would skirt the wilderness boundary or dead end somewhere out there. There are lots of ways to find that out, and we were going to use one of them. Face-time with some fence posts; in an hour or two – we'd know. But first, it was time to field test the Bridgestone M59 front and the D606 rear, both with Bridgestone Ultra Heavy Duty tubes...

I'm barking along the county dirt and I see my purple line heading off to the left, on a super-obliterated two-track. A dude should have known better – it was not my first time in the desert. My brain simply pointed "that-way" and like a dog panting at a freshly painted fire hydrant, I just followed the track into the scenery, content to be facing the mountains with desert under my wheels. Then came 3rd gear as I was ramping up to take a stronger position in the cockpit and play Andy Grider in Dust to Glory across this section towards Silver Creek Road, when all of a sudden.... WHAM! "Holy Mongolian Butt-Clutch, Batman!" THUMP! POW! Phhhhhht.... "Mayday – Mayday – Mayday"

Mount Moriah

With less than zero time to react, I just slammed into and through a prickly pear colony about 18 to 20 inches tall and the size of a laundry basket. My front wheel literally exploded the colony and the rear bumped its way through behind – both wheels, and thence both tires, went cactus smashing before 10 o'clock in the morning. "THAT is gonna leave a mark…" I thought to myself, and turned the bike around, motioning to Keith that this was a bad call and we needed to get back on the county road. That would be a good place to find a rock or a ditch to replace both tubes too.... And so between the sinus meds in the Tylenol taking my personal RPMs down a few hundred, and the mochachinos adding some replacement revs; the early morning frost slowing things down and the scenery mellowing things out… this here cactus whack brought things more or less back up to level. I was now pretty much wide awake.

On the harder surface of the county dirt road I was able to eyeball the running rubber a little bit and all seemed well enough, but everyone knows how a flat develops – either immediately, or slowly over the course of minutes, hours or months. So I knew all I had to do now was to wait. I decided to ride while I waited, and we continued onward to the Silver Creek Road, up Silver Creek into the Humboldt National Forest. (Keith posted a helmet cam video of some stream crossings on good two-track here.) The riding was truly fabulous up this section as we motored under arching canopies of oak and pine branches, inching our way farther and farther along my little purple line into the woods up a canyon. I thought this was another legendary stretch of trail, and enjoyed every minute of it during each meander and throttle blip around tight corners, boulders and a few submarine surges through the creek. The leaf colors were also stunning and the senses were once again filled with all good things of the Fall. It was why we were here, and I was reminded of something my wife has said before, quoting a term from a book she had read many years ago – the idea of "Greensong." It was like floating through Brigadoon…

156

Keith regroups after a whistle through the Bristlecones up Silver Creek.

We passed a party of hunters who were disembarking from a Jeep that had obviously come from the opposite direction, and they just looked at us as we thumped on by on our adventure bikes and waved to them in 2nd gear. A short few turns later and we came out of the woods along the creek and found ourselves up against a USFS sign in front of the path that the little purple line went through, and got denied for non-motorized restrictions into the Mount Moriah Wilderness Area. Oh well, this is where this path detours and we find our way out of here in another direction. We had two options – go back exactly the way we came; 23 back miles down the canyon to the highway, or try and proceed up a steep Forest Service road right there, that switch-backed like a confused meth addict straight up out of this basin. The map and GPS advised it was a "go" for this option, and we climbed out of the basin and made a run through the mountains toward Miller Basin Road and Old Highway 6 toward Sacramento Pass. It was a neat ride with eyeful after eyeful, and good views of snow-covered Wheeler Peak in the Snake Range to the south where we had just camped; where the National Park gives tours to Lehman Caves.

Wheeler Peak inside the Great Basin National Park boundary.

Camp 6 in the Currie Hills on the outskirts of the Dolly Varden Wilderness.

A few miles of slab on Highway 6 got us to a dirt two-track cutting across the Spring Valley floor, and we railed some berms along that to make it to Route 893 on the west side of the valley, and turned north to get back on route. We bumped into a road construction crew on the way, and the fella with the STOP sign told us there was fuel ahead at both Schellbourne and Lages – music to my ears. So we punched through the Schell Creek Range farther up ahead and made for the sprawling metropolis of Schellbourne. We found the place consisted of a ramshackle saloon with a broken gas pump, but they had a bag of chips for sale, and a root beer for me, something else wet for Keith. We asked about gas at Lages, and they said sure they sell fuel, but word on the street was that somebody hit a power pole in their car, and the power was out. So, we had that going for us. I reckoned that a guy could get a whole lot of fouled up in that bar with just a ten-spot, and we waved goodbye and headed north on dirt two-track that paralleled Interstate 93, into Lages Station.

At Lages we not only found the power on, and fuel running, but were able to get water and cold man-killers for the evening, as the day had gotten long in the tooth, and the rays were beaming more horizontally at us. After a few more tan lines on the GPS, which could mean either a road or a wash (a few were indeed washes) we made our connection back on my route, and headed off into the sagebrush through some gates. Route-finding was interesting as everything here was almost completely obliterated, and our path forced considerable hunting and pecking to stay on course. We did that though, and motored through some rough two-track, no track and washes to navigate through the Currie Hills and make a camp to the south of the Dolly Varden Mountains; our last camp out on this legend in the making.

Dolly Varden Range

The knoll we found to make camp had everything, as usual – juniper shelters and flat spots to share with the creatures of the ground. So we shut the engines down with plenty of light left to do housekeeping and collect up some dead branches for another conference under the Milky Way. I killed my last freeze-dried dinner in a bag, and Keith handed me his Verizon bars to chat up my wife while sitting warm around the fire glowing; a cold man-killer nearby. Having made fuel at Lages was a stroke of good luck, and I was more than pleased that both tires stood round and firm at this point in the raid. Would I be changing them cold bastards the first thing tomorrow morning? I'd have to wait for dawn for the answer to that, and the answer would come for sure. For now, I was in my Crazy Creek eating M&Ms – not a cloud in the sky.

Casper standing guard while Stovey wrestles Big Agnes into submission for the last time.
(Keith Briggs photo)

Darkening skies to the north, and that's where we're headed. All day long.

Currie Hills / Wells / Twin Falls

Morning brought some sunshine, but not before I had a chance to wake up on my own and view Orion hunting his way across a perfectly starlit sky while answering the call of nature, and obeying the command to hose off a dusty rock or two. Some time before all the stars had vanished, I stayed up and began scooping nearer the bottom of my coffee can, and enjoying another hot thermo-tumbler of go-juice to accompany a Clif Bar and some oatmeal. It wasn't long before I heard rustling inside of Keith's nylon castle as he contemplated another metamorphosis from slumberjack into legend-making adventure rider. The seeds of our last day on this trail were being planted while long shadows raced across the tan rocks and dry washes of this moonscape.

With Day 7 about to make some progress, I thought I'd rub a cold hand across an even colder tire, and try to give one a squeeze — just for fun. A couple of rubs, squishes and push-downs on both ends of Casper's rubbery bottoms yielded some useful data — the tires were both still fat and puffy. Nice! A respectful glance at the rear wheel that I paid a million dollars for got me a sturdy nod back in return, and the black Excel Superlaced to an orange RAD hub with a cush drive just sat there in the dirt, all round and rugged looking. It would take much more than hitting a few trenches at Mach 1 to even get that Dakar-ready wheel's attention, and my continued thanks to Woody at Woody's Wheelworks remained

Stovey drops down into Independence Valley from the pass on the crest of the Pequop Range. Wells out of the image, to the far right. *(Keith Briggs photo)*

staunch on this Friday morning. Someday, when I am particularly flush with greenbacks, I'll buy the front wheel with a Superlaced A60 rim, and drive this bike straight down the crack of Satan's ass with not a care in the world. Might not even need tires at that point — his wheels are that good.

After packing camp and a map reload in the BarPack, I was about ready. Keith was administering to our "green needs" and giving the fire site the once-over for a Leave No Trace exit, and I sighed a little sigh thinking this was our last day on this tremendous riding adventure across Nevada. My comfort here comes from daydreaming the dream that future rides may still come true, and I'll be able to continue exploring on yet another rolling journey in the Silver State, and beyond. For now, as I spied the skies to the north and straddled Casper, I thought of the goals for the day and wondered if the building clouds I could see in the distance would gather in force and add to the treasure of challenges yet to come. "Where will my head rest tonight?" I got the bike started after a few kicks to clear and a spark on the button, and hoped that the buffet at the truck stop in Wells would be in full force. Keith pulled out ahead and we motored off, leaving no fire trace and only a hint of having recently stayed — but you'd have to dig for that. It's off for a mountain range or two, and a couple more valleys for this morning.

Independence Valley from the Pequop Mountains, looking north.

The route gave us nice riding through two-track that hadn't seen much traffic in a good long while it seemed, and we could continue enjoying the pleasure of having the entire land to ourselves. In six full days so far we hadn't seen another off-road vehicle on our journey, save for local traffic in and around the immediate vicinities of major towns and cities we passed through. We were "it," as if starring in a post-apocalyptic motorhead feature – riding away from one zombie-attack after another. But, since I've seen my share of zombie-attacks, I knew I couldn't let my guard down because as soon as you do, they are right there to get you. Better to stay frosty, keep my wits, and rally forth with some focus like I mean it, just in case.

The riding was excellent on the west side of the Dolly Varden Range and I was having a blast in the twisties on great two-track. Jumping in and out of washes in lower gears was fun on this dirt bike, and for me it was perfect riding for a long-range trip where luggage needed to be hauled. Without camping gear, it would be fantastic but hell – even with saddlebags there was no real suffering. I'd hate to do this kind of ride with zero survival equipment – it would be do-able, but stressy. Nope, things were rolling great, and the tires were full of air and Keith seemed happy to trail behind and wasn't sucking too much trail dust and the weather was good. So we continued around the Dolly Varden Range on our right as we headed northbound, and made a left across the first valley of the day to make a connection at Indian Creek. This would be another pipeline across one more Nevada mountain range.

The desert was flat-out and we took full advantage of the lack of speed limit signs, and left some dust trails for an hour as we navigated our way in the Goshute Valley to the hook up at Indian Creek. The turn was right where it was supposed to be, and as we made our entrance into the Pequop Range the two-track quickly began to take on new character – we were losing one of our two tracks for sure. As we continued west and got some canyon country alongside us, the tracks shared some deep washout back and forth, until there was only a thin line to ride above a four-foot-deep channel that had been chiseled from a fast moving watercourse. Flash flooding had made this trail a hazard – but only if I crashed into it, so my take on this as I'm coursing upstream through the dry washes and sagebrush is to keep my eyes on the thin tan line, even if it is only imaginary at some points. Best not peer too long or hard into these close-by chasms... "bike follows eyes... I follow bike..." can end in tears!

A few turns in the sage-mazes while checking for zombies kept us on route and got us onto the trails above, and as we climbed higher off the valley floor, we got away from the deep trenches from washouts below, and really enjoyed the ride to the top. There we found great views of the Steptoe Valley below and the Cherry Creek Mountains to the left – and got a peek at the line that would shortly bring us into Wells. It sure beat slabbing it on I-93, off to the left and parallel to our course north. We can end this morning with some high-speed dirt roads, looking forward to a truck stop buffet, and an afternoon coup de grace to the east of the Jarbidge Wilderness as we head back to the truck. It was nice to not have to worry so much about fuel on this leg after finding gas in Lages yesterday, and with all pleasant things like this inside my helmet, I dropped down from this last perch of the morning and found the valley floor waiting for big wheels and big legs. Keith joined me in twisting his handle all the way to the stop and we maxed the bikes out for a short bit like Johnny Campbell. It wasn't until we came to within three-quarters of a mile of our connection with Highway 93 that we encountered anything but fast hardpan. Then, it was time for Keith to face the demon silt beds once again.

There was a breeze coming directly at us from the north, and so nothing to blow my dust trail out of Keith's way. At the speeds we were running, I was glad to see Keith had taken the option to hang back rather than go for the close proximity formation to try and keep out of the dust trail I was leaving. But as I looked back a couple of times to check my partner, I was astounded to find his headlight visible in my rearviews! He was back there in it, a few hundred yards, and keeping pace. I hit 88 mph across this section, and he stayed right there with me – unbelievable! As we came to the silt beds though, and I waddled my way through them in 2nd and 1st gears, I realized that his XR was going to be more of a challenge – more like trying to park an oil tanker with tugboats, only without the tugboats.

So after waiting a short bit, I went back and found my friend righting his bike in the midst of the talcum sea – a splash of gasoline covering the far right bank of this powdery man-trap where the impact of a low-speed tumble ejected some fuel from the custom mason jar lid we were field testing. Keith managed to keep good control and got his bike set down nicely, and kept from getting hurt and kept his bike from any damage – skills only a good rider could pull off in this silt bed. After a deep breath, we motored through the rest of the beds, and out onto the highway for Wells. We made the Flying J by noon exactly.

I grabbed extra fuel for this last leg, thinking it would come into play, and we both had a good meal for the road. My thinking at this point was that we were within striking distance of the trailer parked in Twin Falls, but we had to plan carefully and keep mindful on the fly the rest of the afternoon, because this bike goes down at twilight, no matter where we are. That headlight ain't gonna cut it, and my recent nighttime sojourn into a herd of cattle a few weeks prior to leaving for this trip is still on my mind. (Crash thread here on ADV Rider forums: http://www.advrider.com/forums/showthread.php?t=621710.)

The ominous black squares of the jet engine intakes the size of me and my bike on either side of the streamlined fuselage of the first Eagle-driver really got my attention.

If we're going to make the trailer, we're going to have to stay on course, ride smoothly and keep a steady pace. And we need to not hurry, but rather leave time and space to keep focused and stay loose during the witching hours of an adventure ride when you tend to let your guard down and make foolish mistakes. "We're not home yet – Ride my own ride." It's like I have these words taped to my handlebars or something....

Brunch was good – I had one of each from the menu, gobbling all the breakfast menu items I found like a condemned man. After getting a call in to my home base in the parking lot, to let my better half know I was okay and still under my own power – not an ambulance or helicopter in sight (no small relief to her ears...) I lit that bike up and moved off. It was the last purple line on the GPS to try and follow, and we were soon on the Upper Metropolis Road headed north from Wells toward Jarbidge.

We screamed along on a major thoroughfare kind of dirt road, and came up alongside the Jarbidge Wilderness to the east, and went through places like "Dixon's Ranch" and "Choke-A-Man Draw." The Fall colors were stunning in some of the canyons we had to switchback up, and as the skies were building with storm clouds the farther north we rode, the contrast between the yellows and oranges in the leaves were stark against the gray backdrop that continued to develop throughout the late afternoon. The only "incident" we had on this final leg that brought us to home plate was being lit up on the HUDS of two F15 Eagle pilots.

It was easy to spot the aircraft pointing in on me as they exited a canyon somewhere near the "Choke-A-Man" draw; the ominous black squares of the jet engine intakes the size of me and my bike on either side of the streamlined fuselage of the first Eagle-driver really got my attention as I crested a knoll on a twisty. As soon as I saw him, I knew he had already seen me, and he was still turning hard at me to point in and train up – guns or missiles – it wouldn't matter.... Since I was on friendly soil, he was just using my bright yellow jacket as a training target of opportunity, and I was glad to oblige him in his teachable moment. Love to help the troops. Just gladder still that he and his wingman didn't go 'rocket's hot' on either me or Keith when they both pointed in on us, and flew over fast and low; turning sharply then up and out to the west. A squeamish ninny might have browned out.... But not two "buzzards on a legend" like me and Keith. "Tally ho!" my friends, and good hunting....

Stovey supports the troops.

Captain Blohm in the sandbox, showing Team Ruptured Buzzard colors!
(Photo courtesy Captain Michael Blohm, USAF)

Casper about to make a turn back onto Blue Hills Road, northbound to Twin Falls. End of the dirt.

A few more hours of riding on dirt roads put us back on the Three Creek Road, only instead of yarding it around to the west and heading back into Jarbidge, and starting this great ride all over again from the beginning, we veered hard to starboard and made for Rogerson on the little slab. As we rolled underneath the few raindrops that would splatter on my faceshield over the course of the whole trip, the clouds got thicker and the wind got stronger, but nothing ever came of it. What few drops there were blew away, and the clouds did nothing but puff their chests at us, and we got closer to Twin Falls near the magical 5 o'clock hour, and shut-down time for Casper and his stock anemic headlight. We passed a sign indicating "TWIN FALLS – 12 miles" and we rode in formation back up along the Blue Lakes Road that took us south a week ago, and the rolling hills and farm country were giving way to views of the city off ahead on the northern horizon. Just then… another "phhht," cough and sputter, and a slight "brrrrrrrpppp" came from beneath my tank. Without missing a beat this time, I had my hand on the valve and kept the flames burning underneath that spark plug. Eight miles south of the city limits, I ran out of gas. Coming in on reserve – it's the only way to fly.

A few corners inside the city limits and we found our way through the streets to the truck, still parked at our spot Jeff had arranged for us. Tired, happy, relieved – I dismounted with the melancholy familiar to all of us who put great rides in the can. A sweet farewell to another legendary ride.

Epilogue

Page 4 data from Garmin 60CSx:

Max Speed - 89 mph

Max Elevation – 8,608 ft.

Total Ascent – 72,639 ft.

Moving Time – 33 hrs 09 minutes

Stopped Time – 19 hrs 40 minutes

Moving Average – 40.5 mph

Total Distance Traveled – 1,342 miles

Casper heralds the memory of a fallen motorcycle legend, Cliff Gullet, a world land speed record holder.

Pros and Cons of the week-long ride:

PROS:

• I guess the short list would have to include the fact that the weather was great! These tracks simply could not be laid under rainy or wet conditions – silt would have been slicker than eel snot, impassable altogether. Had it rained on us while we were on certain paths, we'd have been pooched – still be out there.

• Not a single flat tire – unbelievable!

• No major crashes. And I had zero of any kind.

• Route finding was right on, no navigational debacles.

• Hot Springs was a total plus!

• No alien probing, that either of us can remember.

• Met good people along the way.

• Got to explore tons of prehistoric country.

• Did not have to eat Keith.

• Witnessed cool show at Ash Springs, got my IDAHO UFO License.

• Water truck and groomers were out on the course just before we rode it.

• Eagle pilots were in a good mood, or they were out of ammo – or both.

• Makeshift gas cap held.

Stovey likes the forums, and Ride Dual Sport is one of the best.

CONS:

Next year's ride is already being planned, but this one will be hard to beat. After all, this one had a little of just about everything. Made for a good story that included high-rev cross-country machines, desolate places, mountain lions, cannibalism, UFOs, Superheroes, abandoned mines, zombie attacks, dust devils, an ancient stone henge, maniacs with a chainsaw, and aliens.

Gunny Highway said, "You can beat me, and you can starve me – just don't bore me...."
This ride was anything but that. Until next time, Rally On.... Stovebolt ■

Route of Legends of the Fall #3

Map of Nevada in the public domain obtained from the National Atlas. (Nationalatlas.gov)

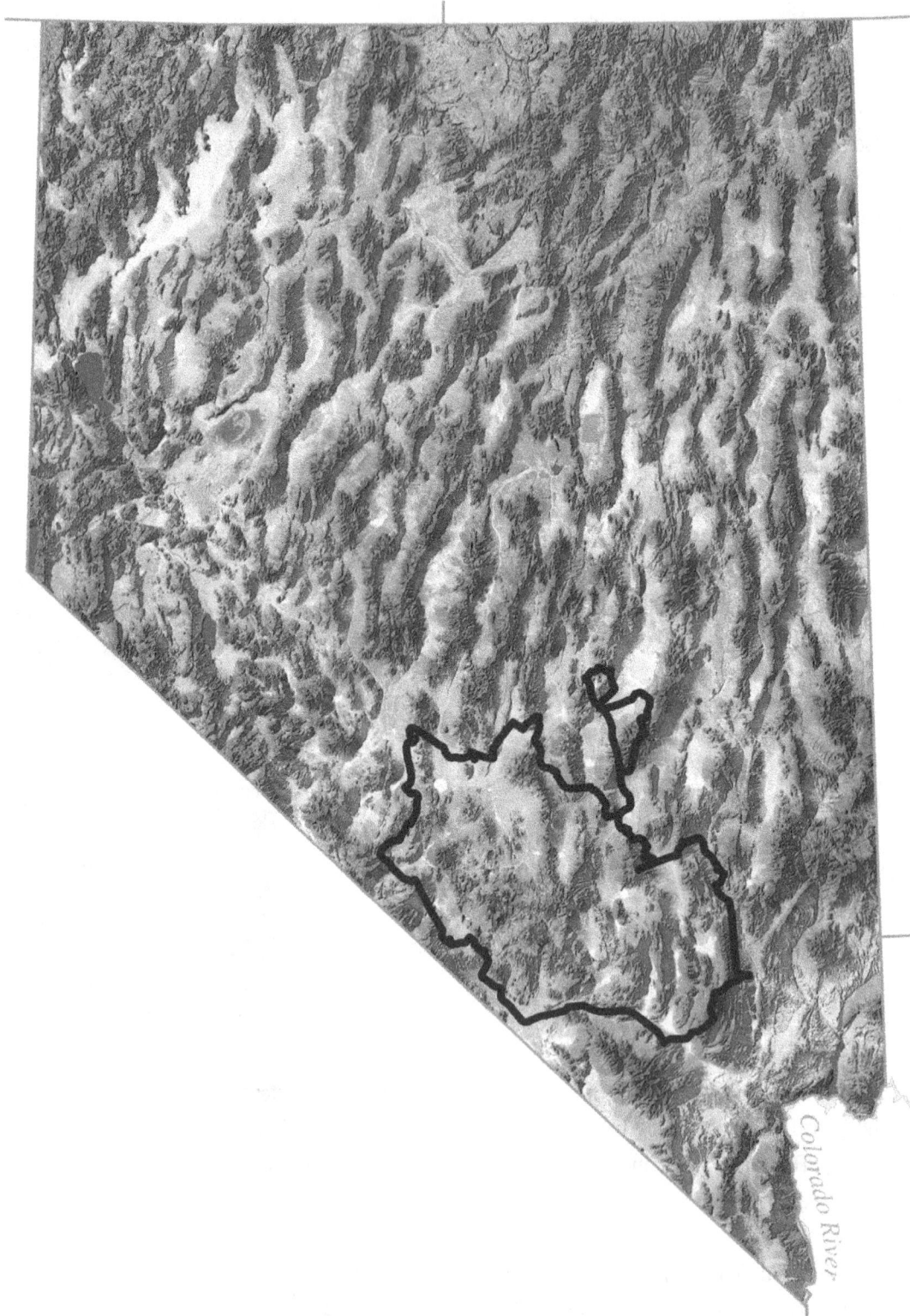

Colorado River

3rd Annual

Legends
of the Fall

Area 51 Circumnavigation and Myocardial Mayhem Rachel-to-Rachel Rally Raid

October 2011

Prologue

There once was a man from Nantucket...

No, no – here it is; "It was a dark and stormy night, when all of a sudden – there came a KNOCK at the door, and..."

No – seriously, begin here...

Where to begin? Dunno, but riding around in circles in the Nevada desert almost has no beginning. No middle and no ending either – it's a "circle," right? But I have wanted to ride around in the vicinity of the Nevada Test Site, Area 51 and the Tonopah Test Range for a long while, and a dirty dual sport bike with Sidewinder missiles and a six-pack seemed like a great way to go. As with many things, though, what seems at first like a great idea often morphs as you go along, and as it played out for me, I had to drop the notion of both AIM 9's on KTM Hard Parts Pods and carrying a cooler full of icy tall boys. So, after editing the equipage down to just Casper and me with some good soft luggage for a sleeping bag, pad and some GORP, all I had to do was to come up with a route and grab hold of my ManBasket and head to Nevada. Good enough.

Reckless driver caught on tape.

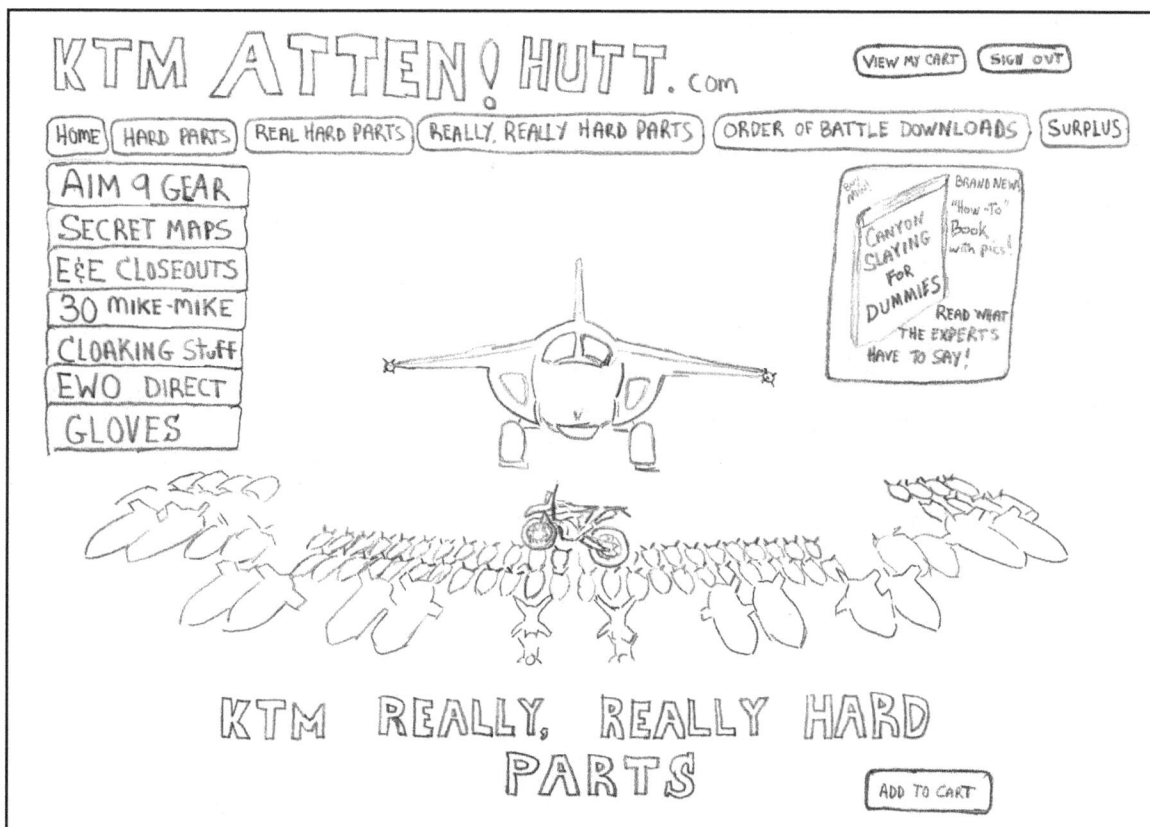

Original setup for my bike, but abandoned after logistical anomalies.

Here then, is my story. Ladies and Gentlemen, prepare to get your money's worth...

This year's ride was pretty short, but it was nonetheless a pretty sweet motorized perambulation. I had routed out a loop circumnavigating the perimeter of Area 51 that penciled out to only approximately 475 miles via dirt roads and obliterated road tracks and single track along the outskirts of some of the most hotly guarded ground on planet Earth. It was simple enough to do, and I had looked time and again over many years at road, track and trail on Google Earth and other map resources, and had a good idea of the lay of the land. I didn't have detailed enough data to make it easy on myself to run a precision razor's edge knife cut along some of the areas I would have enjoyed playing in though, but for the time I ended up making for trip routing, I did alright for my purposes. I had, in fact, even played a bad route through the 18th hole on the course from Ash Springs to Rachel by my routing, and tracked right past the perimeter entrance and through the site into restricted territory – a route that if followed, would have ended badly for me and anyone who followed. The A51/Nellis Air Force Base Security Forces would have intercepted any such folly right away quick, and ended the track, causing us to be DRT (Dead Right There.) But, having realized this was likely, and also that certain 'wheels on the ground' navigational decisions would be expected once en route, I took that in stride and loaded up my Garmin 60CSx. Ain't nuthin but a thang....

The beginning of the journey commenced on Sunday morning, October 9th from the base camp parking we had established in front of the Little A'Le'Inn, Rachel, Nevada. At the behest of several staunch protagonizers on the forums,

Rider1 = Dave

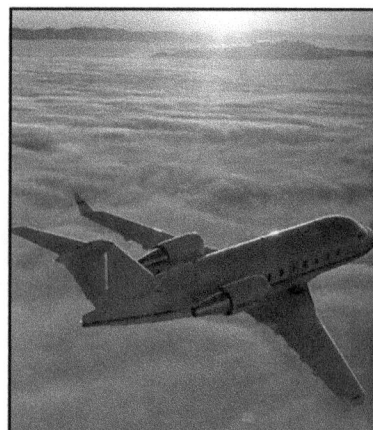

Here is Dave's daily driver.

I posted a ride announcement a full two months ahead of time, and let the candle burn. There had been at one time, seven adventurous souls who signed on with full intentions of participating in these shenanigans, but as things developed, we lost a few to the various circumstances that come up in life. One contracted bubonic plague, one fell victim to acute wienerism; another went shoe shopping at the mall. Still another got hit by a meteorite in Brazil, and another decided to stay home and watch reruns of Project Runway. For whatever reasons, I was gradually playing host to fewer and fewer co-riders, and looking at running this by myself this year. (Actually, some very solid Brothers were suffering from injuries, and had to back away from the table – but I know it pained them to do so. Cal and Peter – you were dearly missed my friends. I hope both of you are coming along better and would love to ride with you guys again. Peter – I've been subscribed to your eyeball thread on ADV, and I hope the doc gives you some excellent treatment for that eye injury! See you out there again, I sincerely hope.)

... as things developed, we lost a few riders to the various circumstances that come up in life. One contracted bubonic plague, one fell victim to acute wienerism; another went shoe shopping at the mall.

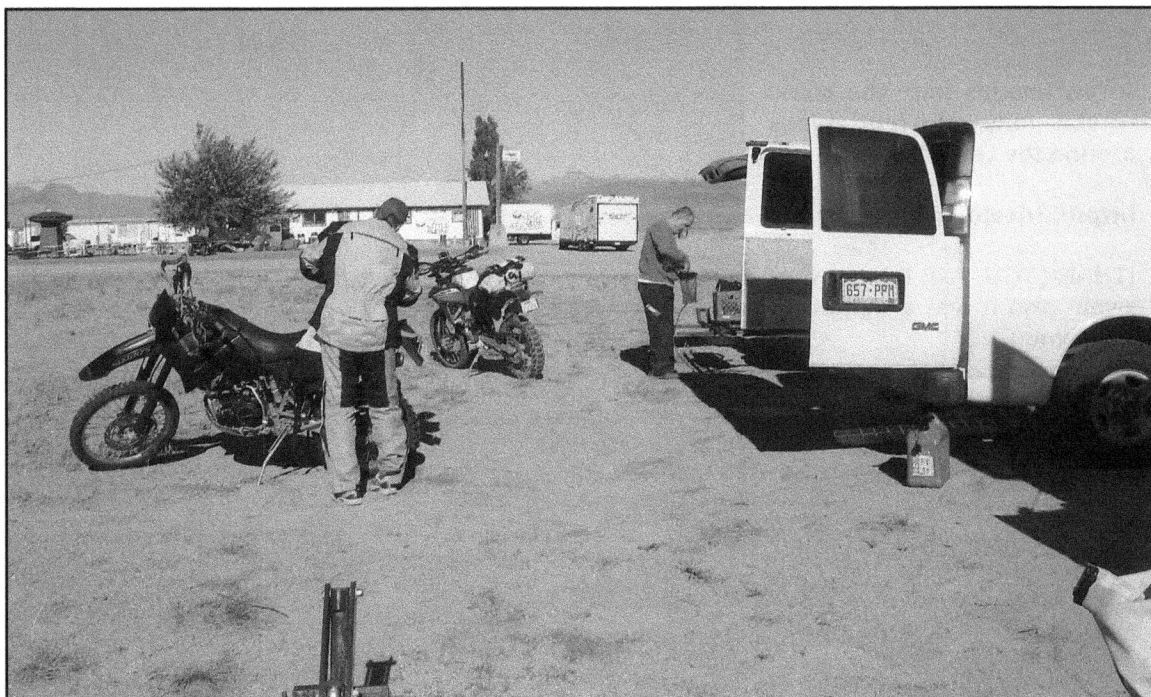

trail717 = Marshal

This left three of us standing together alongside motorcycles in front of the Little A'Le'Inn on a Sunday morning; Trail717 (Marshal), Rider1 (Dave) and myself. Marshal is a former motocross and desert racer from back in the day, and he has recently reignited the dirt riding passion with a bent on dual sporting. He also is an accomplished veteran long-distance mountain bike and road racing bicyclist with many years of training and competing experience. His recent acquisition, a 2000 KTM 640 Adventure, got him back into the game and onto this ride.

Dave is a Nevada resident with some years on bikes and ATVs, with both road riding and dirt biking experience under his belt. His daily drive is a Bombardier Challenger 604, arguably the most critically maintained of all the machines that any of us on this ride would ever see a picture of, let alone get to travel in. For Dave, hi-tech is ho-hum as he pilots his employer at the edge of low-earth orbit altitudes for a living. He was mounted on a new Husky TE449. Shiny and red to boot.

Both of these co-riders are former USAF personnel, and so I felt in extra strong company as we rode off toward the "Back Gate" of the Nellis Air Force Base and Gunnery Range. Me? I have no such creds, save for the fact that Dennis Hopper once bought me a Margarita, and I sat next to Buddy Hackett one time on a flight in a Dash 8 from Aspen to Denver. That and five dollars could get me a cup of coffee. The inane and most vacuous tale of how I came to imbibe such a welcome concoction at Mr. Hopper's expense is extolled in Chapter 1.

I had spent some time readying my rally steed, "Casper the Friendly Punkin" in preparation for this ride, and a general build thread surrounding this folly may be found by pasting this link in your browser, if interested in details on my 2010 KTM 450 XC-W Six Days: http://ridedualsport.com/forum/index.php?topic=1086.0

A few images from the scene of this rally raid rendezvous around the Little A'Le'Inn...

http://littlealeinn.com/

(THANK YOU, PAT! You are very sweet and it was a delight to meet you!)

Above: Camp Zero, outside of the Little A'Le'Inn, Rachel, Nevada; Below left: A view from the inn.

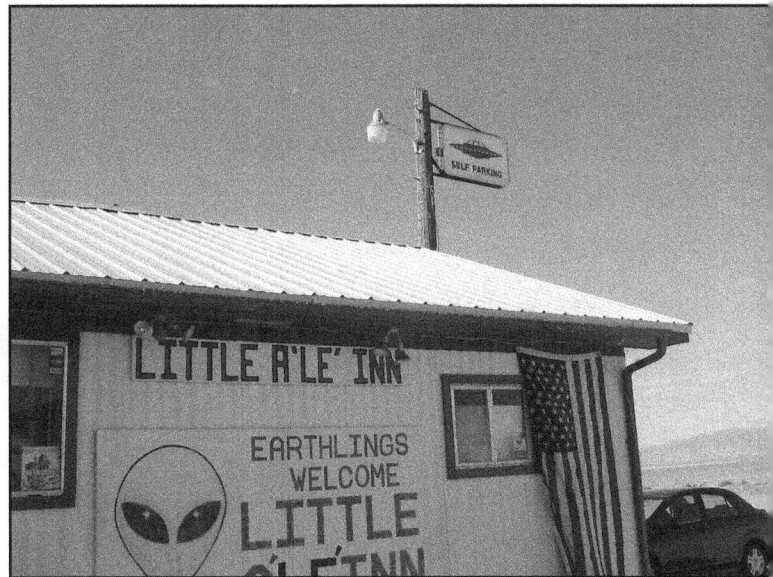

And so, I'll recount these 750-plus arid miles across 'no-man's land' that took place during the second week in October 2011. My camera did a nose dive off a cloud into a volcano, and the LCD view screen went tango-uniform just before the shutter cover also committed ritual suicide. Between the two ailments there, my terrible photographic skills and my desire to ride more than take pics, I'm afraid the chronicle will be sorely lacking in higher quality pics. My bad.

Proceeding on then, when and as I can....

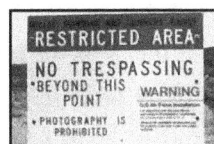

More later, when DAY 1 brings us from Rachel to Tonopah.

Day 1

Rider1 (Dave) on his Husky TE449 out near the Reveille Mill; trail717 (Marshal) running sweep.

Rachel / Tonopah   156 miles

There's not very far to go heading westbound from Rachel before running into the Nellis AFB/Gunnery Range and Area 51 perimeter boundary, so it wouldn't be a long haul out there on dirt road before we hooked a right and headed due north. The three of us got to know each other a little tiny bit over our Alien Breakfast at the Little A'Le'Inn, and we made the usual chit chat before a ride. After a few pictures taken at the start point in front of a captured flying saucer hanging like a trophy on the back of an old tow truck, we set out on the adventure. We used the same dirt road that a small handful of "locals" use to commute to their work inside the Site to Groom Lake, which is also used by a handful of local ranchers to get back and forth from their alfalfa ranch to town and so forth. Just a beautiful sunny day to be riding! And, just like last year, and the year before that, the weather was in a clearing pattern after a week of nasty low pressure had come in and terrorized the mountains and deserts. The paths ahead were likely to be less dusty and more loamy. Me likey!

Our route today would take us along the extreme northeast corner of the A51 perimeter and cross the entire northern perimeter boundary along the Tonopah Test Range. Tonopah Test Range is where a lot of aircraft test flying goes on, in terms of actually testing aircraft in flight as opposed to testing capabilities in mock aerial combat, like what goes on in Red Flag training out of Nellis AFB more to the south inside the Site. There's also considerable high explosive ordnance stockpiled and handled at the TTR, the aircraft operating out of TTR actually consuming lots of combat ordnance. Once around the northern perimeter to Tonopah, we hope to hit a pile of rocks or something out in the desert to the south of a late day fuel/meal stop somewhere, and just crash out in the middle of nowhere along the downbound route. No reason we shouldn't be able to make a 150-mile day out here in the desert; that's only like three hours of heavy petting as far as I'm concerned. Stretch those miles out over a whole day and it's pretty much a day on the couch — with better scenery! Let's light these bikes up and patrol this boundary for God's sake!

We're on some gravelly dirt road to ride on at first, and some fresh air and sunshine to gleam across these shiny bikes as we head out and toward the Belted Range to the west, inside of Nellis/A51. We take a right turn on more dirt road at the extreme western edge of Lincoln County, Nevada — prostitution still illegal here. Over in the hills to the south, in the Groom Range, which we'll come flying underneath the radar (literally) on the last leg home in a few days, prostitution is still illegal, as well. Inaccessible to the public, and no prostitution. Gaming is legal though, just can't play cards on Bald Mountain because it lies inside the Nellis/A51 perimeter. But out there in the Belted Range, it's Nye County — and one of the few areas within Nevada where prostitution is legal. Just not going to find any such operation up there, as it's inside the Site boundary. Just mental meanderings as I lollygag my way across the desert on a dirt road on a Sunday morning. Just junk bumping around inside my Arai XD. Bumpity-bump, throttle blippety-blip.

Some folks have alfalfa under pivots out here, for Nevada and California customers, and we ride by the ranch making that happen. Right about when we get dead even northbound with Sharp Peak to the west, we take a left from this dirt road, and get on some two-track that makes a connection to the pavement on Highway 375 — the "Extraterrestrial Highway." It's a crystal clear day with blue skies on an October Nevada morning... just jet fighters in the skies. (They always seem to be fighting each other or fighting something.... Why can't they just 'get along?') Ha, ha... We make our left and run some nice two-track out to the highway to hit pavement just southeast of Queen City Summit. ("Summits" are mountain passes in Nevada. Pennsylvania, too...) A short few miles through the southern terminus of the Quinn Canyon Mountain Range over this pass puts us on a western shot back out along the Nellis/A51 perimeter, and we leave the pavement after just a very short patch. We won't see asphalt again today.

Riding up to the Cedar Pipeline Ranch gets us to a right diagonal and we take a northwest course on smaller dirt up through the Reveille Valley. We'll be bracketed by the Reveille Range on our right and the Kawich Range to the left for a while, as we make our way through some good-looking country toward a canyon that we'll eventually need to hook a left into. For now, we are content to ride some neat off-road country and get this ride jacked up!

We saw a herd of wild dirtbikes banding together on the side of the road. Each one has peculiar distinctive markings, but they run in packs together out there...

Marshal is mounted up and manufacturing a legend.

Aliens seen walking about, in their uniforms.

We pass by a livestock well and take a helmet-off break, and I water a local rock formation while my two partners get busy with paper maps. There is discussion between them about "where we are" etc. and I overhear the banter and slip a helmet back on over my ears. I'm ready to keep riding and these two guys seem pretty happy. That's a bonus, because we don't know each other and just agreed to get together on the Ride Dual Sport forums, based out of Austin, Texas. An Internet adventure ride meetup. It could be interesting! It could be horrible... it could be deadly, or even fantastic — anything in between. It's a blind date for off-road adventure, and the first one I've been responsible for. (By that I mean that I was the guy posting up the ride, and offering up spaces available to share in the experience.)

Dave and Marshal tending to the herd.

Ruins at old Reveille Mill site.

So far, so good, and these two fellas seem to be very good company. They brought capable machines and have some background, experience, enthusiasm and great attitudes. What more could you ask for? I'm happy, too, and we light the bikes up and blip our way northwest through country with cactus and sage. Welcome back to the desert, Stovey! The course eventually takes us through some fairly obliterated two-track in the shadow of the Kawich Range, and I stop to turn up my steering damper a click, as I feel the need for a little more speed. The track is great and it feels good to be running in the desert once more, and into some really good cross-country style navigating. This old road has been rained on a lot more than driven on, which is to say it doesn't see much traffic. There's little evidence of any road for

Kawich Range in the distance.

Alien in Full Battle Rattle - they were everywhere. I saw lots of things I just couldn't explain...

miles, and you've got to search for it in places. My kind of "road." We make the connection to our left turn on developed dirt road that will take us through the Kawichs and into Bellehelen. Man, that was a nice little run though...

The dirt road into Bellehelen is a perfect, and I mean PERFECT groomer! It's about two compact cars wide and full of twisties, railed with berms on either side, and has hills and rollers. Packed with juniper on both sides and mountains to run a pass through and you can't beat it for some flat-tracking like Dave Aldana.... (I'm old.) There's visibility enough around most of the corners to get a look for oncoming traffic, and so I look and drift the wheels on a perfect Sunday in Nevada! Sweet Sister Sadie this is a fun stretch... can't wait to kiss the trophy girl. (Hope she's not just another antelope with a face like a ripped sneaker.)

Bellehelen is a beautiful hole-up inside the Kawich Range, and the entire area is no exception to the Nevada paradigm – it's mining, mining and more mining. It's also a scenic treasure and we lament our having to only pass on through and not be staying for longer. But, more scabland awaits to the west, and we must make some miles before the sun sets.

Above: The herd waits sheepishly for Rider1 to tell them what to do.

Right: Rock formation in the Kawichs.

Below: trail717 enters Bellehelen.

Looking north from Bellehelen Canyon.

Sons a' bitches were discussing the dreaded 'Plan B' – I just knew it... and it was only the first day!

Bellehelen

The dirty groomed berm-boomer gives way to a left turn heading back down toward the Nellis/A51 boundary again, and farther west toward the Tonopah Test Range. We begin some desert navigation again as we leave the mountain beauty and trade for a ride to the north of these peaks and hills, and track out across desert terrain again, with rollers and twisties on good two-track. On the way down toward Golden Arrow, we pass through a big number of abandoned mineshafts and wild mustangs. . . . Riding WITH the wild mustangs was supernatural. We did exactly that, and ran with the herd as they trampled and galloped and streamlined. They followed their leaders as each dominant male would rear up and leap into action, "Lone Ranger" style, only sans masked fat white Kemosabe. It was really quite something to thunder with the herds as they appeared and disappeared across the floor of Stone Cabin Valley.

Rider1 entering Bellehelen.

Kawich Range

Horses roaming free and wild in Nevada.

Wild mustang north of the Tonopah Test Range.

Stone Cabin Valley to the north of Tonopah Test Range and Area 51.

Rider1 mans his nylon castle.

We netted a side trip straight to the security gate at the Tonopah Test Range, but I foresaw the guards having none of my particular sense of humor, and made a 180 right at the guard station to go back and try and reconnect a purple line on my GPS in the cockpit. Time had taken away the obvious sign of the old obliterated road track, but Marshal put us back on the trail to Tonopah. We scampered here and there like jackrabbits in the sage and cactus for a while and hooked into our final drive on course straight towards Tonopah proper for the end of the glistening desert day, and an evening camp respite. The last bit found us rolling knobby rubbers over top of countless badger holes in good two-track that went on for miles and miles, to finally wind up at a perfect 'hole in the wall' to lay up in for the night, just two miles short of the city limits. We would unload saddlebags here amongst the white ashen rocks of volcanic ejecta, and sit tight and cozy amid the furniture provided inside our moonscape.

trail717 marks out a spot for the night near Tonopah.

Stovey playing 'peek-a-boo' with Rider1 through Cyclops rock.

Above: Rider1 makes camp and stretches his legs after a long day mounted on the Husky.

Right: Cloud-viewing through old one-eye.

Above: Stovey's fortified camp-site amongst the 'rock-scape.'

Left: Hide and seek among the rocks and sage.

When the moon came up shortly thereafter, several gourmet freeze-dried meals had been emptied, and I was enjoying a nice peppermint tea with my new friends, content in my Crazy Creek chair under a perfect desert sky. On the outskirts of Nellis/A51/TTR and only two miles from whatever civilization might have to offer in the morning, I felt very rewarded for having laid this route and met two new friends to ride with. All seemed right with the world according to Stovey, and Big Agnes embraced me once again into her bouncy bosom. Sleep well my friends! Good job today – tomorrow we ride again...

Rally on, Stovey

Day 2

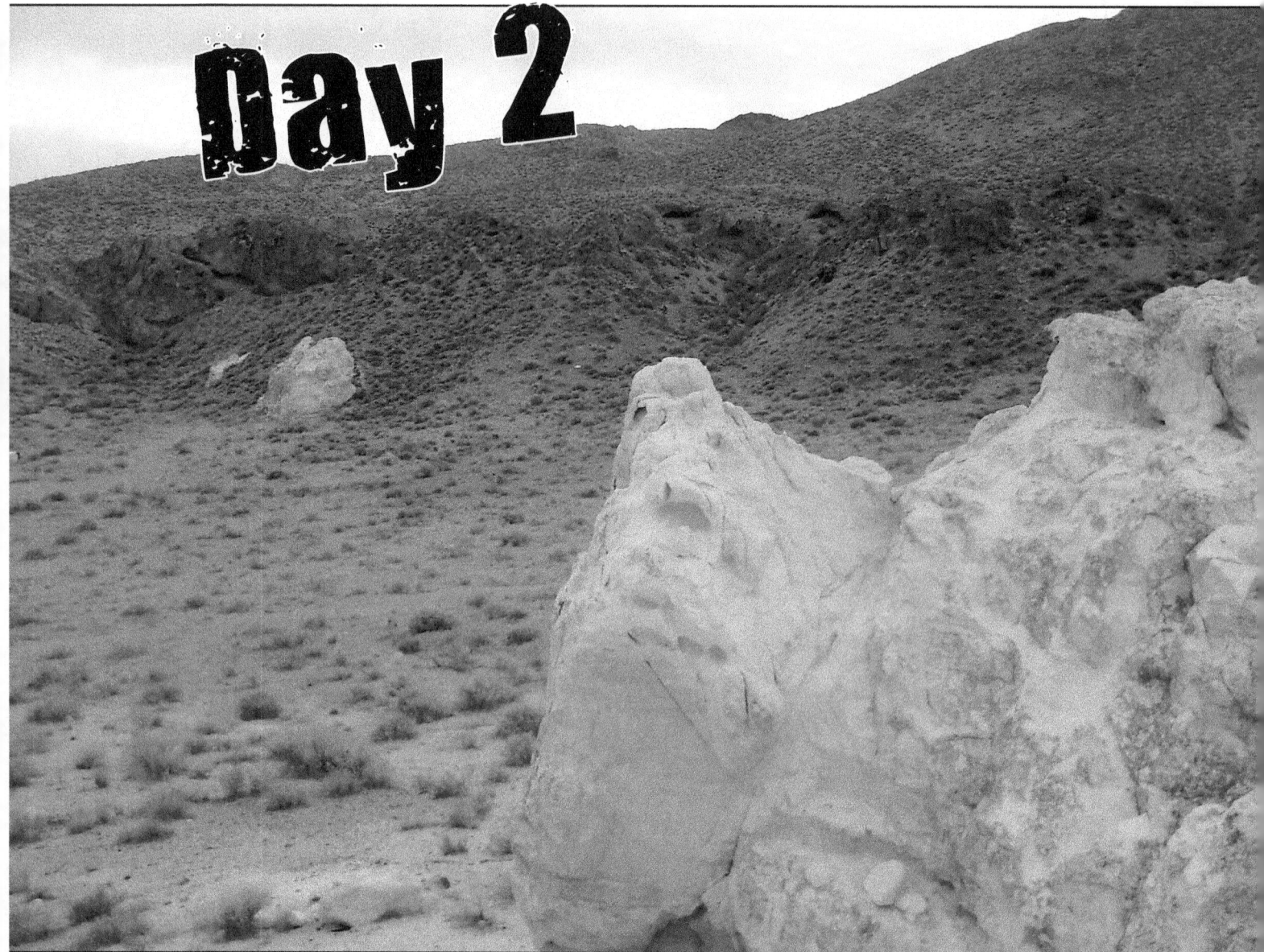

Ghostly echoes from long-dead appliances waft over the floor of this cirque.

Tonopah / Death Valley / 'FYYFF Ridge'   125 miles

Monday morning, and I wake up in a dump....

Well, no, not a landfill – but definitely a wasteland that in the waxing daylight of an emerging sunrise is beginning to reveal itself in unusual splendor. Imagine the merry glow of early morning shadows glancing from the surfaces of a decrepit old Frigidaire or a crumpled microwave laying catawampus in small piles here and there on the ground. Some appliances are disturbingly like small shrines, and occupy a special "throne" of sorts, having been set at just the right angle on just the right mound or anthill – presenting itself exactly the way some dude with a Ruger Mini14

190

Above: A view north from a couple miles east of Tonopah.

Left: "Casper" in Camp Stovey outside of Tonopah.

or a guy with a cowboy hat on his head and a Colt .45 on his hip liked it.

There was broken glass just about everywhere, small bits of shattered bottles hiding in plain sight on high points of dirt or scattered around rock piles where they had been executed.... Only glass ghosts remaining, hidden from view by a sagebrush as soon as you turned your head and changed a viewing angle across the desert floor. No, if I were an appliance on the fritz, or an empty bottle of Budweiser, I wouldn't want to live in Tonopah. We had gathered ourselves up in an adventure rider camp in what was obviously an appliance and glass bottle graveyard – and had pulled up in fading light the evening before to share the land with many deceased kitchen appliances, and laid our heads to rest on the same desert dirt as the bullet-ridden refrigerator doors and shattered ovens and blenders. At least for us, we rise again, whereas the Hotpoint or Kenmore with its doors blown off via 12-gauge... unlike the raven's wingbeats overhead; it would be 'nevermore.'

All of the details coming into focus on the beginning of this Day 2 showed not just the dead fridge that got dragged out here to meet Jesus...

Marshal erected his nylon Man-castle on the desert floor outside of Tonopah, Nevada.

...but also the shades of tan, gray and white coming alive from the sun on different colors of earth.

Rider1 piloting his Husky Te449.

All of the details coming into focus on the beginning of this Day 2 showed not just the dead fridge that got dragged out here to meet Jesus, but also the shades of tan, gray and white coming alive from the sun on different colors of earth, and the sage amid the rocks we spent the night fortified within. It was all in all a very pretty scene, and since the appliances were relatively few and far between, your eye had to scan in every direction and near-to-far to pick up all the junk. Mostly, the eyes are filled with morning desert glow; contrasting colors from the vibrancy of our camping gear and bikes against the sage and tan of the desert hills. It looked like it would be another beautiful day to go ride across Nevada!

We were only a few minutes from town, and we packed up with an easy enough pace. I am the last one ready — my hands are weak from six months recovering from bilateral carpal releases and a level 2 SLAC wrist reconstruction. My dominant wrist (throttle side) is not only relatively weak, but still painful and partially fused from the procedure. It will take a full year to recover fully and realize the most range of motion I'll achieve as a result. For the time being, the dexterity to get camping gear stuffed and poked into saddlebags and all the little things one normally might take for granted — I certainly never gave it much thought. I am slower than I used to be, and slower than my riding companions. Even though I am up early and poking around before anybody else, my hands slow me down getting out of camp, and my friends are patiently waiting for me as I light up Casper the Friendly Punkin to get to town for fuel and breakfast. Thanks guys....

Coffee and something to shove in my pie hole at Mickey D's for us and fuel for the bikes.... Toggle up some southbound route information on the GPS and it's off into the morning sun, the restricted areas of Tonopah Test Range on our left as we go. It's a beautiful sunny morning as we ride solid two-track out of town and head south, but we don't get far before Dave senses some kind of trouble with his bike during a quick trailside stop to water a bush and take in a short view of Mud Lake which lies predominantly inside of the restricted area within the Tonopah Test Range. Mud Lake is a dry lake visible to the east/southeast as we ride out through the hills this morning.

Above: Mud Lake in the distance, lying mostly within the TTR boundaries.

Right: Our path meanders through rising mounds and rocky hills.

Rider1's naked Husqvarna under field repair. *(Marshal Bird photo)*

Dave chased a small leak from a cooling hose clamp a half hour prior to this stop, back at the gas station, and rechecked the area again, finding some oil mixed in with the goo forming on the outside of his cases and hoses. An hour and a half later, with the source of goo having been established as some engine oil overflow coming out of the airbox from a tip-over yesterday afternoon, we're off again and heading through sage, cactus and hills past Ramsey Well toward Goldfield. It was cool blasting down several dry washes on the way, and there was interesting and fun cross-country exploring as we punched our way through a ranch gate and blasted straight down into the hilly meanders on dirt roads through the mines surrounding Goldfield. I sure enjoyed the riding and the great weather and the views of mountains around the western boundaries of the restricted Nevada deserts and mountains. Coolio...

trail717 preparing for relaunch toward a Goldfield lunch stop. The Tonopah Test Range is to our left as we go through these hills along the boundary.

We made Goldfield with no drama, and pulled into town for fuel and a bit of lunch. At the fuel pump I asked Dave how life was going, and he looked dismayed while examining a blank space on the back of his luggage where his camp footwear and Nevada Gazetteer used to be. It was at that point that he looked at me and said, "Ya know, I am thinking that this ride may not be for me just now. . . . I think I'm done."

"What ho," I thought, and accepted his statement and offered my best look of compassion back through the confines of a visage-hiding full-faced Arai. We de-helmeted and Marshal suggested a lunch break at the café inside, at least, and maybe Dave would have another thought or two to share as he was finalizing his decision to call the ride to a halt for himself, and redirect his efforts to something else during his rare week off from normal work duties as an on-demand Challenger 604 pilot. We did just that, and enjoyed some good food at what looked like the only place in Goldfield to get some lunch on the fly. We had wrung Dave out pretty good during the first day out, and he was thinking that maybe he would enjoy a different pace on a ride like this, with less camping setup and teardown demands and the grind of a daily movement regime than he was used to, but that he was liking the riding. He said that he may track us down later on and try to join up with us for the last part of the ride from Rachel to the Lunar Crater and back, if that was something he could swing toward the end of the week as he shifted gears and regathered his schedule. We had enjoyed each others' company

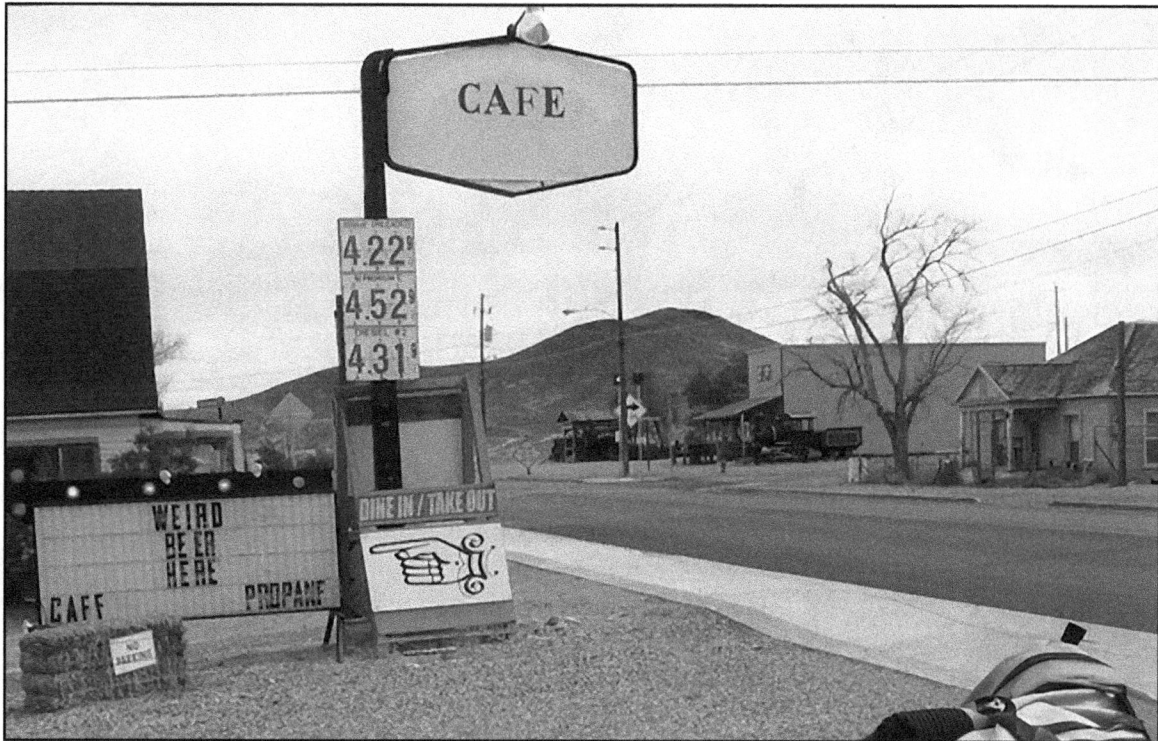

Downtown Goldfield, Nevada. *(Marshal Bird photo)*

in the short time we were out together, but respecting his wishes to sign off, Marshal and I each shook his hand sincerely, and punted ourselves back out onto the dusty trail, southbound toward Gold Point, Death Valley, and Beatty — come what may. "Take care, Dave — catcha on the rewind..."

As I beeped my horn and waved "Farewell" to Dave, I could not help but think that this may all be an implementation of an elaborately concocted 'Marshal/Dave PLAN B' in progress.... And my mind reeled as my gimpy throttle hand twisted. Hmmm... a scene of the three of us somehow standing together in the Nyala Wadi — chainsaws and mayhem abounding — flashed across my radar in front of the Garmin in my cockpit. "Focus... focus..." I find my way out of the imaginary fog in my make-believe dread, outrunning the gut instinct to head for Mexico on the spot. Rallying on, then...

There were great circuitous mine roads to travel as we headed out of Goldfield, and we made some excellent tracks during the building heat on an abandoned railroad grade. It was a good track, and offered some high-speed runs intermingled with the occasional slow down to negotiate a washed-out section here and there, to climb down and then back up to the grade. It was fun following Marshal's dust cloud as he really found some desert legs out on this stretch, and it was here that I discovered my camera LCD viewfinder had exploded. Now, useless and unable to see, track or change any camera settings or details, I resigned myself to shooting pictures even more blindly than I normally do. Good luck to me on that!

We hammered our way off this section of desert through the Chispa Hills west of TTR/Nellis AFB Bombing & Gunnery to Ralston, and Highway 93. It was here that we needed to make a 100-yard run down the asphalt to cross into more BLM through a gate, if we could find it. We did, and we did.

Gate wrangling. (Marshal Bird photo)

We got onto more two-track to bypass Lida Junction and ran a diagonal through the warm winds to the southeast of the Cuprite Hills, toward Gold Point. It was good and easy and a short connection to another short section of asphalt – only about a minute or two down Rt. 266 - then back off the tarmac to the left and into some pretty beat up two-track. We had to get through a few miles of bombed out ruts that were clearly created by 4x4s running through gumbo in the wet weather, so we just augered our way through a few first-gear sections, and stayed on the 'purple line' in the cockpit. More fun and dry washes came along and intermingled with the two-track as we made our way eventually to Gold Point, paralleling the main gravel road, Rt. 774, into this mining town from another age. Gold Point looked pretty cool, and for sure called to mind images of some post-apocalyptic zombie village – "Zombie Apocalypse Headquarters" even. But a really cool place, and the outstanding groomers began right from town, forming another perfect riding course to rail berms on! This was superb dirt road riding, and as an off-road single-tracker, I was fast becoming a believer in the fun factor potential of these groomed Nevada roads! Might just be the place for an old bastard who can't hack the trail anymore to retire to. Get my "Zombie Apocalypse Union Card" and set up shop in an old single wide above a wash in a ghost town, and call it good.

Zombie Attack Vehicle. *(Marshal Bird photo)*

Zombie

Apocalypse

We ran past Mt. Dunfee, the Dunfee Shaft and Alberto and Big Blossom mines on our way through Hell's Gate in the Gold Mountains. The groomed berms and fantastic tight sweepers gave way to views toward more straight and flat as we lost elevation heading toward Bonnie Claire. Bonnie Claire is nothing but a dot on a map and a whisper from the sagebrush on the ground – probably an important dot and whisper at some point back in time. We saw no reason to stop and set up shop there, though, and pressed on into some big straight flats in approach to the extreme northeast corner of Death Valley National Park. There were MILES of endless whoops, straighter than a grizzly's dick and three times that deep to ride through, so in the fading light of late afternoon, we coursed on – keeping the remote KTM PDS shock reservoir's warm to the touch, and the needles pegged on the 'bounce-meters.' And it was great fun as well! The end of a day's riding wasn't far off, though at any given moment, everything in the world seemed pretty damned far, far away. . . . Some radio/microwave towers from a peak between us and Beatty a small growing landmark in the distance straight in front of us, for hours.

There were MILES of endless whoops, straighter than a grizzly's dick and three times that deep to ride through...

Self portrait by Marshal Bird.

A view of Death in the Valley from trail717's cockpit.
(Marshal Bird photo)

No guard shack at this entrance. *(Marshal Bird photo)*

Death Valley ran a boundary right across our tracks, and so we entered into the Park over a cattleguard and continued on over more miles yet of whooped-out two-track that you had to keep focused on. If 4th gear got snicked, it wasn't for long, and there would be a down-snick coming immediately thereafter.... The sun was thinking about dropping out for the rest of the day over the hills near Currie Wells and Gold Bar as we made our exit from the Park near Bullfrog Mountain, and began scanning for a campsite that could house two intrepid desert interlopers. We found a good one on a ridge with some rock outcrops below Busch Peak in the vicinity of Ryholite.

I like my campsites with rocky fortification and natural furniture provided, so when I spied this place it seemed like a no-brainer beacon, and beckoned me to climb up and drop saddlebags. Marshal was game, and in fading light he found a lower gear on his 640A, twisted his throttle, and piloted his bike and portable castle up the ridge and parked it. We were home for the night. Marshal snagged a photo and christened our site "ADV Rider Salute Ridge." I didn't notice it until he posted the pics.... Couldn't have planned that any better – uncanny! Perfection – sometimes you just can't fight it...

"FYYFF Ridge" *(Marshal Bird photo)*

Stovey fights for a landing zone on "FYYFF Ridge."
(Marshal Bird photo)

The Eagles have landed – Casper in the peregrine perch.

Marshal's nest next to "FYYFF Rock."

Moonrise over the falcons' nests…

A beautiful lightscape kept unfolding in all if its desert drama as we proceeded to set up camp on the ridge, ("FYYFF Ridge" in shorthand and to save ink) and the harvest moon appeared in full force. As the sun dropped the full moon rose from behind high bluffs to our east, and it was a picture-perfect evening. My Crazy Creek never felt so good, and the beef stroganoff was going down real good. Logistics didn't grace me with a solid opportunity for a cold man-killer to top off the day with my meal, but I didn't miss it. The day was ultra-fine, the company was excellent and the setting was fantastic. Big Agnes still held my breath for me, and there was little else a right-minded man could possibly ask for (without getting struck by lightning for his greed…) Marshal and I held court around our campstoves for a while, and I investigated the night sky until about 10 p.m. before giving way to the serenity of a Feathered Friend in my slumber. The SPOTcast was "off" and my wife knew I was "in" for the night, if she was watching. I hoped "Rider1 Dave" was all set, wherever he was, and let the stars beat me to death. That took all of about 30 seconds.

Petcocks OFF

Day 3

Stovey leaves the nest. *(Marshal Bird photo)*

Rhyolite / Desert National Wildlufe Refuge   161 miles

I slept like a peregrine in a rock nest all night; high on my cliffy mattress overlooking Death Valley to the west and the Amargosa to the south. Smooth and hot orange mochachinos were flowing once again, and as I pack up this morning after moonset, I reflect that things are going pretty well in life. I am a lucky man to be here.

My hands had been giving me trouble for a couple of years; real trouble for that long, and minor trouble for longer than that. And as I'm stuffing and pushing and packing my things away into Wolfman saddlebags here in Nevada, about six months after the last surgery for what came out to be four separate procedures to my hands and one wrist, I can't help

This whole thing could have gone a whole lot worse... reflections this morning as I recall both hands bound in bandages and unable to handle even the paperwork required in this day and age just to snap a steamer.

but notice both the pain and the progress. It's been so long since I've not had pain in my hands and right wrist, I can't even remember when I didn't. It's been years. It got so bad that after last year's 'Legends of the Fall' ride down here with Keith, that I immediately checked in with a physical therapist to see what he could do. Six weeks and lots of rubbing and ice and ultrasound and all this other feel-good voodoo later, my wrist swelling was down, but not gone. I needed a surgeon. You can't fix broken ligaments and arthritis and tweaked bones with ibuprofen and ice dipping. Huh... who knew?

This morning as I pack up camp I still have pain, but I notice the changes in where it hurts and how bad. Things are changing, growing, healing. Another six months or so of this and I'll have crossed another milestone in life, and will be living with this partial fusion. At least I'm out here riding a dirt bike! This whole thing could have gone a whole lot worse... reflections this morning as I recall both hands bound in bandages and unable to handle even the paperwork required in this day and age just to snap a steamer.... Yes, I am a lucky man at this point, and there is reverence in this mystery to me and I pause to notice while I watch the last stars get chased back into the heavens by an early rising sun. This reminds me a lot of my mountaineering days – haunting glacial or rocky perches in Colorado, Washington or British Colombia.

Marshal is up and visiting me – he's a pensive man and bringing me cheer with his enthusiasm and intelligence. It's a great combination and his background in engineering gives him an analytical viewpoint to things. He asks me a lot of questions and we enjoy talking about riding plans we have with friends and family, and I like hearing about his two sons and the way he talks about them. He talks about his wife too, and I can tell he is a well-grounded man, and he's a strong man. He's been rescued by SAR when a leg injury left him unable to self recover, and he's a successful bicycle endurance racer. He's had to grieve over the loss of one of his sons. He spends long hours at his job and travel duties keep him from his home half the time. His lifestyle demands resolve to keep him on track, and his intelligence adds to his perspective. Marshal is a man of experience, strength and resolution – somebody who can 'get the job done' and will "Never Give Up." He is a 'ruptured buzzard' if ever I saw one! It's a privilege for me to be out here with him, and this is the guy I'm about to cross the Amargosa desert with, as we round another corner on this Area 51 circumnavigation. Pack 'em and rack 'em, let's roll!

Marshal on Secret Pass, in between sheep.

Marshal is the first peregrine to falcon-off this ridge and dive down into the wash towards the track we laid out, and hit the dusty road again this morning. I light Casper and let him warm up for a couple minutes before taxiing out of my rocky hangar onto the apron above the wash — my little helipad on "FYYFF Ridge" below Busch Peak. Like an Apache helicopter pilot, I throttle up and nose her down along this steep bank and into the wash, gliding down through the sage and pucker bushes amid the rocks. This KTM has the suspension to flatten out the nasties, and hitting the wash ruts in the bottom is no thrill, just a course in navigating another washout and embankments to drop into and climb out of. The Apache pilot uses his cyclic and rotor controls to pull his nose up; I use my fused throttle wrist welded in place with a carbon fiber brace… and it's a light front wheel that nudges rocks and hovers over the lip of the uphill bank, and clears the way for a Dunlop D606 rear wheel — I never even feel it. Out of the nest, back from the bushes and back on the trail. Heading for civilization and a fuel stop, then more purple lines on the GPS.

Around the corner right away is the old townsite of Rhyolite, and we zoom past that for a couple more miles into the town of Beatty where a gas station/convenience store will take our money in exchange for food and fuel. We buy a few water jugs too, and refill Camelbaks and bottles, and drink heartily with our breakfast of ratty muffins or breakfast burritos. Another coffee for me as we repack our packs for the trail, and I re-sync my cockpit with fuel-point info on the computer, and I'm good to go. We're off to explore around some more mines in the mountains before hitting open desert again. Somebody's gotta do it!

We follow our route out of town and get on the slab for a minute, then yank on the bars, hard to starboard in good pirate fashion, taking us around a giant pit mine that leads straight to the center of the earth. Marshal leads up "Secret Pass" near Meiklejohn Peak on a piece of two-track, and I find him shored up in the middle of the trail butting heads with a ram on the way. He points out a giant sheep that had crossed his path, and he had to tell it a joke to make it get out of the way. A few short moments later, and he had meandered into a herd of them in a canyon, and we stopped to take a few pictures

of them before throttling off again. It was good riding under bluebird skies, and we commenced to hammering down the mine roads for a while as we navigated around the Diamond Queen Mine towards Steve's Pass. We made Highway 95 again and crossed it to make our connection to Race Track Road, where we would face many miles of sandy whoops!

Above: Marshal coursing through Steve's Pass.

Right: trail717 is a good photographer. *(Marshal Bird photo)*

Amargosa sand dunes. Marked and mapped as "Big Dune," elevation 2,731 ft. ASL.

Race Track Road got its name from something, and I don't know who named it. . . . But I know for damned sure the local boys use the area for lighting up their trophy trucks! I hadn't been on anything like this since riding on portions of the race course of the Baja 1000 and the parts of this "road" that were used by trophy trucks were really whooped out. And sandy. Pretty much sandy whoops, for miles. And miles again.

Marshal on Race Track Road.

Right: What ants make after several million generations of exposure to radiation inside the Nevada Test Site. Quarry to the west of Mercury, Nevada.

Below: Out in some unGodly wash in the Amargosa.
(Marshal Bird photo)

Predator drone barely visible in the center of the image above. Indian Springs Auxilliary AFB west of Las Vegas. *(Marshal Bird photo)*

We continued on it southeast all the way until it dumped us out at the Amargosa Speedway, and picked up another section from there that was partially obliterated from that point onward. We spied snow-capped Mt. Charleston in the distance as we steered through sandy dry washes and turned lefterly at the Ash Meadows National Wildlife Refuge. This turn put us smack into the middle of nowhere, and the route was on completely obliterated road/trail – we were absolutely cross-country. It was supremely fun, but it was pretty hot out in that Amargosa Desert. Early in the afternoon we hit Highway 95 again, and superslabbed it from there into Indian Springs.

The big highway was fine because the bikes were running lean way down low and the temps were high, so it was good to get some air flowing over those radiators and cases. As we wheeled into the Shell station at Indian Springs for food and fuel, we were treated to in-flight displays of Predator drones executing maneuvers over the air base across the street. I stopped Casper after refueling, and noticed some colorful crap ringing his exhaust tailcap, and I thought to myself, "…huh – I must have melted my jacket on that thing bounding along in those miles of whoops!" No matter, the jacket was nowhere to be found, so the fact that it was burned up and melted didn't really make any difference at that point. If anybody reading this finds an Acerbis rally jacket in the sand wash south of Highway 95 between Mercury and Amargosa, it's got my name on it…

We made Corn Creek Road turn-off after lunch via the big highway that leads into Las Vegas, and we jumped on the Mormon Wells option because the Alamo Road is closed. "How closed" Alamo Road is remains a matter of conjecture, but it is officially closed, so we opted for the sure thing through the Desert National Wildlife Refuge on our way back up on the northern leg. Dave had sussed this out for us ahead of time to confirm that the road was indeed closed, and that we should plan on taking the Mormon Wells Road instead. It was a fine choice, and we enjoyed great late afternoon riding on pebbly dirt through the largest NWR in the Lower Forty Eight.

Above and right: Desert National Wildlife Refuge

Yuccas, rocks and Gila monsters lurking in DNWR.

Peek-A-Boo Canyon in DNWR.

We jabbed through "Peek-A-Boo Canyon" on our way up to Mormon Pass, gaining elevation once again as we rode through giant yucca forests and crossed a few washes. It was another great day winding down as we made our way north toward what would be the final leg back to Rachel the next day. At Mormon Pass we made camp at the only

Above: Stovey rolling through Peek-A-Boo Canyon, DNWR.

Right: trail717's mighty KTM 640 Six Days in Desert National Wildlife Refuge.
(Marshal Bird photos)

Mormon Pass, Camp 3. *(Marshal Bird photo)*

camping allowed in a developed campground there at 6,600 feet in some truly beautiful country. We had plenty of daylight left to really stretch our gear out and settle in before nightfall, and prepare to hold court once again – this time around a really nice fire under the ponderosa and juniper.

The evening meal was great and the fire superb. Marshal and I compared notes and sure enough – we had found the secrets of the universe and discovered a cure for cancer and world peace. Alas, the next morning I would be unable to remember these things as usual, and I would be forced to rinse and repeat! Ah, well. feisty peregrines are fast and smart, but they have bad memories. What they lack in mental retention they must make up for in speed and grace. And so it goes – falcons nested under the Nevada skies, cedar embers wafting…

Night court at Mormon Pass. *(Marshal Bird photo)*

Day 4

Peak off in the distant Arrow Canyon Range.

Mormon Pass, DNWR / Rachel 158 miles

"F-16s of the desert floors…"

Morning is here! What a thrill… can't stand waking up dead. Time to pop my Big Agnes and brew some mochachinos – and pack up some Wolfman Rolie Bags, maybe take Marshals temperature and see how life is treating him this morning.

All is well on the other side of the campground, and Marshal is doing well about 15 feet away. No lions or aliens got him. Life is good so far, and we're soon on our way after a nice leisurely breakfast of coffee, GORP and beef jerky for me, God-only-knows what healthy crap for my co-rider. I know it included some Red Bull.

The trail is fine and the weather is gorgeous – another moonset chased down by el Sol, and we're down the road again through some mighty fine scenery in this wildlife refuge. Losing elevation slowly all the way, we pass through this valley in between the Sheep Range to the west, and the Las Vegas Range to the east, into Sawmill Wash, and hook a right. Sawmill Canyon is pretty sweet, with a nice feeling of enclosure as we run down through the rocks and rollers toward the exit of the DNWR and our intersection with Highway 93 – "the Great Basin Highway," and into the wash south of Lower Pahranagat Lake.

As we make our way down from the higher valley in DNWR, and I approach the highway under some power lines, I spy some dude in a bright red shirt standing next to a silver SUV and looking straight at me. Hmmmm…? "Alien public representative" on the loose? Perhaps an errant "Dakar Rally Spectator Impersonator" who can't wait for New Years?

Marshal piloting his mighty 640A through the last of Desert National Wildlife Refuge.

Better go to full flaps in any case, and scrub some speed — the highway is coming up fast anyway... and it wouldn't do to slam a culvert in this ship at speed.

I wave to this fella, and rocket right by him, but I only reach a few feet past where he is standing when a couple dusty synapses fire in my soggy noggin... "...I KNOW that guy! (from somewhere?)" "But where?" Aha! It's Dave — aka "Rider1" the jet pilot! But he's out of uniform and no bike in sight — where's the Husky? Where's his Challenger 604 corporate jet? I mean, if he's here to rejoin the ride, he's missing a bike, and if he's here to take me to lunch, he's missing my airborne corporate coach... "What gives?"

Rider1 and Stovebolt. *(Marshal Bird photo)*

We meet up for a bit, and discuss his desire to rejoin the ride tomorrow, and get in line behind our bikes with his ATV on our way to the Lunar Crater from Rachel. Logistical matters are contemplated for a few moments after Marshal pulls up – they had me bracketed with Marshal coming in behind me on what was left of Sawmill Canyon Road, and Dave blocking my exit to the pavement; in the event that this was an actual "Plan B Activation" by these two guys in cahoots! I ended up turning my back on both of them, and no nets were deployed or alien communiqués transpired where I might have been auctioned off to some green bastards in shiny suits to a Beta Reticuli fart-mining colony, and so all was good! We planned to meet in the evening or on the morrow, right next to the captured spaceship in front of the Little A'Le'Inn, and attack the final legs of the weeklong riderfest together – Marshal on his 640A, me on Casper

A view east from DNWR. *(Marshal Bird photo)*

the Friendly Fighting Falcon, and Dave on his CanAm ATV. Splendid!

There is an old abandoned roadbed that shows on several maps and databases due east of this position, and heads north and parallel to the highway for some miles, and we figured it was worthy of investigation to keep off the slab. Marshal and I said our goodbyes to Dave, and railed off across the pavement towards this potential off-road connection, but found it shut and locked and signed "CLOSED" when we got there. For the second time we were good off-road ambassadors, and elected to be lawful and good sports — abiding by the closure with no attempt at any kind of a bypass. It was back to the highway for a short pavement slammer north. The ride up to our turnoff near Lower Pahranagat Lake came up quick, and we made our way through another wildlife refuge to connect with the Delamar Road, and thence to another connection that will take us through Hell's Half Acre, into Ash Springs.

... no nets were deployed or alien communiques transpired where I might have been auctioned off to some green bastards in shiny suits to a Beta Reticuli fart-mining colony, and so all was good!

Stovey in his undies. Yes, it's a thong… *(Marshal Bird photo)*

Marshal in his undies.

See this sign? We didn't go this route…. We're too dirty.

The berm-railing was great on each of two dirt road sections into Ash Springs, and I enjoyed straightening out a few corners. I admit to exceeding the hull speed of Casper more than once, and there was no comparison to the flight of my bike through these canyons, to the desert tortoise we encountered a few miles back near where we met up with Dave. Getting into Ash Springs at mid day meant we would only have an abbreviated rest stop here for hot spring soaking and barnacle scraping, while at lunch break. The stop did afford a luxurious bathing opportunity though, and I thoroughly enjoyed my time in the city park hot springs, and my lunch.

Cell phone signal is strong here, and both of us managed quick calls out to our home bases as we got dressed and reassembled after food and fuel. This next leg was, to my mind, what this ride was all about, and I was bumming that we had burned up so much time at our stops and investigating the old abandoned roadway option – I wanted the maximum amount of time for this leg from Ash Springs to Rachel – it's the juiciest section on this leg, and on the entire circumnavigation. Big desert, special navigation skills, boundary issues, waning daylight, security concerns and the exploration of the unknown in the Tikaboo Valley next to the most publicly known and notorious of the Area 51 access areas all wait ahead. I wanted to get it going, so as not to lose any more daylight.

We elected to hit a dirt road just north of Ash Springs that runs parallel to Highway 93 – "The Extraterrestrial Highway" – and we should intersect our route again on the pavement just underneath Hancock Summit. We manage a ranch gate with signage of stern warning for people NOT to disturb any animal control trap equipment encountered out on the landscape we are about to enter into. Under pain of torture, death or Beta Reticuli deportation, or at least a big fine or something, we mentally note to abide by yet another rule, and sally forth. The two-track diminishes rapidly, but maintains some semblance of its formerly navigable self as a two-track, for miles toward the mountains that form the southwest side of Hancock Summit.

As we gain ground and elevation toward this juncture, and at the pinnacle of this jaunt through BLM land tracking along the top of a ravenous ravine, we run out of two-track. For good. It's an ancient memory or never existed. On the maps it shows the connection here never actually physically existed, but since "Stovey knows better" I presumed a solution prior to launching this mini-expedition, in the form of connecting a couple of dots that are only about a centimeter apart, on the map. A good reconnoiter from the top of this ravine yields some info, that the drop into the ravine will connect

Wreckage cleared, Marshal gone and already underway behind me. This was the slope he vaulted down...

us to where we might oughta be, and it will be a cross-country drop through some sage, rocks and a little washed-out terrain. Casper is panting, he wants to tear off a hunk of this. Marshal is game, and even though his 640A is a virtual aircraft carrier by comparison, he's up for it, and glides off behind me, into the wash.

I make the drop, and come up short of the little hillclimb on the other side, and extinguish the flames underneath the Six Days spark plug, turn my head to spy my co-rider's progress. He's skiing down the slope with his engine off, and makes good until the front wheel of his KTM gets in an argument with a sagebrush. It's a low-side entry and a high-side exit for him, and I clearly heard the message, "EJECT-EJECT-EJECT" come over the intercom as he performed an "adverse yaw" in the middle of his "Low Yo-Yo" maneuver. He was a goner...

Ass over teakettle he went, and it was as elegant a highside as I've ever witnessed! A spectacular bit of air was gained, and Marshal would have stunned the floormat judges at the gymnastic Olympics with his fine height, speed, style and recovery! Add to that his stunning rebound, coming up without so much of a scratch – no bone showing and the bonus of that freshly bathed and now-entombed scent of desert sage to boot! What a guy....

224

...and the view from the bottom of the ravine toward our connection to the slab under Hancock Summit.

We got his bike righted together, and he finished poaching that ravine slope, thumbing noses at the impasse as we left it in our rear-views. Daylight was waning – no time to tarry. The pavement connection was right at hand after climbing out of this wash, and we popped over Hancock Summit to rejoin our original routing, and the connection below in Tikaboo Valley. We spy the long 13.8-mile dirt road off in the distance – the 13.8 miles of publicly allowed access, toward the gate entrance to Area 51 – Groom Lake. Dust clouds waft for miles from a vehicle making its way east from the Site, coming toward the highway as we approach our turnoff and we can see the entire valley and our route into it and out as we crest Hancock and down in. We are about to commence our run in to the boundary, and "touch the holy wire" as it were, and amscray the hell back outta there before the Cammo Dudes decide to make sport of us, and take us prisoners. The ride down and in is filled with fun, dust, anticipation and sun in our visors...

Does this image need a caption? Seriously?

The last bit of roadway has signage to slow us down; first from 45 mph to 35 mph – then to 25, then again to 15. Bingo! We're around the last corner and facing the infamous "Go No Further Or You Die" (at taxpayers' expense and completely-legal-to-kill-you fashion.) Sure enough, as we stop the bikes and take in the boundary area at this juncture before turning around to grab some primeval Tikaboo Valley floor on the last leg to home base, there is the tan Jeep Cherokee on the hillside not 250 yards from us, and he flashes his headlights at us as a warning. It's a gesture I appreciate, and I take the opportunity to engage the occupants in a short but civil one-way conversation. (Marshal is looking at me like a blackbird just flew out of my nostril. . . .) But I say in a normal tone of voice that we are big fans of "Delta and the SEAL Teams" and we're on our way back the way we came. "We're heading across the Tikaboo Valley floor on BLM roads, northbound through the Medlin Ranch, and over the pass near Andies Mine back to Rachel where our trucks are parked. We're not intending to cross any base boundaries. Keep up the good work!"

I told Marshal I was convinced that "they" can hear every word we are saying, and it won't hurt our cause any to just backfill a little info to the powers that be, in anticipation of our cross-country jaunt across the valley. Personally, I was hoping to negate the need to perform my ground-based "JINKOUT Maneuvers" en route north, and this was my last ditch effort to give me some leeway. I have not chaff, flares or any other countermeasures to try and defeat these Cammo Dudes if they decide to light me up – and I'm thinking I'll probably come up way short in the defense department if I have to try and outrun or out maneuver a Blackhawk or an Apache helicopter.

Whitesides to Freedom Ridge - now closed to the public. (Taken from Groom Lake Road.) The privately owned and still operated Groom Mine lies behind these hills on the right, but lie inside the Nellis/A51 boundary, and restricted access to mine owners is granted on a case-by-case basis. Cammo Dudes lurk in this area, and are not to be trifled with...

Above: Tikaboo Valley

Left: Views of the Pahranagat Range from the west, looking southeast from inside Tikaboo Valley.

A little farther down this road, and you better get your paycheck from the CIA, USAF Edwards Flight Test Center, or someplace else that probably pays in bags of cash....

"Tally Ho..."

We make the turn just short of the scary signs proclaiming "Deadly Force Authorized" (for trespass or photography) and get these "wild weasels" headed back away from the sun, and on course for our final blast across a desert floor towards home base. It's been a fantastic ride so far – and I'm feeling like a million bucks even if my wrist has swollen inside this carbon fiber support brace. "Fight's ON!" and we're gone like a bad check, heading back out Groom Lake Road. There are several turn opportunities to take us into and across the Medlin Ranch where we will navigate several obliterated road tracks and washes northbound, and I pick one. I'm navigating on the fly now, no purple line to course as my routing was in error when I set this part of the leg up. But, I had studied hard in my preflight to this ride, and had lots of data memorized and stuffed into my noggin – I was hitting it hard and loving every minute!

The hills on the left are danger-close to the Site boundary, and we ride north on the flats to the right, skirting the perimeter and paralleling these hills in the Groom Range.

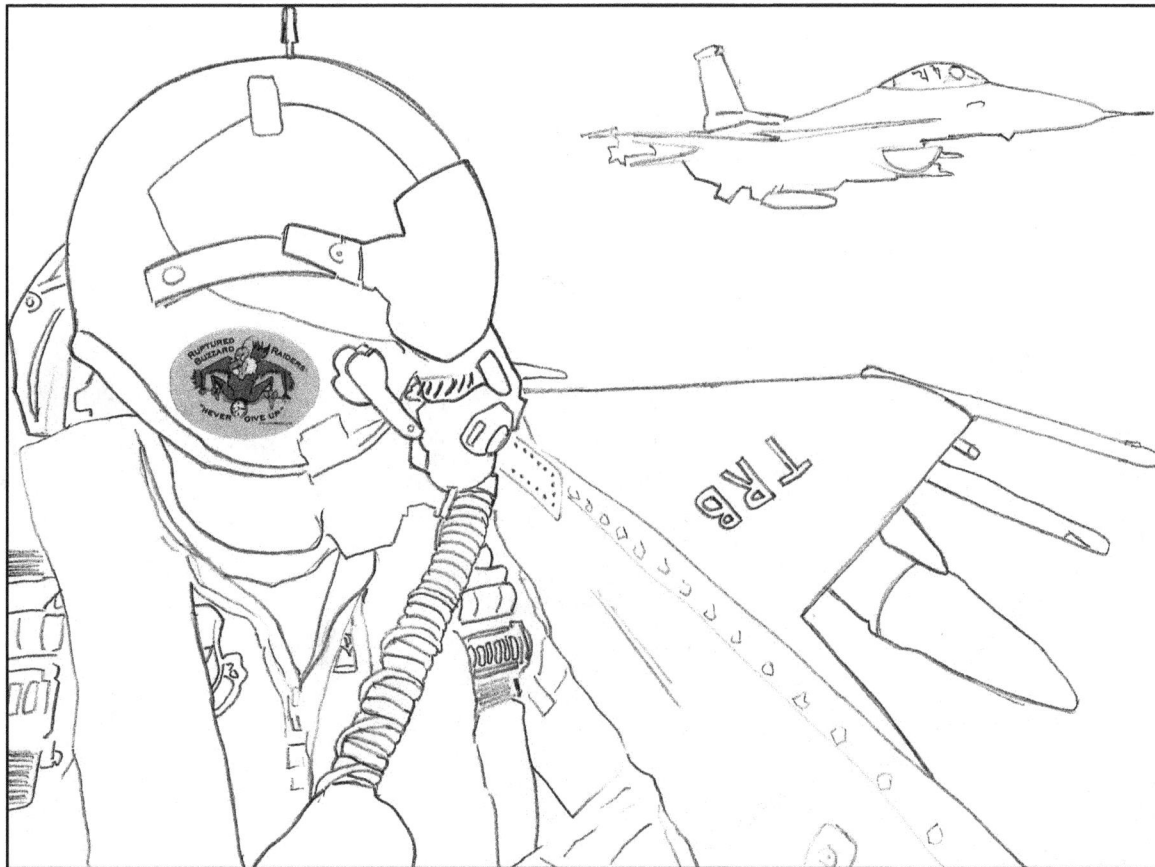

"trail717 - this is Werewolf2, how copy? <OVER>"

The zig-zags through and out of the Medlin Ranch bordered on notorious and approached the glorious as Casper negotiated each turn – pulling Gs and leaving a slipstream for my partner to chatter through – and this is the stuff I live for.... The GPS is glaring at me; the two-track has diminished to nonexistent and we're tracking through obliterated desert to the point where there is zero visible track or trail left. Zero. There were miles of track we laid out there that if you stopped your bike, you lost the route on the ground. Nothing but the brown trail whispering up from the glow of a GPS nav screen on my KTM heads-up-display. The terrain itself had to be "in motion" to give any appearance whatsoever of passage through what once was a two-track roadbed or wagon trail gone extinct. Like the movement of a deck of cartoon cards where each symbol or image is static until the deck gets "shuffled" and each static image becomes part of a simulated movement, or a movie, or a cartoon effect. We blazed mightily across this navigational abyss toward the north end of Tikaboo Valley, and the mountain passes in between the Nellis Air Force Base/A51 boundary and the Extraterrestrial Highway.

Under the watchful eyes of electronic perimeter surveillance out in the sagebrush and the optical power stationed above us on Bald Mountain inside the Site, we throttled on for mile after cactus-laced mile, dodging spiny landmines and foot-deep washouts in our paths. A quick check over my shoulder now and again was all I could afford to see if my wingman was still with me back there somewhere, or if he'd gotten splashed by one of the many terrain hazards we were blazing through as the sun began to give its last to this earth for the day. Damnation if this wasn't the coolest high-speed run I've ever made! This hour could go on for days, and I'd call it Heaven – if only it could last for a little while longer!

Long shadows forming up in the wake of our Tikaboo slipstreams.

But, it is the witching hour – and the bush gremlins are just waking up – ready to come out and do their best to take a wheel out from under me, and give me a push down into the dirt. "Controlled Flight Into Terrain" or a C-FIT might be the best I could hope for if a get-off was imminent... at best a crash-landing might yield a survival if a screw-up commenced at the speeds I was carrying. Admittedly, I was going fast, but I simply could not pry either my hand from the throttle stop, or the grin from my face. "Crash my ass! Crashing is for pussies!" I rallied on. And on. Through the sunset toward Andies Mine south of Rachel.

We crossed the mountains at the northern Groom Range spur into the Sand Spring Valley, and negotiated a cool technical wash to a gate. Last gate out – homefree to the Little A'Le'Inn.

Bald Peak right of center – high tech communications array on summit operated by 'you-know-who' for the purposes of 'you-know-what' and if that ain't good enough... you don't need to know. We exited Tikaboo from the passage in the foreground, through this gate.

My Wingman as we exited Tikaboo Valley, and coursed through the mountains near Andies Mine and back into Sand Spring Valley - F-111s hot on our tails...

Mountains in the background lie inside the A51 boundary. F-111s flew low over our heads from the direction of these peaks, "herding" us north. We were legal, of course – otherwise the Raven drivers would have fried us, for real. They were just burning some Jet-A on the company dime.

As the sun was setting behind the Belted Range in the west, the range we had ridden toward four days ago, we gathered ourselves back together in formation – two riders exiting the BLM bushes in echelon formation, 24 feet apart from fender to fender, like the Fighting Falcons we had become. And though I take poetic license in the telling of my tales, I shit you not – there, as we roared back into the town of Rachel, Nevada, two USAF F-111s were executing maneuvers low over the valley floors. To the east, I saw one Aardvark/Raven hauling the mail southbound across the Sand Spring

From the last gate of the Tikaboo raid, looking northeast into the Sand Spring Valley. Rachel visible just over the number plate windscreen of the bike, center right in the image.

Stovey gives Marshal a final 'thumbs-up' as he roars by after closing the last gate behind him, inbound to Rachel for debriefing. Away from a setting sun, flat out at nearly XX mph, one of two mere specks on USAF heads-up-displays. *(Marshal Bird photo)*

Valley floor, along the base of the Worthington Range. He pulled up and crossed a pass in the Tempiute Range and disappeared, while simultaneously another Aardvark with its wings sweeping back, executed a hard right turn heading toward this same pass. This second F-111 was heading right towards us before his turn, right out of the Tikaboo Valley and over the mountains we just came from and crossed.... It was a seismic rush to welcome us back to town at the end of the ride! I could just imagine the words over the pilot's comm set, as he "chased us" out of "his valley" along the perimeter boundary of Nellis/A51.... "KNOCK-IT-OFF   KNOCK-IT-OFF" as he "disengaged" from us two lowly dirtbikers encroaching no further under his wings. He disappeared over the Tempiute Range to the east like a bat out of hell... and I thought I saw his wings wag. Just a little....

Day 5 follows, as I lament the passing of this incredible day of riding...

For now, it's back to base, and debriefing by the spaceship hanging from the back of an old tow truck, under the stars.

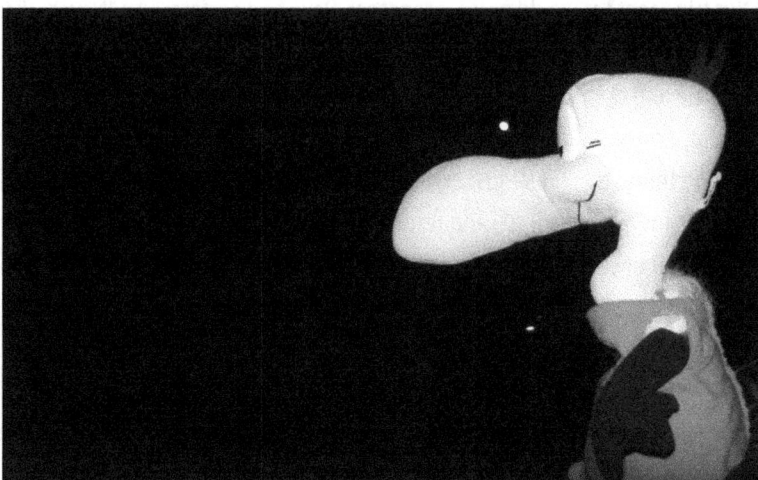

Beaky the Buzzard tracks a moonrise over the Tempiute hills, back at Camp Zero.

Day 5

Tempiute. *(Marshal Bird photo)*

Rachel / Lunar Crater / Cherry Creek Pass   120 miles

Rider1 had shown up with his high-zoot Can Am four-wheeler last night, and we were a gang of three once again. The original 'three amigos' who had started this trip together would finish it together. Dave had performed a "New York Re-load" as I call it, after the term coined by famed NYPD Stakeout Squad leader Jim Cirillo, who referred to dropping a dead handgun in the middle of a running gun battle and drawing another from a separate holster, in favor of spending any precious time or effort even reloading the empty one — a field expedient for staying alive when time was paramount. Since our trip would eventually end as all good things do, Rider1 just exchanged tools and kept on going after regrouping with us, and gave his Husky to a mechanic for a valve adjust, and returned to Rachel with his ATV. His tenacity in this regard earned him my utmost respect for diligence and creativity, and I must admit to having learned a few things from him during this ride. The man simply wanted to do the ride, even if it took a separate machine and rolling with the punches in real time. And he did it with style. Salute to you, Good Sir!

Thursday morning found us at a round table inside the Little A'Le'Inn for breakfast to fuel our bodies for a ride across desert floors to clear a couple of valleys and mountain passes today, so I took full advantage to pack some carbs into

Water Canyon

my cake hole. It was good and I was ready to look at my bike real quick, and take care of some maintenance. A quick oil change for Casper the Friendly "F16 Punkin" made him happy, and I managed some Dr. Bronner's peppermint soap on my head under a water jug off the tailgate of The Mighty Dodge before encapsulating my cranium with a familiar well-made Arai XD. Not that this was a particularly valuable cranium for all of my species, but it's the only one I have to protect. So, black Kevlar and a faceshield gets 'what I got' insured for all its worth, and I'm ready to go. Another combination of solar rays blasts through the desert skies, and bluebirds would be flying around if they were native to the area. For now, it was buzzards and fighter jets… and maybe something else?

We take off eastbound on two-track from Rachel, into the desert across Sand Spring Valley toward the town site of Tempiute, an old mining outcrop that has seen better days but still has a house and marks a place on a map. From there we turn northerly to make some zigzags as we satisfy our navigational requirements to get to the Quinn Canyon Range that helps ring the Railroad Valley to the north. We make Smith Well and stop for a viewpoint opportunity and to get on some lesser single-track after a Sand Spring Valley crossing that included more riding across open country on diminished to mainly obliterated two-track. The dirt road climbing into the Quinn Canyon Range was a hoot! Lots more corners to try and straighten out and berms to rail, and the flat desert floor gave way to more circuitous mountain pass eye candies.

Marshal providing documentation services in a canyon en route through the Quinn Canyon Range to Railroad Valley.

Casper waiting patiently for a relight, one of our only water crossings having just been made, in the background.

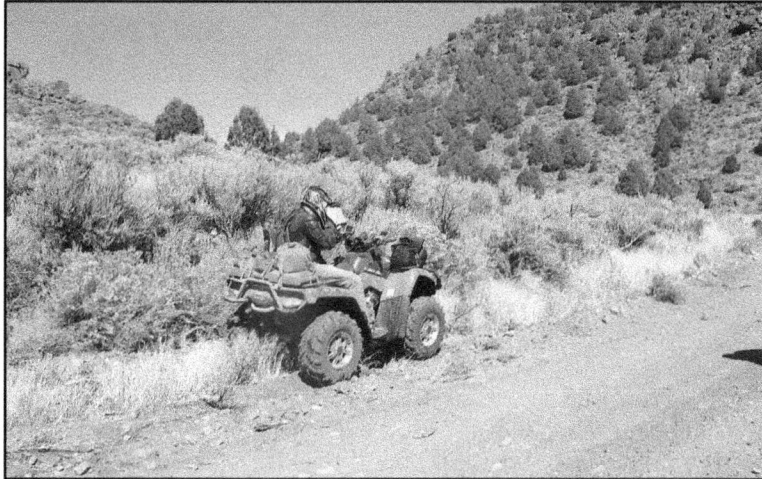

Left: Rider1 going over some navigational instrumentation in preparation for our touchdowns into the Lunar Crater this afternoon.

Below: Southern terminus of the Railroad Valley.

Making great time and enjoying the fresh air and Nevada views we cruised through the pass and went by some more rock ruins from an old-time settlement before dropping into the vast Railroad Valley – a place of desolation and eternal "begotten-ment." Our route takes us across this southern end of the Railroad Valley and rises to the toes of the Pancake Range that serve to ring the Lunar Crater Dry Lake – a place we'd like to ride into, and out of under our own power I might add, just to see if we can. After all, it's a Thursday, so what better thing to try and do, right?

"You're taking us to _where_?" _(Marshal Bird photo)_

The Lunar Crater is designated a National Natural Landmark by the Department of the Interior, but the land is under BLM stewardship. Astronauts used to train here for Apollo missions, and you can see why — if you use your imagination and convince yourself you are on the surface of the moon. Eating some ancient 'space food sticks' that were available in the 1960s before there were Clif Bars and PowerBars, and maybe huffing a line of Tang off your saddlebag might help. I wonder what worked for Neil Armstrong? We performed a continual rock-dodging 'jinkout' en route to the top of the southern Pancakes along some great two-track, and entered the Lunar Lake landscape like three riders on a mission to the moon!

Looking northwest from the bottom of Water Canyon toward what will be our eventual exit from the Lunar Crater, through The Wall.

Above: Entering the Lunar Lake landscape from the south.

Left: Dust clouds from Rider1 and trail717.

Looking west across the dry Lunar Lake, Easy Chair Crater in the background.

trail717 and Rider1 slamming the southern Pancakes.

Left: Rider1 carving desert along the Lunar Lake en route to The Wall.

Below: Stovebolt on the far side of the moon.
(Marshal Bird photo)

Volcanic cinder cones and ashen hills dot the landscape as we skirt the actual Lunar lake bed and ride in between the lake and the craggy mounts of the Pancakes that form the geological "Wall" boundary to the east, and ride some great starkness along our paths. I ride by a parched cattle carcass lying amidst the sage, and perhaps a desiccated wild burro boneyard or two as I journey northward to a hard right turn that will take us 'over the edge' and out of this moonscape and into another. I let the actual Lunar Crater escape me, and we didn't make our way across the other side of the lake and back to jump to its precipice, or visit the Easy Chair Crater again on this ride — but I think we should have. It's my fault for not taking that initiative to make the short detour to take in this viewpoint. I must apologize to my co-riders for this oversight. With any luck, they will both go back there at some time, making a point of visiting the crater rim to look at this hole in the ground on yet another Lunar adventure. Stovey is nothing if not an imperfect riding companion. . . . My bad.

Cinder cone marking the southern end of the Pancake Range.

The Can Am is hauling the mail with Dave at the helm, and he's making big dust trails with Marshal on the approach to The Wall. If the drop through The Wall is too marbly with a sidehill component for a safe squirt through on the ATV, we're going to get out the 'Moab Straps' and tag team this red four-wheeler down the other side, and back into the Railroad Valley. We'll leave no man behind, whatever it takes.

Rider1 checking for scorpions or something.

Above: "Tranquility Base; this is trail717 – come in please. <OVER>"

Left: Lunar probers... "probing."

Left: How many times has this sign even been *read*? Right: Gap in "The Wall."

Shooting through the gap in "The Wall."

Left: A "gap-scape."

Below: trail717 goes through a gate in the gap at The Wall. A view east above the Railroad Valley.

"Casper" listens in as Marshal and Dave discuss strategy for dropping The Wall.

With that idea in mind, we crest the rise from the Lunar Lake to the passage through The Wall, and take in a reconnoiter of the droppage – and decide it's a non-issue for Dave and his ATV. I had remembered from last year that this section was a little marbly, and had compared the scenic experience with a Moab-esque type of landscape, but it posed nowhere near the technical challenges to be found on some of Moab's tougher trails like Behind the Rocks or Pritchett Canyon. Ah, better to have a solid rider and terrain that is no match for his skills, than the other way around. Dave throttles over the edge on

trail717 studying more moonscapes in anticipation of a touchdown at Stonehenge.

Left: View across the Railroad Valley from the notch in The Wall, looking east toward the Grant Range (left and north) and Quinn Canyon Range. Our passage through those mountains will lie in the middle of the image, up Bordoli Creek to Cherry Creek Summit.

Right: A view toward Water Canyon from The Wall.

his Can Am with a yawn, stopping wherever he damn well feels like a photo op, and tears it up! No ride compromises are made with the intermixing of four-wheeler and motorcycle, and we drop down the slickrock passage from Lunar Lake heading east and back into the Railroad Valley a little to the north of where we had just ridden through a few hours before. The view from The Wall eastward toward the Quinn Canyon and Grant Ranges that form the east edge of the Railroad Valley are stunning, and we can spy our far-off pathway through these ranges in the distance as we crest and drop. The Railroad Valley continues to offer an other-worldly desert experience in its vastness running north-south, with no signs of civilization save for a pinprick of green under pivot barely visible to the naked eye across the valley in the Nyala Wadi.

Rider1 contemplating something as he drinks in a large Railroad Valley view from The Wall.

Left: trail717 at The Wall. Right: De-biking at The Wall for photos.

Rider1 commencing the drop.

Stovey makes a sweep of The Wall. *(Marshal Bird photo)*

Marshal finishing his Wall.

Right: The "Pillars of Hercules."

Below: "Leaving The Wall Be-hind"... sounds like a Johnny Cash ballad. (*Marshal Bird photo*)

Above: Marshal looks back at The Wall.

Left: The view that Marshal sees when he stops and looks back at The Wall from the east.
(Marshal Bird photo)

Right: Rider1 storming desert floors on his red Can Am ATV.

Below: Rider1 on his final approach into Stonehenge.

But before we cross this valley once again, we will encounter the "stone henge" that Keith and I had passed by on last year's ride, and this time we are going to stop and explore! Ancient druid ritual slaughterhouse? Alien abduction holding pen for humans under the influence of Martian cough syrup? First Nations sheep corral? An old hardware store whose owners hadn't internalized "LOCATION — LOCATION — LOCATION!?" We will soon stop and drop a kickstand, and try and figure this out. . .

Left: trail717 follows behind Rider1's slipstream.

Below: Marshal doing a little trials riding as he rolls into Stonehenge. No toe-touch. No bike drop. No lie. Impressive...

"Casper the Friendly Punkin" waits outside the henge. No way he's going in there... that's for caged animals, not for thoroughbred raiders!

I am the last man down from The Wall, with Marshal and Dave trailblazing ahead; dustclouds in the wakes of the Mighty KTM 640 and cherry red Can Am. It's only a few minutes from here to the site of this stone circle that we plan to stop at and visit, and perhaps call it a day and spend the night. The thought of a night under the stars at this site was definitely on my mind, and we had been thinking it would be a great campsite, especially if it was as inviting as we thought it could be, and of course, alien-free. Around a few rocky buttes and long desert corners later, and soon the rock structure comes into view at the base of a butte – the "Stonehenge" at last from radar scope to 'right here, right now!'

We pull into this dual sport traveler stop and jump down to have a walk-around, just to see what we can see... the place is really cool! Dave and Marshal speculate that it is in fact a relict livestock corral of some sort, and it's impossible to disagree. The stones are piled three-and-a-half to four feet high, and form a perfect circle with a single opening. There being a small scrap of wire fencing piled near the opening, as might be handy for a rancher to use for a gate to control access in and out of the circle, it seems a no-brainer that we are standing in the middle of an abandoned sheep corral out here, with some kind of useful stone structure attached that might serve an old rancher well – for what I have no idea. But I've never been a rancher and couldn't even play one on TV if they held a gun to my head, so I simply marvel at the entire thing. What an engineering and manpower accomplishment to have built this henge up from the desert floor, and you can see where all the construction material came from; the rocks apparently tumbled down from the hillsides of the adjacent butte. Need a rock? Go up the hill and tip one over. Need another? Keep tipping them over and heaving them into place as each building block trundles down, one after the other, thousands of times. I bet the builders wouldn't have turned down a cold beer or two during this project. Under those conditions though, it's hard to say whether this henge would have turned out this well and perfect, or if the cold tallboys would have contributed to the erection of a giant ancient white elephant, suitable for abandonment as a corral, and more like Modern Art... so much rubble to the eye of the beholder!

Left: Rider1 inspects the henge perimeter. Right: Source of stone henge building materials.

This stone circle is visible on Google Earth. I left a message inside of it for my wife, but it's in code.

Marshal recalculating the pi R squared situation, to verify circularity.

Opening to the inside of 'Druid Circle?'

What a captured sheep might see.

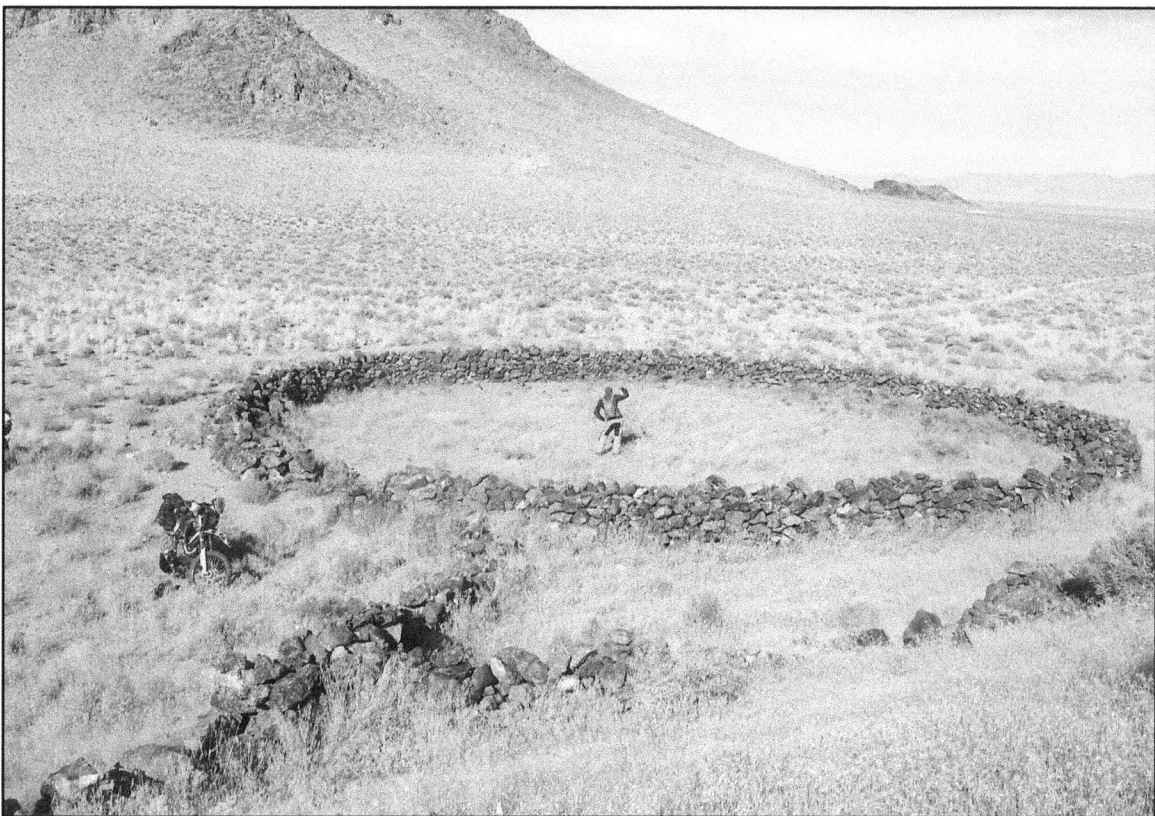

trail717 communing with the desert spirits.

Right: A message for my wife.

Below: Saddling back up at Stonehenge... way too hot to spend more time here waiting for the sun to set and aliens to show up with cold beer.

Recrossing the Railroad Valley, heading southeast toward Nyala in late afternoon. *(Marshal Bird photo)*

It's a cool place, and 3 p.m. — and hot as the hubs of hell. We all nod in agreement that with no breeze, sitting it out here to wait for sundown to do an alien dance at our newly discovered secret ritual site would be an exercise of varsity foolhardy proportions, so we think it best to keep rolling, and make our beds in a cooler setting, way off across this valley floor and into the mountain pass en route back to Rachel. Making miles before sundown is what we opt for, and we roll out of Stonehenge with nothing but photos and mystic memories as we had paused to try and listen to stories whispered from ghosts long passed. It's off to Cherry Creek Pass, via Nyala. Great builders of stony monuments, "Adieu!"

A view from the middle of the Railroad Valley floor looking northward.

Quinn Canyon Range from the west. *(Marshal Bird photo)*

"The Marshal's" quarters. *(Marshal Bird photo)*

Before long we were into and out of Nyala – a place I still envision as a spawning ground for a chainsaw-wielding, mask-wearing clan of cannibals.

Last year Keith and I crossed this way and jumped across the ranch into Nyala via a crisscross of two-track that was definitely a more direct approach toward the Cherry Creek Pass, but we butted heads with a couple of gates and ended up too close to a residence on private property than we would have liked. This year, I routed us around the ranch with less concern over time and fuel than we had before, and with a focus more on comfort with regard to the route we were treading. Before long we were into and out of Nyala – a place I still envision as a spawning ground for a chainsaw-wielding, mask-wearing clan of cannibals. 'Home Sweet Home' for somebody, just not for me, and we're soon leaving dust trails alongside this wash and the community of Nyala is once again a memory – neither Marshal nor Dave met me there in advance, to execute "Plan B." My good fortune not taken for granted, I rallied on to the northern connection that would be a right turn up toward Cherry Creek Pass, near the Bordoli Ranch.

This road up Bordoli Creek Canyon is as sweet to ride on as last year, and twisties are offered to us in abundance! Berms are at every corner, the scenery is awe-inspiring and the shadows from the mountains now beginning to envelop us in this elevation-gaining approach sure shut down the rays from the nuclear reactor some 93 million miles away, and we're soon feeling more chilly than the heat from a mere few minutes before! Add a little adventure-riding velocity to this section and it's beginning to feel downright cold! Nevada riding – simply surreal. The Bordoli Creek approach from the west gives up another "summit" and this mountain pass is yet another candidate for 'scenic spot of the ride.' Cherry Creek pass is drop-dead gorgeous, and we know that our camp will lie only a few miles distant, down in the trees and valleys of this complex geological jumble of holes and drainages on the east side of the Grant and Quinn Canyon Ranges. I even coast a while with the engine off, just like last year, in order to take it all in with the benefit of a quieter drop into the ethereal embrace of these verdant pinions – a stark contrast to the post-apocalyptic zombie zones of the valley floors.

A right turn a few miles down from the pass and we're yards from an official USFS primitive campground, a beautiful setting just on the outskirts of the Quinn Canyon Wilderness boundary. It's time to cool Casper's powerplant for the day, and find a cushion of pine needles to lie on top of for the night. What's this? Aahhh, a great place to be. Let's stop right here, alongside the hushed babble of Little Cherry Creek, and call it a day!

The area is stunning, so we have no trouble finding three good footprints for tents – one for each lunar explorer, and set up camp. There's a fire ring and wood is abundant. The hot meal will be forthcoming and we are in a great hole in the mountains, sheltered from any big winds should they come, and the heat is gone. We'll be bundling up in warm fuzzy after-ride duds and sitting by a campfire, ready for a last-night-out gather-up, Rider1 handing out chocolate bars in preparation for counsel! Damn – that Can Am was also hauling treasure, pretty hard to beat; thanks, Dave!

A tremendous warm glow is pushing welcome heat out in all directions from around our firepit as we consume our gourmet meals once again, and the light babbling of the stream alongside is tough to beat as accompaniment to a literally "Stellar" night out. Dave and I spy the biggest shooting star I've ever seen in my life, and we're left with our jaws dropping trying to describe it to Marshal who may have only caught a glimpse of the last part of this giant, brilliant streak of something burning up in our atmosphere.

Desert tracks across open country with long views and daydreams of running the Dakar intermingle with visions of ancient lava beds and cinder cones as I drift off a few feet from the ebbing coals. Last night out on this Legend. . . I will miss this journey. Fuel for my dreams, and fodder for the next imaginings when Mapsource and Google Earth collide in my mind. Where will my next ride take me? What will I see and what will I learn? Embers to drift away by, and I do just that, all night long by a creek.

Above: The last night's courtroom... beautiful! A rock hangs like a spark plug on the cliff face in the background, daylight visible all around the big oblong boulder! . *(Marshal Bird photo)*

Right: My camera, taking a dump.

Day 6

Heading down along the Pine Creek and back out of the Quinn Canyon Range. *(Marshal Bird photo)*

RTB / Cherry Creek Pass / Rachel 50 miles

Perfect. Simply perfect... The orange mochachinos are flowing and my bed of softness beneath this archway of giant cedars has cushioned my trail-weary hulkiness to perfection overnight, and Casper stands firmly en guarde; my sturdy sentinel in this cirque of craggy shelter in the Quinn Canyon Range. A quick tear across the top of a bag of instant oatmeal gives way to the grainy goodness that will soon be flooding my fiber tube, and the dawn is breaking as it should be — nice orange sunrise bathing these canyon walls and gendarmes as the moon is once again forced to retreat. If you've got to face the end of a fantastic sojourn, this is the kind of day to do it. At least I won't have to bid farewell to this 'legend' all on my own, my co-riders will help me take it home as we return to base.

More great zoomer-groomers!

The Little Cherry Creek runs along a course out of the southern end of the Quinn Canyon Range, and back down into the Railroad Valley to the north of us. We leave this little creek but join another, the Pine Creek, as we follow along its drainage that leads from near our campsite and out of these mountains toward the Sand Spring Valley. These are beautiful mountains, and we cover our ground this morning starting at around 9 a.m. on more fantastic dirt roads. Veritable super highways out here with groomed surfaces – makes us all wonder out loud later on how in the world they manage to keep them in such great shape, or why?

It's a gorgeous sunrise beaming through each gap in the canyon walls and over the ridgelines here and there – my bike continues to run strongly and smooth, such a pleasure to ride this thing.... We've only got a short distance of easy ground to cover this morning, so we won't be long in the saddle before the whole ride is over and this 'Legend of the Fall' comes to a halt. But, the riding here is fast, fun and furious if you wick it up and drain the last bit of pleasure out of these hills – I can do that! There's a left turn here and a right turn there as we pilot our bikes and ATV farther and farther down from the mountains and through the pinions and sage. Soon there are less and less hills in the way of our view toward the valley floor to the south, and the Worthington Range to the east looms closer and closer. As we pop down out of the foothills on great groomed dirt toward the valley once again, the mirage over a dry lake bed is already vibrating on a jiggly cushion of hazy air between us and Tempiute. It's as if we are about to land the Space Shuttle at Edwards Air Force Base when we come flying down out of these hills at speed and witness the patch of flat tan dry lake way out there between us and Rachel, just before losing this last height of land.

Above: Rider1 gives a thumbs-up en route back to base.

Left: A loping Stovebolt, from the rear. *(Marshal Bird photo)*

Above: Stovey on Casper, not sure he wants to give this ride up and go back home...
(Marshal Bird photo)

Right: Tempiute, straight ahead – a dry lake hushed below the surface of the sage sea...

Left: trail717 coming out of the Quinn Canyon Range on his 640 Six Days.
Right: Rider1 emerges from the Quinn Canyon foothills, the Worthington Range to his left.

The connection onto the main dirt road from these secondarys is here all too quickly, and it's all 6th gear now until the bitter end, unless I can figure out a way to do something about it. I decide to take the obliterated track back across the middle of the valley to Tempiute the same way we went up north yesterday, so I can get a little more challenge by dodging more badger holes and sagebrush. Dave is electing to keep to the main dirt en route back to home base on his Can Am, and Marshal decides to go on ahead of me across the obliterated two-track, as I take one last jab at my flailing camera and pan around pushing this infernal button. I hadn't realized until just now, that my lens cover is malf'ing on me, and that it is intermittently not opening or closing all the way. Cripes.... This camera needs a "New York Reload."

Pit stop at Smith Well, our camp was in a pass in the background.

Cemetery on a ranch in the Quinn Canyon foothills. *(Marshal Bird photo)*

We arrive back in Rachel at 11 a.m., and turn the fuel valves "OFF." The eagles – or "Falcons?" – have landed... or is it "Buzzards?"

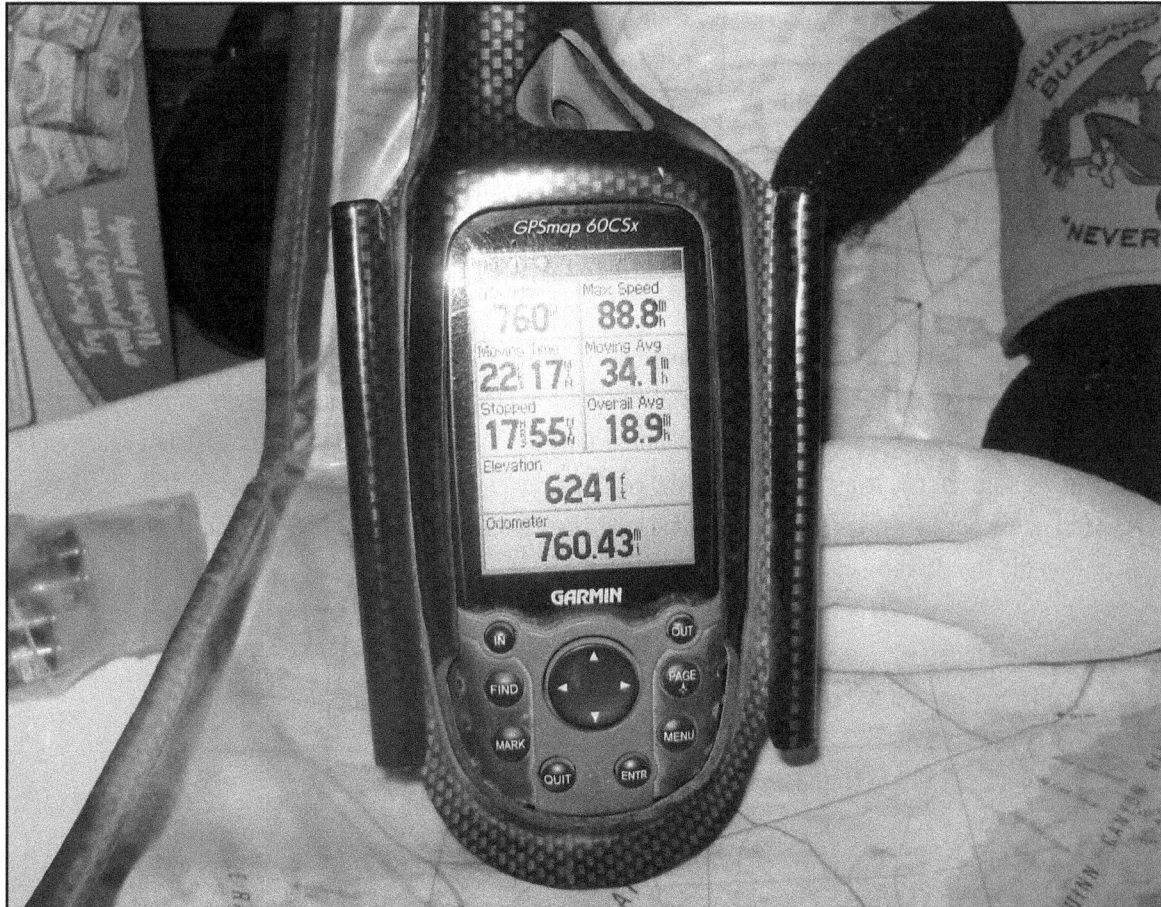

This short blast only lasts for two hours from saddle-up in Cherry Creek campground to kickstands down in Rachel, and we arrive back at our trucks after a left and a right turn in the middle of the Sand Spring Valley. Cruising past Tempiute townsite is a wistful non-event, recalling that the end is only a couple of miles away, and after that, a few minutes on the top end leaving dust clouds like contrails, and the ride is history. A really, really damn good ride – and I hate to put it away like this, but when it's done, it's done. (Insert "Taps," here....<sniff>)

We arrive back in Rachel at 11 a.m., and turn the fuel valves "OFF." The eagles – or "Falcons?" – have landed.

Page 4 from the Garmin reads:
Trip Odometer = 760 miles
Max Speed   = 88.8 mph
Moving time = 22 hrs 17 min
Moving Avg   = 34.1 mph
Stopped time = 18 hrs 01 min
Overall Avg   = 18.9 mph
Max Elevation = 7,552 feet
Total Ascent = 39,779 feet

It's not escaped me that I've thought a lot about my Dad during much of this ride, and one wistful treasure of a memory after another crept its way back from the past and hovered in my mind as I remembered him in his day, a proud and capable New York Air National Guardsman. Each fighter jet that "strafed" us or dog-fought its way through a mountain pass; every sonic crack from a bomb run and each glint from the canopy of a passing jet got me to remembering my time growing up around my Dad, his friends, and times spent around an air base. A circumnavigation from my dream, this run was a happy trail around in my past, as much as it was a ride around one of our most top secret air bases and military installations. If he were alive today, I would hope that we could do a ride like this together.

In closing this report on what was one of the coolest rides I've done, I'd like to recognize and thank my co-riders Marshal and Dave, for their good natures and able companionship. And for their prior military service as well. I'd also like to salute the men and women serving behind that line creating the boundary around Nellis, Tonopah Test Range and Area 51, and dedicate this ride report to you guys. And especially to the PJs who I know are stationed at Nellis. To the guys who respond to our airmen in trouble; who go and bring them home. And to my Father – this ride is dedicated you, and to all who still stand guard and keep the watch.

I leave this ride report with the best tribute to a lost airman I know, that written by Pilot Officer John Gillespie McGee, Jr., himself an airman lost to a crash in his Spitfire during a training mission during World War II.

High Flight
"Oh! I have slipped the surly bonds of Earth
And danced the skies on laughter-silvered wings;
Sunward I've climbed, and joined the tumbling mirth
Of sun-split clouds, — and done a hundred things
You have not dreamed of — wheeled and soared and swung
High in the sunlit silence. Hov'ring there,
I've chased the shouting wind along, and flung
My eager craft through footless halls of air. . . .
Up, up the long, delirious burning blue
I've topped the wind-swept heights with easy grace
Where never lark, or even eagle flew —
And, while with silent, lifting mind I've trod
The high untrespassed sanctity of space,
Put out my hand, and touched the face of God."
– *John Gillespie Magee, Jr.*

Thanks everybody, for reading along and sending your kind words and compliments. See you out there, as we all

Rally on, Stovey

(On station, until the next Legend of the Fall, wherever that may be. . .) ■

The Poetry of Adventure Riding

A Journey Under Starry Skies

A Glimmer, a Heartbeat — a desert landscape with castles of stone. Side views of a galaxy still swirling; ancient light arriving after long-spent journeys — from stars and planets. Tiny lights, wandering lights; find me on a dusty plain beneath this night's sky — all dark and quiet. Desert winds have gasped to gone, and sleep will find me soon.

Spiritus

Miles of desert crossed; rock and sand beneath my wheels, long days passing through windswept 'scapes — stark and remote, the look of the moon. Miles and miles through old stone castles; cliffs and spires. Miles and miles. Ancient stone and golden light, now waning as the night tides flow over cracks and fissures — desert dust ensconced in starglow. Gone the Sun, the close star hidden.

Eyes are filled with dreams inside my helmet — coming true 'round castle bridges, sandy washes. All day moats to cross and dragons to find — beware. Wheels have stopped and boots touch soil, ancient light above. A darkened 'scape yields to ancient lights, a stillness within our Milky Way. Sleep will take me soon...

Sancti

When Hope arrives, where will you be? Will you bring your hope with you on your journeys, under starry skies?

Hope and Dreams to you now...

— a poem by Stovey

Left: New bike with an MSO. Center: Secret fabrication laboratory comes complete with my own mad scientist, Berg Briggs. Right: A machine evolved.

The Money Pit – "Farkle-Fu in Stovey's Dojo"

What	Where Got	Retail Price
2010 KTM 450 XC-W Six Days	Bill's Cycle Shop	$8799.00
DC HO Stator upgrade	Trail Tech	$195.00
7" Rally Headlight	Cyclops	$399.00
(Included Brake line guide, Dash, H4 Plug)		
Osram Rallye Bulb	Candlepower	$19.00
LED Flasher Relay	RMATV	$24.99
Husaberg Turn Signal Switch & adapter	KTM Hard Parts	$100.00
Tusk LED Turn Signal Set	RMATV	$24.95
Grip Heaters	Symtec	$50.00
Handguards /Top Clamp/Front TS	Highway Dirt Bikes	$299.65
(Included 4-LED Dash kit, Spoilers, Front Turn Signals, Mirrors, anodizing, 12v Horn, LED TS Flasher)		
Rear Turn Signals	Highway Dirt Bikes	$49.00
Brembo Brake Light Switch	Highway Dirt Bikes	$16.95
Computer Protector	Highway Dirt Bikes	$50.00
GPR v3 Stabilizer	GPR	$495.00
Garmin 60CSx Handheld GPS	GPS City	$282.50
Buzz-Bomb GPS Cradle	Rogue Dog Communications	$75.00
Buzz-Bomb SPOT Cradle	Rogue Dog Communications	$75.00
SPOT Personal Tracker	SPOT	$99.00
GPS Power Cable	Backroads Moto	$19.00
RAM Mounts	Backroads Moto	$50.00
CycoActive BarPak	CycoActive	$52.00
White Plastic	RMATV	$125.00
Shock Sox Fork Seal Protectors	RMATV	$24.99
Carbon Fiber Fork Guards	E Line	$69.95
Header/Exhaust Heat Shields	E line	$99.95
Header wrap	New Level Motorsports	$50.00
Woody's Rear Wheel/Cush hub	Woody's Wheel Works	$939.00
Woody's Front Wheel	Woody's Wheel Works	$715.00
Myers Valve Stem Caps	RMATV	$.78
Dunlop D606 18" DS tire	RMATV	$89.99

Lef: Casper in a full-battle-rattle. Center: "Beaky" is Team Ruptured Buzzard's mascot. Right: Into and out of the pits.

2010 KTM 450XC-W Six Days Build

Bridgestone Ultra Heavy Duty Tubes	RMATV	$48.00
Motion Pro Rim Locks	RMATV	$16.99
50T Stealth Rear Sprocket	KTM Hard Parts	$78.99
Rear Sprocket nuts & bolts	KTM Hard Parts	$17.00
Rear Brake Rotor	KTM Hard Parts	$99.50
Rear Brake Rotor Bolts	KTM Hard Parts	$6.00
14t CS sprocket	KTM Hard Parts	$26.99
CS bolt & pressure washer	KTM Hard Parts	$4.99
Graphics	KTM Hard Parts	$109.99
Acerbis 3.4 gal Fuel Tank	KTM Hard Parts	$319.00
Fuel Tank Petcock	KTM Hard Parts	$32.00
Z-Ring Chain	KTM Hard Parts	$104.99
Rear Disk Guard	KTM Hard Parts	$80.00
Clutch Slave/Case Guard	KTM Hard Parts	$55.00
Giant Loop Original	Giant Loop	("Original" discontinued – price a Coyote)
Wolfman Rolie Saddle Bag System	Wolfman Luggage	$250.00
Wolfman Water Bottle Holstersx4	Wolfman Luggage	$80.00
PC Racing Stainless oil filter	Bill's Cycle Shop	$29.99
Tuggers	Highline Recreation	$50.00
Renazco Seat	Renazco Seats	$469.00
Antigravity Battery	Ironman Dual Sport	$180.00
Radiator Guards	Ironman Dual Sport	$105.00
Dirt Tricks Cam Chain Tensioner	RMATV	$82.99

Stock Motorcycle	$8799.00
Aftermarket Parts and Accessories	$6737.04

Does not include all taxes, title, fees, registration, insurance or shipping and handling fees for parts ordered.

Original build thread on Ride Dual Sport forums, here: RideDualSport\\Motorcycle Gear\\Farkles\\Farkled Bikes
http://ridedualsport.com/forum/index.php?topic=1086.0
2010 KTM 450 XC-W Six Days build... Farkle Frenzy in Progress, send help...
May 7, 2010 at 4:06.54 pm

A Ride Announcement Thread – The Folly Starts HERE...
(How does it get this outta hand?)

A planned ride might get an announcement on one or more of the forums, and riders do it all the time to gather in friends and make new ones. At the time of this writing I had a ride announcement posted in a thread on the Ride Dual Sport forum announcing the 4th Legends of the Fall ride. Below is what it looked like from my post #1, but if you want to read how it grew and developed, you'll have to log on to that forum and take a peek for yourself!

The post as it appears on the Ride Dual Sport forum:

4th Annual "Legends Of The Fall Trans-Nevada Cactus Slasher and Badger Basher Team Ruptured Buzzard Rally Raid"

Ride announcement details and route information pending. Put this on your calendar in advance if you want to. Sunday morning 0900 October 7th (2012). CPR, hematomas, concussions and sucking chest wounds all week. Petcocks "OFF" by end of day Saturday, October 13th.

Flex date(s) are: Start on Monday October 8th in Rachel, Nevada, and end on or about sometime Saturday, October 13th. Basically, blocking off the second week in October. Some people will ride all and some people will ride part of the route. Some may die trying, I dunno. I'm not an AMA promoter. I'm just Stovey.

Teasers are the Ride Reports/announcements from past rides.

LOF3 Ride Report
http://ridedualsport.com/forum/index.php?topic=2365

LOF3 ride announcement
http://ridedualsport.com/forum/index.php?topic=2277.0

LOF2 Ride Report
http://ridedualsport.com/forum/index.php?topic=1378.0

LOF2 ride announcement
http://ridedualsport.com/forum/index.php?topic=1327.0

Still just Stovey

Rally on...

Acknowledgements

Credit needs to go to the following people whom I've had the good fortune to meet, learn from, ride with, receive help and guidance from, or otherwise receive the blessings of fantastic equipment, support, photographs, advice and companionship from. Without these folks, my adventure riding thus far would have been more about trying to find my way home on foot due to broken gear and injuries than it has been a journey of two-wheeled delight!

Name they go by for real	Forum screen name	Name they go by for real	Forum screen name
Jim Craner	"Yimmy"	Steve Sergei	
John Craner	"Swinerider"	Ricardo Cota	
Eric Edelstein		Jorge Sandez "Coco"	
Berg Briggs	"bbriggs"	Mike Row	"mikerow"
Joe Watsabaugh	"Jwats"	Peter Harris	"MasterChief"
Jay Cunnigan	"advjackass"	Rod Peterson	"Stinky"
Lincoln Ramsey	"bumpylogz"	Ronald Steele	
Tim Thomas		Marshal Bird	"trail717"
Kelly Hart		Dave Ricker	"Rider1"
Mike Murdoch		Patrice Ninaud	"KosmicKLR"
Renee Murdoch		Jack Daley	"DR_Jax_650"
Michael Blohm, Captain USAF	"Spooky510"	Tracy Stiehr	"Frostbit"
Keith Briggs	"950transalp"	Charlie Ketchum	"DRZCharlie"
Steve Phillips		Christian Ninaud	"DoctorXRR"

Berg Briggs of BACKROADS MOTO in Jackson, Wyoming
Paul Degarate of HIGHWAY DIRT BIKES in Niwot, Colorado
Darryl of CYCLOPS ADVENTURE SPORTS in Kent, Washington
Eric Haugen of WOLFMAN LUGGAGE in Longmont, Colorado
T.G. Witte, aka "Woody" of WOODY'S WHEELWORKS in Denver, Colorado
BILL'S CYCLE SHOP in Idaho Falls, Idaho

Since the online forums have served as such an inspiration to me over the years, I wish to thank the owner of the Adventure Rider Forums, Chris MacAskill "Baldy" and his moderators, as well as Ride Dual Sport Forums owner Patrice Ninaud "KosmicKLR" and his outstanding moderators for their kindness, patience and wisdom over the years. And to the forum members who have given such wonderful feedback, information, guidance, camaraderie and riding partnership opportunities – I owe you all a round of thanks and applause! Salute.

ADVENTURE RIDER forums here: http://www.advrider.com/forums/index.php

RIDE DUAL SPORT forums here: http://ridedualsport.com/forum/index.php

Photography is a weak spot for me, and that includes all the effort it takes to document a ride. I have a lot of respect for the high quality images people get on their adventure rides, especially since they convey in such profound ways the spirit of these journeys across the hinterlands of the world. While my rides haven't yet taken me to such far-flung places as Mongolia, Ushuaia or Greenland, the photographs of so many riders has sparked many dreams for a lot of us. The guys who provided the images for this book, and who so kindly granted me permission to use the images, are a special group of people in their own right, and it's been my pleasure to ride and spend time with them. Many sincere thanks must go to the following good fellows for allowing me to publish their pictures, in support of this effort; Berg Briggs, Lincoln Ramsey, Jay Cunnigan, Joe Watsabaugh, Keith Briggs, Mike Row, Rod Peterson, Ronald Steele, Captain Mike Blohm-USAF, Dale Gullet and Team Bozeman, and to Marshal Bird. Marshal took the image that graces the cover of this book, and it really captures for me the sometimes outrageous spirit and vast commitments that enrapture all of us during these very intimate, very personal adventure riding journeys. Marshal also supplied most of the photos (and all of the really good ones) that I used in the "3rd Annual Legends of the Fall" ride report when he and I circumnavigated Area 51 together in 2011. A special thanks also to Keith Briggs for use of his many pictures, and, of course, for his companionship. Thank you all sincerely for sharing your rides, your visions and your images with me and all the readers of my book. And thanks for the good times!

To my wife, Dorothy, I owe a great deal for the undying support I've received from her over all these many years. She has encouraged me to follow my dreams and ambitions and has watched me ride off into so many sunrises and sunsets on my way down one fool's parade after another for over 25 years. Her professional editorial expertise during this project was invaluable, and without her I wouldn't have done it. She also gets full credit for all the design work, and any errors in copy are strictly on me. Thank you, Dorothy. Always...

And, to my sponsor, Captain Fur-illo. Without him, my compass would be truly busted.

There's almost always something more to look at, read through, or follow a SPOT-cast on at my website:
http://bustedcompass.com. Rally on... Stovey

David Jankowsky's Biography

A sixth-grade English teacher conferred an award for "Excellence in Composition" to David Jankowsky when he was still in the fifth grade. A love of language as well as off-road motorcycling led David to publishing adventures on websites since 2003, and he's been at both writing and riding for over 40 years. A short motocross career ended in tears in 1975, but his spirit of adventure was undiminished. A skier, mountaineer, rock climber and competitive combat shooter, Dave has managed to fill in an adventure resume to his heart's content while carving out a living in the mountain states since 1986. A dose of Catholic schooling as well as an early career track in emergency services and "all things 911" gave the author early starts to forming a values-based moral crucible, and forged the needle on his compass. Still, the author drinks from a rogue's well, and he makes his home in the Tetons where his adventure journeys are either taking place or being conceived; oftentimes while ensconced in a remote cabin that lies at the crossroads of many a GPS track laid between Canada and Mexico. Find him with his wife of over 25 years, running with his dogs in the hills.

ADVrider and Ride Dual Sport forums are both free of advertisements and spam, and no paid subscriptions are required to view the posts, join, post and receive information and solicit help from the membership – all adding value to these enormously helpful and extensive resource bases. ADVRider has a formal channel in place for members who wish to make a donation by sending funds in any amount to the forum owner to help defray costs of bandwith — real out-of-pocket expenses for Chris MacAskill (aka "Baldy"). View the information on how to help sustain ADVRider forums by entering this URL address, here:

http://www.advrider.com/Donate/Donate.html

Ride Dual Sport forums are also currently free of charge to wander around in, lurk, learn, plan from, shop, post and develop contacts and friendships. At the time this book went to press, there was no express way to formally contribute to the operation of the RDS forums. I hope in the future there will be contact information for donations to RDS forum owner/administration. As it is, many people contribute there in real and tangible ways already. It's as productive and friendly as forum members make it for themselves!

Thank you to Chris MacAskill of ADVRider and to Patrice Ninaud of Ride Dual Sport forums!

Follow Stovebolt live on his SPOTcasts
via the live feed link on his website!

Go to http://bustedcompass.com

and find the live link on the homepage of Team Ruptured Buzzard to see if Stovey is out and running, or maybe just home, licking his wounds. Spying is fun, especially if ya can't be out riding yourself.

"Team Ruptured Buzzard" swag is available for sale directly from the Café Press. Caps, shirts, mugs, stickers, mousepads, stadium blankets, sweatshirts, journals and more are for sale at the "Never Give Up" storefront.

Go to www.cafepress.com/teamrupturedbuzzard to shop at "Never Give Up"

"Until one is committed, there is hesitancy, the chance to draw back, always ineffectiveness. Concerning all acts of initiative and creation, there is one elementary truth the ignorance of which kills countless ideas and splendid plans: that the moment one definitely commits oneself, then providence moves too. All sorts of things occur to help one that would never otherwise have occurred. A whole stream of events issues from the decision, raising in one's favor all manner of unforeseen incidents, meetings and material assistance which no man could have dreamed would have come his way. Whatever you can do or dream you can, begin it. Boldness has genius, power and magic in it. Begin it now."

— Johann Wolfgang von Goethe

www.ingramcontent.com/pod-product-compliance
Lightning Source LLC
Chambersburg PA
CBHW080457110426
42742CB00017B/2915